MW00709478

THE
LOGAN GUARDS

The Civil War's First Defenders
from Lewistown, Pennsylvania

FOREST K. FISHER

COVER IMAGE: Design from the 1961 Civil War Centennial replica of the Logan Guards' company flag. Central feature of the reverse depicting Logan, the Mingo Chief, and namesake for the Lewistown company, also appeared on the original 1859 flag. Mifflin County Historical Society Museum, McCoy House, 17 N. Main Street, Lewistown, PA

All photographs by the author, unless otherwise noted.

THE
LOGAN GUARDS

The Civil War's First Defenders from Lewistown, Pennsylvania

FOREST K. FISHER

Published by the
Mifflin County Historical Society
Lewistown, Pennsylvania

Copyright 2011 by Forest K. Fisher

All rights reserved. No part of this book may be reproduced or transmitted in any form by any means, electronic or mechanical, including photocopying and recording, or by any information storage and retrieval system, except as may be expressly permitted by the 1976 Copyright act or by the publisher. Requests for permission should be made in writing to the publisher listed below.

Published by The Mifflin County Historical Society
1 W. Market Street, Lewistown, PA 17044
Telephone: 717 - 242 - 1022
FAX: 717 - 242 - 3488
E-mail: info@mifflincountyhistoricalsociety.org
www.mccoyhouse.com

ISBN -10: 0-9763433-4-7
ISBN - 13: 978-0-9763433-4-9

Library of Congress Control Number
2011937206

First Edition

Printed by

1124 Oneida Valley Road Route 38
Chicora PA 16025
www.mechlingbooks.com

The lines aptly dramatize the action of the First Defenders in the following verse, written by Edgar Downe, April 18, 1938 on the 77th Anniversary of the five companies going to Washington. — Attribution confirmed by the Historical Society of Schuylkill County, Pennsylvania.

There's a stirring satisfaction in the First Defenders' action,
On the 18th day of April in the year of '61,
As we tell the living story with its everlasting glory
Of the first to reach the Capitol and form its garrison.
They had heard the call to battle in Fort Sumter's deadly rattle,
And Lincoln's call for soldiers sped them onward to the war;
For they saved the nation's honor with the darkest day upon her
And sustained the war's first bloodshed in the streets of Baltimore.

This medal was authorized by an Act of the Legislature of Pennsylvania and signed by Governor Robert E. Pattison, May 26, 1891. It was made in the United States mint in Philadelphia, and presented to each member of the five companies comprising the First Defenders. On the face is a picture of the U. S. Capitol and the words: "First in Defence of the Capitol, April 18, 1861." On the reverse are the words: "Medal of Honor, Presented by the Commonwealth of Pennsylvania." Then the engraved name of the First Defender and a list of the names of the five companies. Two of these medals are on exhibit in the McCoy House Museum, Mifflin County Historical Society.

Acknowledgment

A special thanks to two individuals at the Mifflin County Historical Society: Research Librarian, Jean Aurand Laughlin, who aided with comprehensive historical and genealogical materials, presented in the most organized, coherent fashion, as well as checking my local historical facts. To Karen Aurand, MCHS Executive Secretary, for working with me on research in the Society's vast archives and helping with photos, documents and other resources. The expertise of these ladies made wading through the historical record of Mifflin County's Logan Guards an enjoyable, learning experience.

Special thanks for research assistance from: the Historical Society of Schuylkill County and its president Dave Derbes; Kimberly Richards, Director of Special Collections and Archive, Henry Janssen Library, Historical Society of Berks County; and Historical Society of Dauphin County, Ken Frew, Research Librarian.

Managing Editor of the Lewistown *Sentinel*, Frank Jost, and Sergeant in the 148th Field Hospital, provided invaluable help with identifying individuals appearing in the author's Logan Guard March photos, as well as extending permission for use of *Sentinel* photos in this book. Frank's shared historical knowledge as a Civil War reenactor provided insight into the life and times of the era. Along with wife Crystal and their children, the Jost family imparted their enthusiasm and unique understanding of the Civil War period through the living history experience.

Thanks to Michael A. Walters, First Sergeant in the 148th Field Hospital, who provided invaluable information on his 3rd great grandfather, Logan Guard Henry A. Walters. Michael had a unique opportunity to march in his ancestor's footsteps during the 150th anniversary remembrance of the local company.

Susan Sillence of Hamburg, NY provided genealogical information on Logan Guard, Henry Printz. Every clan needs a "Nancy Drew" to follow the clues along an ancestor's trail, and Susan fills that role for her family.

Freda Richard provided background information on the Lewistown Community Band and member names. In addition, Freda shared the finished commentary for the July 2011 concert honoring the Logan Guards.

In addition, thanks to Neil Scheidt, Find A Grave researchers, for documenting the graves of First Defenders, including almost all 105 Ringgold volunteers from Berks County. Neil provided additional data on Elias Eisenbise, last of the surviving Logan Guards. Additional volunteer genealogists and researchers at the Find A Grave web site, (www.findagrave.com), also aided with cemetery marker photographs and additional biographical data for Logan Guardsmen interred in cemeteries outside Mifflin County. These individuals have been credited with shared photographs.   F. K. F.

Table of Contents

Dedication

This book is dedicated to Willis R. Copeland (Jan. 1, 1899 - July 20, 1962). He was an officer and member of the board of directors of the Mifflin County Historical Society, and took the lead in the late 1950s and early 1960s in Mifflin County's participation in the Civil War centennial celebrations. Willis chaired local efforts surrounding the First Defenders' centennial, including the program and events in Harrisburg, PA in April 1961, and authored the only book on the Logan Guards up to that time. He was considered a preeminent military historian of all things Mifflin County, with a special knowledge of local military units in all wars, but particularly the American Civil War. A veteran of the First World War himself, he was a leader in area veterans' groups, including the Lt. Earl W. F. Childs Post 1667, Veterans of Foreign Wars; and World War I Veterans' Barracks 1015 of the American Legion; and served as commander of the Mifflin County Veterans Council.

In a resolution passed by the Mifflin County Historical Society general membership on December 6, 1962, the organization memorialized the historian by resolving, in part:

Whereas, Willis R. Copeland as an author, had written the history of the Logan Guards, the First Defenders of our Nation, which publication was sponsored by the Mifflin County Historical Society and which is recognized by the public as an outstanding work, and

Whereas, Willis R. Copeland brought credit to Mifflin County and its citizenry as well as the Mifflin County Historical Society by his acts and deeds as a member of the Armed Forces of the United States of America, and Reserves, and in federation organizations;

Now, therefore, be it resolved... that this resolution be published... in Mifflin County, Pennsylvania, calling to all its citizens' attention the untimely passing of our friend, member, author, historian, and leader in keeping alive the patriotic conscience of our community.

Sadly, Copeland is little remembered today, due to his untimely death the very year his history of the Logan Guards was published. It is in the spirit of Preserving the Past for the Future that this book is dedicated to the memory of noted veteran leader and Mifflin County historian, Willis R. Copeland.

Introduction

History tells that this company of volunteers answered President Lincoln's call for emergency troops in April 1861. History also tells that with their three month's of Federal service completed, the patriotic spirit of the age led most of the original Logan Guards to join the ranks again, where dozens rose to command positions.

Willis R. Copeland wrote a history of the Logan Guards for the Mifflin County Historical Society, published in 1962, titled *The Logan Guards of Lewistown, Pennsylvania - Our First Defenders of 1861*. His Civil War centennial work was the first book written specifically about the Logan Guards. Copeland tapped primary sources including access to the unit's Roll Book for 1858, 1859 and 1860 and the Morning Report and Muster Book kept throughout the company's three months' Federal service. Soldiers' letters and diaries play an important role, too, with an extensive use of excerpts to impart a feel for the life and times of those who lived during those turbulent years.

This book also builds upon the broad foundation of knowledge Copeland revealed, and to share with a new generation the events that were so important locally, yet intertwined with state and national Civil War history. Mifflin County played a unique part in that war. It has the Lincoln Stone from Lincoln's tomb in Springfield, Illinois in the base of the county seat's 1906 Soldiers' and Sailors' Monument as testament to that role, due in no small part, to Lewistown's Logan Guards answering the call for volunteers in 1861.

2011 begins the Sesquicentennial of the Civil War. The 1861 march to Lewistown Junction by the Logan Guards was reenacted during this year; joined by Civil War reenactors, history buffs, military veterans and county citizens, tracing the footsteps of those 19th century citizen soldiers. Additionally, during the 2011 Fourth of July weekend, the Lewistown Community Band presented a Logan Guards memorial concert under the marquee of the Embassy Theatre on South Main Street, Lewistown.

The overwhelming magnitude in blood and treasure of the war years that followed overshadowed the actions of those first volunteer companies of April 1861. Historians speculate that the quick response of those volunteers saved the nascent Lincoln government. During this 150th anniversary of the Civil War, it is again time to remember the story of the county's own – The Logan Guards – First Defenders of the Nation from Mifflin County.

- 1 -
GENESIS OF THE LEWISTOWN COMPANY

In the early afternoon of April 18, 1861, volunteer soldiers from Mifflin County found themselves on the gritty streets of Baltimore, a pro-Southern city that favored the secession of states below the Mason-Dixon Line. Five Pennsylvania companies from the eastern part of the state marched together: the Ringgold Light Artillery, Berks County; the Allen Infantry, Lehigh County; the Washington Artillery and the National Light Infantry, both from Schuylkill County; and the Logan Guards of Mifflin County. A fuming mob of Confederate sympathizers roamed Baltimore's thoroughfares, armed with bricks, pistols and even paving stones. They cared little for the lives of these Pennsylvania volunteers. The troop train from Harrisburg dropped the men at one Baltimore station; the soldiers then had to march

THE MINUTEMEN OF 1861
from *Hardtack & Coffee*, 1887
– Courtesy MCHS Archives

through the city to another station and from there on to Washington, D.C. to protect the new President and the United States' capital city.

Although the Lewistown company numbered 92 men, they carried only 34 muskets, and had no ammunition. Weapons, powder and ball, and proper uniforms, were promised first at Harrisburg, then upon arrival in Washington, D.C. Some of the officers may have had loaded side arms, but in reality the company stood ill equipped to face this festering mob on their two-mile march through Baltimore. The jeering crowd taunted them, laughed at their ragged appearance, derided them: "Is this the best Lincoln can summon to his defense, ragged Northern boys?"

Hearts were pounding, hands gripped the 34 empty Springfield mus-

BALTIMORE OR PRATT STREET RIOT April 19, 1861 involving the Sixth Massachusetts Regiment. The Logan Guards and four other PA companies passed through the city and faced a mob the previous day. – Courtesy MCHS Archives

kets, commands were issued, "Steady... Steady... Hold you temper... Make no reply to anything said to you... Company, forward...march." The assembled troop moved toward the mass of rioters, estimated in the thousands, while the outcome was quite unsure. The only thing that stood between this angry mob and the lives of these volunteers, was the bravery and courage each man brought with him from hearth and home. By then, that sanctuary was far behind in the Keystone State.

THE CITIZEN SOLDIER

How did these militia companies, and in particular the one from Mifflin County, come into existence? The story of this volunteer company begins before April 1861. The Logan Guards evolved from the military tradition of the citizen soldier – the volunteer, the Minute Men of the War of Independence – a tradition extending back to the militia of colonial Pennsylvania.

Serving in the militia was different than military service, in that the regular army asked for a commitment for a specific period of time, usually in years, with an established pay scale. The militia was intended for emergency service, for short periods of time - days, weeks, months - and individuals were expected to supply their own weapons, ammunition, equipment, plus incidentals. Reimbursement might be forthcoming later from higher authorities. The existence of volunteer units, forefathers of Mifflin County's Logan Guards, can be traced to Benjamin Franklin.

In 1747, Franklin was able to persuade the Commonwealth's Quaker government that self protection was a necessity. The Pennsylvania National Guard history notes that some 600 "gentlemen and merchants" of Philadelphia were guided by Franklin to sign "articles of association" to provide for a common defense against Indian raiders and French privateers. These "Associators" are recognized as the foundation of what would become the Pennsylvania National Guard, according to the organization's history.

Less than ten years later, in 1755, the Pennsylvania Assembly passed the first Militia Act, formally authorizing a volunteer militia from among the Commonwealth's citizens. This militia saw service during the French and Indian War. In the days of the Revolutionary War, over a decade before the creation of Mifflin County, eight companies of militia were formed locally in 1777 under Col. Arthur Buchanan. These companies reorganized in 1780 for frontier defense, composed of volunteers who lived on land destined to become part of Mifflin County.

Two Federal Militia Acts, both approved in 1792, formalized the system. These acts gave the President the authority to call out the militia of the several states,

... whenever the United States shall be invaded, or be in imminent danger of invasion from any foreign nation or Indian tribe... whenever the laws of the United States shall be opposed or the execution thereof obstructed, in any state, by combinations too powerful to be suppressed by the ordinary course of judicial proceedings, or by the powers vested in the marshals by this act...

The Acts further stipulated:

That each and every free able-bodied white male citizen of the respective States, resident therein, who is or shall be of age of eighteen years, and under the age of forty-five years... shall severally and respectively be enrolled in the militia, ... every citizen, so enrolled and notified, shall, within six months thereafter, provide himself with a good musket or firelock....

The Acts specified each member's required equipment - a bayonet and belt, two spare flints, a cartridge box with 24 bullets, and a knapsack. In addition, men owning rifles were required to provide a powder

The Iconic Minuteman, 1775 — The terms militia and minuteman may be considered synonymous today. In the 18th century, minutemen were citizen-soldiers in highly mobile units, able to assemble quickly, usually selected from the roster of the regular militia. This image depicts the farmer answering the call. – From *Battle Fields of the Revolution*, by Thomas Y. Rhoads, 1857. – Author collection

horn and 1/4 pound of gun powder. There were some service exemptions based upon occupation. Ferry boat men and stagecoach drivers were excused, for example, and so were congressmen.

STATE MILITIA & BATTALION DAYS
During the nineteenth century, the states maintained their various militia units under quite dissimilar rules, lacking standardized regulations. Under the Militia Acts, states could call up their own militia as needed to meet state emergencies. Before the Civil War, the southern states used their militia to control slaves, as in the case of a Virginia slave revolt in 1800; the 1811 slave uprising near New Orleans, suppressed by volunteer militias and a detachment of the United States Army; and the 1831 slave uprising known as Nat Turner's Rebellion, crushed by militias from Virginia and North Carolina.

Two years into the Civil War, the Militia Acts were amended by Congress to allowed African Americans to serve in the militias of the United States. This was a major development of the war. Historical background accompanying the PBS landmark series *The Civil War*, states that African Americans constituted less than one percent of the northern population, yet by April 1865, made up 10% of the Union Army. A total of perhaps 180,000 men of color, more than 85% of those eligible, enlisted.

The "free able-bodied white male citizens" named in the Militia Acts of 1792 were expected to attend and undergo training, officially twice a year. These sessions were called "Battalion Days" or "Militia Days." In 1793, Pennsylvania Governor Thomas Mifflin established the Adjutant General's Office to provide for "a new system for the regulation of the militia."

In 1794, President George Washington invoked the Militia Act to quash the Whiskey Rebellion in western Pennsylvania. Almost 13,000 troops were raised in Pennsylvania, New Jersey, Maryland and Virginia. This Federalized militia was personally led by President Washington, with some 4,000 Pennsylvanians participating in the action. The experience pointed out weaknesses in the States' citizen militia system, especially in army organization, and poor officer training. Washington stressed the importance of well prepared officers to the end of his life.

During the War of 1812, local men left their homes to join militia companies destined for action on the Niagara frontier in New York. The Thompsontown Patriotic Blues marched up the Long Narrows from the part of Mifflin County that became Juniata County, then joined Captain Millikin's Troop of Horse formed at Alexander Reed's home in the Kishacoquillas Valley. Both traveled to Potter's Mills and on to the Lake Erie region during the war.

The Mexican-American War, 1846-48, drew volunteers from the Juniata Guards under Captain William H. Irwin and the Wayne Guards under Captain James Caldwell. Irwin and Thomas F. McCoy (both later served during the Civil War) were commissioned captain and first lieutenant respectively in the 11th U.S. Infantry by President James K. Polk. Within 30 days Irwin and McCoy recruited a company, with the Juniata Guards as the nucleus, for service in Mexico. Other local militia groups to serve in this war included: the Washington Guards of McVeytown, the Lewistown Guards and the Lewistown Artillerists.

H. L. Fisher wrote about "Battalion Day" in his book *Olden Times: Pennsylvania Rural Life* published by Fisher Brothers, York, PA in 1888. This reminiscence of Fisher's volunteer experience some fifty years earlier places his stint in a local Keystone militia in the 1830s. Fisher's recollections run some eighteen pages on the topic, all in poetic form. He

BATTALION DAY AROUND 1830 — All "free able-bodied white male citizens" were expected to attend and undergo training, officially twice a year, according to the Militia Acts of 1792. – Image from *Olden Times: Pennsylvania Rural Life, by H.L. Fisher*, 1887

recalls in part:

> *The sergeants formed them into ranks,*
> *And from the ranks into platoons;*
> *And by platoons they marched along,*
> *Some stepping right, some stepping wrong*
> *To old-time merry marching tunes-*
> *To tunes that never failed t' inspire,*
> *Or set a soldier's heart on fire.*
>
> *The patriotic marches that*
> *Were played on old-time training-day*
> *Though muffled in the maze of years,*
> *Still echo faintly in my ears,*
> *And with recurring ides of May,*
> *The martial pageant with the sound,*
> *Still, as of yore, comes marching round.*

Militia notices appeared in Mifflin County newspapers over the years. Here is a smattering from the *Lewistown Republican* in 1842:

Attention Volunteer Battalion
The Mifflin Guards, Volunteer Battalion, will parade for
Inspection &c. at McVeytown,
on SATURDAY the 14th of May, at eleven o'clock A.M.
– R. C. Hale, Lt. Col. Comm'g.

Attention Lewistown Artillerists!
YOU will assemble on your usual ground of parade,
on Saturday, the 14th day of May, at 6 o'clock, A. M.
each member provided with thirteen rounds of blank cartridges; arms and
accoutrements in good order.
Punctual attendance of members is requested.
By order of Capt. W. H. Irwin, O. S.

Attention Lewistown Guards!
You will parade on your ground, on Saturday, May 14,
at 6 o'clock A. M. in summer uniform, each member provided with thirteen
rounds of blank cartridges &c. Punctual attendance is requested.
By order of Capt. J. Givler, O. S.

An eyewitness to militia gatherings of the 1840s and 50s was William F. McCay, the official historian of the Logan Guards and a member of that company. His recollections are recorded in Ellis' 1886 *History of Susquehanna and Juniata Valleys*. He mustered in as a private, later transferred to other units and was discharged in 1862 as a sergeant-major, Fifth U.S. Cavalry. McCay wrote about those times, remembering: "Battalion Day…was considered sort of a holiday and brought many people together to witness the evolution of the troops and to admire the showy uniforms…"

McCay describes what the soldiers of militia companies wore in those days, writing:

Who that has ever seen them cannot forget the uniforms then in use.
The heavy leather hat, with different colored pompons thereupon, and
brightly burnished brasses; the swallow tailed uniform coats, with three
rows of buttons down the breast, and which was either red, buff, or blue,
indicating the arm of service to which the wearer belonged, the breast
being padded so as to give a military bearing to the wearer; heavy col-

VALUE OF MILITIA TRAINING IN THE 1840S — "The demoralizing influences of our own militia drills has long been notorious …It has been a source of general corruptions to the community…" - George Cone Beckwith, 1847 – Image from *Olden Times: Pennsylvania Rural Life, by H.L. Fisher,* 1887.

ored epaulettes; the stiff leather stock worn around the neck, to keep the head up in proper position, and in the summer the white pantaloons stretched to the utmost by straps attached, which were placed under the feet.

Another, more or less comical aspect of such gatherings was the "officer corps," of which McCay remembered :

Almost every third man became an officer, addressing one another as general, colonel or captain. The officers especially, and they were legion, were simply grand in gold and silver braid and bullion epaulettes. The staff particularly presented a magnificent appearance, mounted upon spirited horses, with the trappings, showy uniforms and nodding plumes.

Militia training as applied in each locality, McCay notes, became quite unpopular by the 1840s. The military usefulness of battalion days had long become suspect, and was condemned by critics and national leaders. In his 1833 *Commentaries on the Constitution of the United States,* Supreme Court Justice Joseph Story lamented:

And yet… the importance of a well regulated militia would seem so undeniable, it cannot be disguised, that among the American people there is a growing indifference to any system of militia discipline…How it is practicable to keep the people duly armed without some organiza-

tion is difficult to see. There is certainly no small danger, that indifference may lead to disgust, and disgust to contempt; and thus gradually undermine all the protection intended by … our National Bill of Rights.

George Cone Beckwith wrote in his 1847 *The Peace Manual - War and Its Remedies*:

The demoralizing influences of our own militia drills has long been notorious …It has been a source of general corruptions to the community…beastly drunkenness, and other immoralities, were enough to make good men shudder …

Eventually, protesting citizens would show up for militia day carrying cornstalks and broomsticks in place of firearms. As time passed, the laws were no longer compulsory, and most militia organizations disbanded or died for a lack of members, some simply became men's social clubs.

Gilham's Manual for Volunteers and Militia, 1861, and books like it, were used as instruction material for training in the "School of the Soldier" by local units in the antebellum years. – Courtesy MCHS Archives

McCay continues with his narrative:

The old militia law having died, very few military organizations were maintained outside the larger cities. However, in 1857 a new law was enacted by the Legislature which encouraged the formation of volunteer military organizations.

This law authorized the Commonwealth to fund companies of 32 or more volunteers. The Legislature also made generous provision for both officers and men, the uniform prescribed being the one then in use by the United States Regulars, according to McCay. The old, superannuated arms (obsolete, retired from service) were condemned and replaced by the most improved modern weapons of the period. It was under this law that the Logan Guards were organized.

THE CALL WOULD ARRIVE

Over 360,000 Pennsylvanians served in the Union Army during the Civil War, more than any other Northern state except New York, according to the Pennsylvania Historical and Museum Commission. From President Lincoln's first call for 75,000 volunteers in 1861 and continuing until 1865, Pennsylvania mustered 215 infantry regiments, and raised dozens of emergency militia regiments to meet possible Confederate invasions in 1862 and 1863. Mifflin County contributed thousands to the conflict.

Asked to reflect on the Logan Guards in 1996, Daniel M. McClenahen, Mifflin County Historical Society board member and noted local historian, said in a Lewistown *Sentinel* article, "The closest thing we would have today would be a volunteer fire company." Discussing the formation of the Logan Guards, the local historian commented, "It was a social club, yet they did do military things."

McClenahen said that it was doubtful the group had any intention of going off to fight and die for the United States when they first organized. The group, however, was well trained in the military arts. In addition, the quality and character of those men was extraordinary, McClenahen asserted. Following their original three month enlistments, most turned around and reenlisted for longer hitches, or served throughout the war. Three Logan Guards attaining the rank of general, and more than thirty becoming officers, while many would be killed or wounded over the course of the conflict. When the original Logan Guards finally returned home after the war, many would go on to become prominent local citizens and successful businessmen, admired and well thought of in the community. McClenahen concluded, "They put it on the line. What they believed in, they put it all on the line for that."

Mifflin County's volunteer units were among the hundreds of thousands of servicemen to take part in the American Civil War. The first to march away from here were the Logan Guards founded in 1858. The concept of the company itself, some say, actually came after a walk along a local stream.

- 2 -
A STROLL ALONG THE CREEK

The **traditional story** of how the Logan Guards formed was retold in the last century by George R. Frysinger, editor of the Lewistown *Gazette*, and stems from a walk along Kishacoquillas Creek that took place over 150 years ago.

Five young Lewistown men were strolling along the stream bank one warm, sunny day in early June 1858. Walking together were Robert W. Patton, Frank Sterrett, Joseph Ard Mathews, William B. Weber and Jacob F. Hamaker. The group paused under a tree to rest and discuss the affairs of the day. As the narrative goes, one of the five declared, "Boys, there is lots of good material for a first-rate military company in this town; I propose we talk it up among our friends and see what we can do." All agreed, then leisurely ambled back to town along the stream.

Coincidentally, local jeweler George W. Gibson stopped into Robert W. Patton's store on East Market Street the very next day. Patton, a fellow jeweler, greeted Gibson, who told Patton that he just had an idea. What did Patton think about helping him form a local in-fantry company? Patton then told Gibson of the previous day's con-

John B. Selheimer — On June 10, 1858 Selheimer was elected captain of the Logan Guards. A vote held on August 7, 1858 to approve the company constitution and by-laws, also reaffirmed his position as company captain. Selheimer would lead the Lewistown company to Washington, D.C. in April 1861.
– Courtesy MCHS Archives

versation along the banks of Kishacoquillas Creek. He proposed, "Let us get handbills struck calling for a meeting in the town hall to see what we can do towards raising a company of infantry in our town. If you will put up the handbills (around town), I will go up to the Lewistown *Gazette* office and have them printed and pay for them." They shook on it, both left the store and each proceeded to complete his part of the bargain.

The handbills called for a meeting on the evening of June 7, 1858 in the town hall, located where the Lewistown Municipal Building is today, and encouraged the attendance of every able man willing to volunteer. Earlier that evening, fife and drum music filled the main streets of Lewistown, calling the interested to the gathering. Just before 7:00 p.m., the assemblage marched up and down Market Street, and next proceeded from the Red Lion Inn (the Coleman House) to the Town Hall.

An article in the *Gazette* dated June 10, 1858 acknowledged the meeting and announced that John B. Selheimer was elected captain of the company until its formal organization.

A subsequent meeting on August 7, 1858 approved a constitution and by-laws. The preamble to the constitution, probably the composition of J. Ard Mathews according to an 1881 article in the Lewistown *Gazette*, follows:

In a republic like ours, the safety and defence thereof must consist in the people themselves, inasmuch as they are the promoters and supporters of it. Where the citizens are the soldiers, no standing army can be requisite, yet it cannot be denied that too great an ignorance of military knowledge is an evil that now prevails in Pennsylvania. To obviate this deficiency, (being encouraged by a recent enactment of our State legislature), and for the purpose of improvement in the military art, we associate ourselves together as volunteers under the provisions of our State law and the regulations of the United States army, considering ourselves jointly and severally bound thereby, and pledging ourselves to the support of the... Constitution...

After the document was signed, Selheimer was again elected captain. Others elected were Thomas W. Hulings, first lieutenant; John Zeigler, second lieutenant; and John Swan third lieutenant. Non-commissioned officers and musicians were elected and appointed, including:

Orderly Sergeant .... H. A. Eisenbise
Second Sergeant .... J. S. Waream
Third Sergeant .... J. A. Mathews
Fourth Sergeant .... J. F. Hamaker
First Corporal .... E. W. Eisenbise
Second Corporal .... P. P. Butts
Third Corporal .... J. M. Nolte
Fourth Corporal .... F. Hart
Fifers .... S. G. McLaughlin, J. F. Cogley
Tenor Drummers ..... Thomas Elberty, I. Boggs
Bass Drummer .... John Spiece
Color Bearer .... Mitchell Riden

In consideration of contributions to the company, the following persons were elected honorary members: Captain William H. Irwin, Captain Thomas F. McCoy, Hon. John Davis, Colonel William Butler, Major Buoy, Major Daniel Eisenbise, George W. Elder, Esq., Lafayette Webb, Colonel John A. Wright, Hon. Samuel S. Woods, Colonel Alfred Marks, H. J. Walters, Esq. and Samuel Aultz.

THE COMPANY ROSTER

A list of original Guard members was printed in the *History of the Juniata and Susquehanna Valleys*, published in Philadelphia in 1886, and was generally considered an authoritative source for several generations. However, diligent research by local historian Willis R. Copeland in 1960 and 1961 revealed that some of the names on that list of the signers of the constitution did not join the Guards until the following year of 1859. In addition, he found certain discrepancies in what is purported to be the original roster. Copeland attributes the differences to the passage of time, a quarter century between the occurrence of the events and the publishing of the *Valleys*. Failing memories and the loss of pertinent documentary material combined to "produce a certain amount of error."

Copeland's 1962 history, *The Logan Guards of Lewistown, Pennsylvania - Our First Defenders of 1861*, notes that Mrs. James Sterrett of Mifflintown, Juniata County, made the original handwritten roster available for publication. The listing includes the Logans for the years 1858, 1859 and 1860. Mrs. Sterrett's grandfather, Robert W. Patton, was second lieutenant of the Guards, later

List of Names

1858 August 7th

Sergt R. W. P[redacted]tton, x
Corpl E. W. Eisenbise, x
Lieut John Zeigler, x
G. M. Freeborn, x
F. Hartt, x
Henry Walters, x
Jas. M. McEwen, x
E. E. Zeigler, x
Sergt H. A. Eisenbise, x
William Spaulding x
Corpl W. B. Weber x
Capt J. B. Selheimer, x
Henry Comfort, x
Corpl C. M. Shull, 0
Sergt J. Hamaker, x
Sergt B. F. Heisler, x
Ensign J. M. Rian, x
W. F. McCay, x

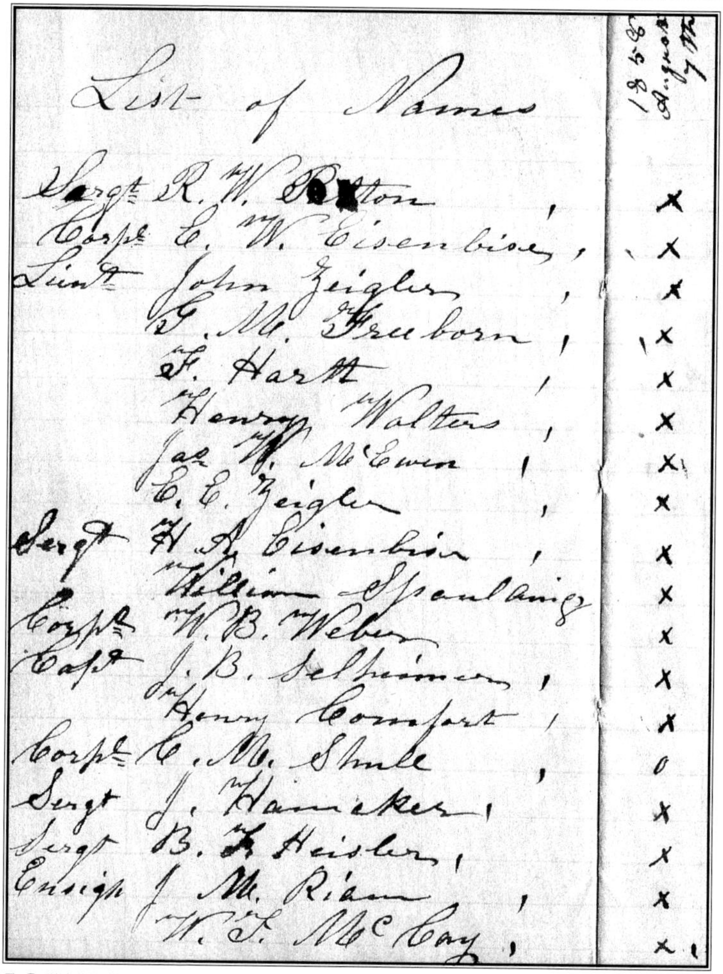

LOGAN GUARDS ORIGINAL ROSTER — The authentic first roster, page one, with "as written" spellings, appears above. The original includes the years 1858, 1859 and 1860. The listing is verbatim from the company roll book of Orderly Sergeant H. A. Eisenbise, dated August 7, 1858. Mrs. James Sterrett, Mifflintown, Juniata County, PA provided the roster for publication in 1961. Her grandfather, Robert W. Patton, was a Logan Guard. – Courtesy MCHS Archives

becoming major of the 131st Pennsylvania Volunteer Infantry. The following is the authentic first roster (with "as written" spellings) of the Logan Guards copied verbatim from the company roll book of

Orderly Sergeant H. A. Eisenbise, August 7, 1858, the date of the organizational meeting of the Logan Guards:

    Sergt. R. W. Patton
    Corp.   E. W. Eisenbise
    Lieut. John Zeigler
        G. M. Freeborn
        F. Hart
        Henry Walters
        Jas. W. McEwen
        E. E. Zeigler
    Sergt. H. A. Eisenbise
        William Spaulding
    Corp. W. B. Weber
    Capt. J. B. Selheimer
        Henry Comfort
    Corp. C. M. Shull
    Sergt. J. Hamaker
    Sergt. B. F. Heisler
    Ensign   S. M. Riden
        W. F. McCay
        John Guiser
        John Nolte
    Corp. Jos. S. Waream
        Samuel Eisenbise
        G. W. Gibson
        J. F. Cogley
        Bronsen Rothrock
        Geo. W. Elberty
        James Yeamens
    Lieut. T. M. Hulings
        John Swan
        Jos. Stidle
        Jos. Hoot
        William Gibson
        John Spiece
        S. G. McLaughlin
        G. W. Hart
        J. Orner

The company was organized, and gave strict attention to matters of military discipline, including squad and company drills, which were held in an unfurnished brick building on Logan Street, Lewistown, originally intended for a church, but which was secured as an armory and drill hall. During these drills, the officers were assisted by Captain Henry Zollinger, an experienced drill officer, who had been captain of militia at Newport, Perry County. He subsequently commanded a company of the 49th Pennsylvania during the Civil War. Also acting as a drillmaster was Captain (later Brig. General) William H. Irwin, Mexican-American War veteran in 1847, then commanding the Juniata Guards of Mifflin County.

The Logan Guards mustered into state service under the supervision of Major Daniel Eisenbise, the proprietor of the Red Lion Inn in Lewistown, described in the *Gazette* as "a warm and enthusiastic admirer of the Logans."

THE COMPANY NAME

Where did the name originate? Modern parlance for an organized military unit would assert "Guard" over "Guards" as in *National Guard*. Yet the title seems to have been known early in the company's existence. The *Gazette* mentions the company by name, Logan Guards, in its August 12, 1858 edition, reporting:

The Logan Guards paraded on Saturday for inspection, and afterwards were initiated into some of the mysteries of a soldier's life by a regular drilling through the streets of Lewistown. Their uniforms, which are in accordance with the new army regulations, look well, although they appear rather warm for sultry weather. As they are now ready for the wars, we have no doubt the ranks will receive a considerable accession.

One account about the name, retold by historian Willis Copeland, explains that in the very early days of the company, the men were assembled in what is now the east part of Lewistown, beyond Dorcas Street. While the men stopped for a rest, conversation centered on the company's name, which according to this story, had not been settled. One of the drummer boys, William Hopper, pointed his drumstick toward a sign on the side of a nearby house, which read "Logan Street." Will shouted, "There's your name, up there. Call the company the Logan Guards."

Perhaps the name was cemented for all time with a not uncommon offering to local military units of the age, a company flag. This particular present came from the women – the mothers, sisters, wives, and daughters of the soldiers – one of the communities most ardent support groups for the men soon to be away from home.

A GIFT FROM THE LADIES

The unit became the highlight of the local scene. Newspaper accounts note that the company fired salutes on the 4th of July, and paraded frequently during social, patriotic and other civic gatherings. In 1859, an encampment of area militia groups took place in Lewistown. $300 was raised to underwrite the Logan Guards' participation in the event, donated by "60 patriotic citizens," according to the *Gazette*. (The title page of the subscription book appears on p. 39.)

During the encampment, the ladies of Lewistown presented an elegant fringed silk flag to the unit. The hand painted standard was produced by a Philadelphia military supplier, Horstmann Brothers & Company. According to *Advance the Colors - Pennsylvania Civil War Battle Flags,* the company's colors had different images on each side. The state's Civil War battle flags and banners were evaluated by the Capitol Preservation Committee as part of an extensive survey of the collection in the 1980s. The project findings were published in *Advance the Colors*, volumes 1 and 2. During the 1961 First Defenders Centennial, when a replica flag was created, it was not known what the exact illustrations was on the flag's reverse side. The flag hung in the old State Museum, part of the former State Library in the Capitol complex. Mifflin County Historical Society researchers visited the flag to confirm details, however the original silk had become so delicate, its unstable condition prohibited removal from the display for a thorough examination.

In fact, the obverse shows a Federal eagle and shield with the details of the presentation inscribed on a ribbon encircling the national bird —"Presented by the Ladies of Lewistown to the Logan Guards - Sep. 19th, 1859." The reverse depicts a recumbent Chief Logan. The iconic American Indian was then remembered for his 18th century residence in Mifflin County's Brown's Mill (present day Reedsville) and became the company namesake, his image encircled with a wreath and the legend, Continued on page 28

LOGAN GUARDS REPLICA FLAG, 1961

This replica was carried during the Centennial of the First Defenders in the 1961 ceremonies in Harrisburg, PA. The original flag hung in the former State Museum in the old State Library at the Capitol complex. Mifflin County Historical Society researchers visited the flag to confirm details, however the original silk had become so delicate, condition prohibited removal from the display for a thorough examination of the side opposite the Chief Logan image. – Courtesy MCHS Archives, J. Martin Stroup photograph

[27]

"Heroic Actions Win Immortality."

A letter published in the *Gazette* from a visiting militia member reveals the setting, and presentation of the new flag. Portions of the letter from the 1859 encampment follow:

Camp Juniata
Sept. 24, 1859

Mr. Editor: Thinking that a few lines from a stranger about the sayings and doing of Camp Juniata — and more particularly about the beautiful and accomplished ladies of Lewistown... with your permission we will give you a few hasty glances. On my arrival on Monday I was surprised, and no less highly delighted, at the magnificent display your town presented. Hard would be the heart that could restrain the feeling of joy and patriotism on beholding the grand reception that awaited the military —the streets gracefully arched, houses festooned and gayly decorated, flags suspended from all points, drums beating, cannon booming, and the Logan Guards out in all their glory, uncommonly precise in all their military evolutions with that gallant old Major Eisenbise and other staff officers on gaily caparisoned horses, whose foaming mouths and

extended nostrils gave evidence that they caught the spirit that animated their riders... About 4 o'clock that eloquent and talented Parker... presented a magnificent flag on behalf of the heaven-blessed patriotic ladies of Lewistown in one of his usual off-hand speeches to the gallant Logan Guards...

THE LOGAN GUARDS' COMPANY FLAG — On the obverse, encircled around a Federal eagle with shield are the words, "Presented by the Ladies of Lewistown to the Logan Guards - Sep. 19th, 1859." – Flag detail taken at the State Museum, Harrisburg, 1998.

Joseph W. Parker, Esq. made the presentation speech in front of the residence of Captain William H. Irwin, on North Main Street. First Lieutenant Thomas M. Hulings received the flag on behalf of the company, pledging in his speech that, if ever called upon in his country's service to defend it, he would do so with his own heart's blood. The future Colonel Hulings would die in action in 1864.

The company flag Hulings swore to defend went with the Guards when they left Lewistown. It was the first flag carried by Union troops through Baltimore in 1861, borne by Private William Mitchell at the head of his company en route to Washington.

THE COMPANY UNIFORM

In an age when photography was the rage, and every soldier wanted photographed in uniform, alas, no company photographs have been found to date that show the Logan Guards as they looked in 1859. There is Captain Selheimer's image shown in this chapter taken about 1861. The uniform of the Logan Guardsmen in the ranks can be gleaned from the few surviving carte de visite images, a popular 19th century format of a thin paper photograph mounted on a thicker paper card, approximately the size of a playing card.

Perhaps their appearance prior to the Civil War may be visualized by referencing the U.S. Army Regulations published by the War Department in 1858 and 1860. The prescribed uniform included: a single-breasted frock coat of dark blue cloth, with a skirt extending one-half the distance from the top of the hip to the bend of the knee. One row of nine brass buttons on the breast, placed at equal distances; stand-up collar, to rise no higher than to permit the chin to turn freely over it, to hook in front at the bottom, and slope thence up and backward at an angle of thir-

POPULAR STYLE — Carte-de-visite or cartes de visite was a thin paper photograph mounted on a thicker paper card, approximately the size of a playing card. This image shows Capt. Franklin H. Wentz, Logan Guardsman, later in his Civil War military career. — Courtesy MCHS Archives

Pre-Civil War leather shako on exhibit at the Mifflin County Historical Society museum

ty degrees on each side; cuffs pointed according to pattern, and to button with two small buttons at the under seam; collar and cuff edged with a cord or welt of light blue (for infantry). Trousers to be of light blue cloth, made loose and to spread well over the boot. In addition, a four-button, blue wool sack coat and a forage cap or "kepi" were authorized for fatigue and field wear.

The forage cap became the most common form of head covering worn by U.S. regulars and volunteers during the Civil War, most often associated with the war in the east, as western troops tended to prefer broad brimmed felt hats. The forage cap is standard headgear in Civil War movies, films such as *Red Badge of Courage*, *Gettysburg*, *Glory* and many others.

The early volunteers' headgear may have been the shako type, the stiffened crown standing about seven inches in height at the back and inclining to about five and one-half inches in front. This cap was equipped with a square-cut visor of black leather and a chinstrap of the same material. When adopted by the Army (*ca*. 1851), it was sometimes referred to as the "Albert" Cap, copied from the British and named for Queen Victoria's husband.

The Model 1858 Army hat in black felt with appropriate branch insignia might be worn. Insignia included the national eagle used to hold up the brim, and branch insignia for Artillery, Infantry, Cavalry, Engineers, and the Ordnance De-

Typical Civil War era forage cap.

partment, with numbers and letters to indicate the soldiers regiment and company. After the war started, many soldiers also wore their insignia on the popular forage cap, although this was unauthorized. In effect, the forage cap was a less-expensive and more comfortable version of the shako with the stiffening removed. Soldiers of the period described it as "shapeless as a feedbag."

The muskets furnished by the National Armory, historian Willis Copeland noted, were known as the "altered musket" for the U. S. Army, being the old pattern musket rifled with a bore of .58 caliber to use the Minié ball (or more commonly, the minie ball). Each was furnished with a bayonet eighteen inches in length. In July 1855, Secretary of War Jefferson Davis, and future president of the Confederacy, authorized the production of the .58 caliber rifle musket. This was the first rifled weapon produced for general issue used by the U.S. Army, while the later Model 1861 Springfield was the most widely used weapon in the war.

For all the speculation about what they wore and what they carried, as strange as it sounds, the Logan Guards

Young volunteer, 1861 — Although not a Logan Guard, Pvt. Edgar A. Walters of Mifflin County, 195th P.V., is shown in his single-breasted frock coat. Walters kept a war diary during his service. This photo and a copy of his diary were donated by Mr. and Mrs. Wilber L. Edmiston of Lewistown, PA in honor of Frederick L. Walters of Shippensburg, PA. – Courtesy MCHS Archives

left their uniforms and most of their weapons in Mifflin County when they stepped off for Washington in April 1861.

THE ANTEBELLUM YEARS
In September 1860, the Logan Guards participated in another volunteer encampment at Huntingdon, traveling by packet boat on the Pennsylvania Canal from Lewistown. Both encampments were

commanded by Major General William H. Keim. He was the commanding officer of the Fourteenth Division, Pennsylvania Militia, in which the Logan Guards were a component unit of the Second Brigade. A bit of military organizational background follows.

At this time, the state militia was mainly composed of several hundred independent companies with the brigade as the tactical unit. The officer structure was top-heavy with brigadiers whose commands consisted of only a few companies. Copeland speculated that this system was adopted on the premise that, in the event of a national emergency, each company would expand into regimental or battalion strength.

By early 1861, the Logan Guards were part one of four companies of the Second Brigade of the Pennsylvania Militia, all from Mifflin County. The other companies were the Mifflin County Dragoons of Reedsville, the Irwin Guards of McVeytown and the Belleville Fencibles.

At this same time, the State militia comprised 476 uniformed and armed volunteer companies, averaging about 40 men to a company; making an aggregate of about 19,000 men. The 14th Division, then commanded by Major General James W. Crawford, consisted of five brigades, organized as follows:

First Brigade (Juniata County) .... four companies
Second Brigade (Mifflin County) .... four companies
Third Brigade (Centre County)   . . . twelve companies
Fourth Brigade (Huntingdon County)   . . six companies
Fifth Brigade (Clearfield County) . . . three companies
Second Brigade (Mifflin County) Field and Staff:
Brigadier General, commanding . . . William J. Furst
Adjutant .... William Townsend
Quartermaster .... John Zeigler
Paymaster .... James J. Cottle
Inspector   .... Daniel Eisenbise
Surgeon .... George V. Mitchell
Judge Advocate   .... James Hassenplug

THE CAPITOL & THE GOVER-NOR — The image of Pennsylvania's capitol building, above, during the Civil War era. The "Hill Capitol," named for the architect, was the site of Lincoln's visit in February 1861 remembered by Logan Guard drummer boy Robert Burns Hoover. Governor Andrew G. Curtin, right, was the Commonwealth's chief executive during the Civil War. – Courtesy MCHS Archives and LOC Prints and Photographs Division, Washington, D.C.

The Logan Guards participated in the ceremonies at the Harrisburg inauguration of Governor Curtin in January 1861, and in the February reception for President-elect Abraham Lincoln. The Lewistown *Gazette* of February 26, 1861, described the latter event as follows:

Washington's Birthday was celebrated at Harrisburg on Friday last by raising a U. S. flag to the dome of the Capitol, the first that was ever flung to the breeze from that point. The display of military was greater than ever seen before at Harrisburg, about two thousand men being in line, comprising companies from most of the counties bordering on the railroads, which transported them free of charge. The

Logan Guards, Captain Selheimer, numbering 40 men, and the Mifflin County Dragoons, Captain Mitchell, 35 men, were in attendance, and acquitted themselves with credit. The concourse of citizens was immense, every train being crowded to suffocation, notwithstanding the large addition of cars.

Native Mifflin Countian Robert Burns Hoover, a career telegrapher, remembered this event firsthand. He wrote to his old friend, George R. Frysinger in 1909, asserting that he spied Lincoln's exit from a Harrisburg hotel in 1861.

LINCOLN IN PHILADELPHIA — The President raised the 34 star U.S. flag at Independence Hall during a 7:30 a.m. ceremony February 22, 1861. He then proceeded to Harrisburg for further Washington's Birthday ceremonies remembered by Logan Guard drummer boy Robert Burns Hoover. – Courtesy MCHS Archives.

Frysinger was editor of the Lewistown *Gazette*, and the Hoover letter was among Frysinger's papers in the archives of the Mifflin County Historical Society. Hoover wrote, in part:

I was at Harrisburg with the Logan Guards at the time referred to. Lincoln was disguised in a long cloak and scotch cap and smuggled out of the rear door of the hotel, while 5,000 people stood in front hoping he would appear and make another speech...

After considerable cajoling by Frysinger, and persuasion that his recollections were of historical interest, Hoover put his memories to paper in 1913. Hoover's uncle (his mother's brother), Chauncey M. Shull, joined the Logan Guards in 1858. Young Hoover became a drummer boy for the unit, but at only age 16, wasn't permitted to accompany the Guards when war came. *Gazette* editor Frysinger shared the story in the newspaper, quoting from Hoover's written account. It follows, in part:

On that day (February 22, 1861) *a large U.S. flag was raised to the dome of the capitol building, run up...by soldiers of the War of 1812...The military display was the most imposing ever gathered in the capital city up to that time...among them our own Logan Guards...and the Mifflin County Cavalry, afterwards know as the First Pa. Cavalry... Thousands of citizens were present... literally packing the streets. Cannons boomed salutes... but the main feature of the day was yet to come. The vast multitudes took up a line of march to the Pennsylvania Railroad depot into which the train carrying the presidential party slowly rolled at 1:30 p.m.... announced by a salute of 21 guns. The president elect, with two chosen friends, alighted and were at once escorted to a barouche* (open carriage) *drawn by six white horses, the entire procession following to the Jones House, where on the portico he appeared in company with Governor Curtin and was greeted with prolonged cheers... While all this was going on railroad officials, detectives, telegraph operators and others were busy trying to discover any signs of suspicion and at the same time planning for the President's secret exit from the city... Robert Burns Hoover, then a drummer boy for the Logan Guards... saw Lincoln partly disguised, hastily making his way through the courtyard in the rear of the hotel to take a cab for a point on the tracks of the... railroad...*

PRESIDENTIAL HOPE — During remarks at Harrisburg's Jones House on February 22, 1861, the President-elect declared, "With my consent, or without my great displeasure, this country shall never witness the shedding of one drop of blood in fraternal strife." - Courtesy LOC Prints and Photographs Division, Washington, D.C.

Recollections recorded decades after the fact lead to doubt about the veracity of a given story. Hoover could have seen the future 16th president slip from the hotel. Lincoln was in Harrisburg, and his safety was in question. There was the Baltimore Plot, a suspected conspiracy to assassinate President-elect

Lincoln while traveling to his inauguration in late February 1861. The founder of the Pinkerton National Detective Agency, Allan Pinkerton, managed the president-elect's security during this journey. Historians debate whether or not the threat was real, but it appears Lincoln and his advisors took the possibility seriously, and made plans to move him through Baltimore and on to Washington with all haste.

The inscription on a Harrisburg city historical marker also describes the event. The marker was erected by The Harrisburg History Project, and is located at the intersection of 2nd Street and Market Street, near the former hotel, inscribed, in part:

On this site, the southeast corner of Second and Market Streets on Market Square, stood the Jones House, a mid-Nineteenth Century Hotel... It was here that Abraham Lincoln stopped on February 22, 1861, en-route to his inauguration in Washington DC. The President-Elect greeted and spoke to city residents in the Square and went by carriage to the State Capitol Building to address the Pennsylvania Legislature as the guest of strong ally Governor Andrew Gregg Curtin. Although Lincoln was scheduled to stay overnight at the Jones House, threat of an assassin forced his unscheduled early morning departure by way of a more obscure train station outside the city.

The Pennsylvania Abraham Lincoln Bicentennial Commission presents these excerpts from *Harrisburg: Crossroads of the Civil War* exhibit, National Civil War Museum exhibit:

After addressing the citizens of Harrisburg from the Jones House in Market Square, and the Pennsylvania State Assembly at the State House, Lincoln attended a dinner given by Governor Andrew G. Curtin. Having told the Governor of his plans, Lincoln left the dinner at the Jones House at 6:00 p.m., donning an old overcoat and a soft cap as a disguise, in place of his trademark stovepipe hat. A carriage waiting outside carried Lincoln to the train station and in the early hours of February 23, the President-elect passed through Baltimore and into Washington completely unnoticed. The newspapers and Lincoln's critics portrayed him as a coward for his unannounced arrival, and he regretted his decision to enter Washington secretly for the rest of his life.

Before his departure from Pennsylvania's capital, Lincoln spoke to the crowd from the front portico of the Jones House, concluding his remarks, saying:

While I have been proud to see today the finest military array, I think, that I have ever seen; allow me to say in regard to those men that they give hope of what may be done when war is inevitable. But, at the same time, allow me to express the hope that in the shedding of blood their services may never be needed, especially in the shedding of fraternal blood. It shall be my endeavor to preserve the peace of this country so far as it can possibly be done, consistently with the maintenance of the institutions of the country. With my consent, or without my great displeasure, this country shall never witness the shedding of one drop of blood in fraternal strife.

Willis Copeland asserted of the 16th President:

Lincoln's words point to the inward anguish of a man caught in the inexorable current of destiny, fervently hoping that war may be averted, but actually resigned to its inevitability.

On March 4, 1861, Abraham Lincoln and Hannibal Hamlin were inaugurated President and Vice President of the United States at Washington, D.C. Seven southern states had already declared

LINCOLN'S CLANDESTINE ESCAPE TO WASHINGTON — Logan Guard drummer boy Robert Burns Hoover recalled seeing President-elect Lincoln, partly disguised, hustled by associates through the courtyard at the rear of the Jones Hotel. There a carriage awaited to whisk Lincoln to a train for Washington. Allan Pinkerton, Lincoln's security chief, suggested the late night trip, fearing for Lincoln's safety. *Harper's Weekly* reprinted the caricature in March 1861 as part of three assassination attempt theories, with the caption: "He wore a Scotch plaid Cap and a very long Military Cloak, so that he was entirely unrecognizable." Another cartoon titled "The MacLincoln Harrisburg Highland Fling", appeared in *Vanity Fair*, March 9, 1861. The newspapers and Lincoln's critics portrayed him as a coward for his unannounced capital arrival, and he regretted his decision to enter Washington secretly for the rest of his life, according to a National Civil War Museum exhibit in Harrisburg, PA. – Courtesy MCHS Archives

their secession from the United States to become part of the Confederate States of America months before Lincoln took office: South Carolina (December 20, 1860); Mississippi (January 9, 1861); Florida (January 10, 1861); Alabama (January 11, 1861); Georgia (January 19, 1861);

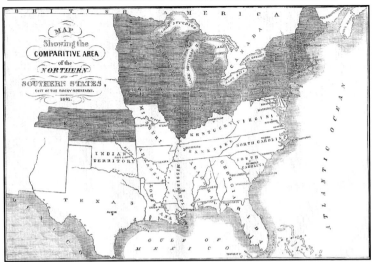

THE NATION AS IT LOOKED IN 1861 — Seven Southern states seceded before Lincoln took office, followed by four more after he was sworn. Copeland wrote: *Lincoln's words* (spoken prior to his departure from Harrisburg for the inauguration) *point to the inward anguish of a man caught in the inexorable current of destiny, fervently hoping that war may be averted, but actually resigned to its inevitability.* – Courtesy MCHS Archives

Louisiana (January 26, 1861), and Texas (February 1, 1861).

After Lincoln's inauguration, four more states seceded, including: Virginia (April 17, 1861; ratified by voters May 23, 1861); Arkansas (May 6, 1861); Tennessee (May 7, 1861; ratified by voters June 8, 1861); and North Carolina (May 20, 1861).

Professor William L. Barney, Department of History at University North Carolina at Chapel Hill writes in *The Confederacy*:

The popular reaction to the firing on Fort Sumter and Lincoln's call for troops unified the North behind a crusade to preserve the Union and solidified, at least temporarily, a divided South behind the cause of Southern independence.

After Fort Sumter surrendered, the Logan Guards were ready to answer Lincoln's urgent call for volunteers, though the event turned the county on its ear, and imbued citizenry here and across the North with patriotic spirit.

1859 MILITIA ENCAMPMENT SUBSCRIPTION BOOK TITLE PAGE — Written by Sgt. Robert W. Patton, a total of 60 contributors signed up to underwrite the cost of the gathering, the first entry states: *We the undersigned promise to pay to R.W. Patton or bearer, the Sum set opposite our names for the purpose of defraying the expences* [sic] *of an encampment to be held her* [sic] *in September 1859.* – Courtesy MCHS Archives

- 3 -
WE ARE COMING!

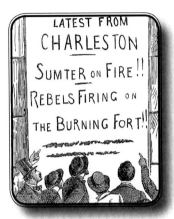

Confederate forces under General P. G. T. Beauregard in Charleston, South Carolina, formally demanded the surrender of Fort Sumter on April 11, 1861. Fort commander Major Robert Anderson refused the demand after lengthy negotiations. At 4:30 a.m. on April 12, a single 10-inch Confederate mortar round was fired. The shell exploded over Fort Sumter as a signal to open the general assault from dozens of guns and mortars that ringed Chraleston harbor, including Fort Moultrie, Fort Johnson (a floating battery), and Cummings Point.

Civil War historian David Detzer, in *Allegiance: Fort Sumter, Charleston, and the Beginning of the Civil War* writes that due to low ammunition, Major Anderson withheld fire until dawn, but was eventually reduced to using only 6 guns, and that ineffectually. Confederate guns fired in a counterclockwise sequence around the harbor, with 2 minutes between each shot. General Beauregard also wanted to conserve ammunition, calculating he had enough to last for about 48 hours.

The cannonade awakened Charleston's residents, who gathered outside and on rooftops in the early morning to watch the shelling of the fort. The firing from Confederate batteries continued for thirty-four hours, before Major Anderson hauled down the United States flag. Fort Sumter endured over 3,000 Confederate rounds resulting in no casualties on either side during the extended shelling. The lack of wounded in this opening engagement would belie the carnage the Civil War would visit on both sides.

On the 12th, Pennsylvania Governor Andrew G. Curtin received a telegram stating: *The war is commenced. The batteries began firing at 4:00 o'clock this morning. Major Anderson replied*

THE BOMBARDMENT — Charleston citizens clambered to roof tops to witness the spectacular bombardment of Fort Sumter in the city's harbor. After the fort capitulated, *Harper's Weekly* published press reports in the April 27, 1861 edition that announced: *The last act in the drama of Fort Sumter has been concluded. Major Anderson has evacuated, and, with his command, departed by the steamer Isabel from the harbor. He saluted his flag, and the company, then forming on the parade-ground, marched out upon the wharf, with drum and fife playing 'Yankee Doodle.* Anderson visited Mifflin County in May 1861 en route to duty in Kentucky. – Courtesy MCHS Archives

and a brisk cannonading commenced. This is reliable and has just come to the Associated Press. The vessels were not in sight.

News of the monumental events reached Mifflin County. In a later age, the general feelings that swept the community might be likened to the outrage of Pearl Harbor in 1941 or the terrorist attacks on New York and Washington D.C. in 2001.

The reality was that in April 1861, the Regular U.S. Army numbered a mere 14,000 men, those scattered across the country. The national capital city lay virtually helpless before a potential Southern attack, as thousands of Confederate troops were within striking distance from across the Potomac River in Virginia. Federal leaders, the very Union government itself, sat unprotected in Washington. Less than forty-eight hours after the fall of Fort Sumter, on April 15th, President Lincoln sent out a call for seventy-five thousand volunteer troops, proclaiming:

Whereas, The laws of the United States have been for some time past, and are now opposed, and the execution thereof obstructed in the States of South Carolina, Georgia, Alabama, Florida, Mississippi, Louisiana and Texas, by combinations too powerful to be suppressed by the ordinary course of judicial proceedings, or by the powers vested in the marshals by laws:

Now, therefore, I, Abraham Lincoln, President of the United States, in virtue of the power in me vested by the Constitution and the laws, have thought fit to call forth, and hereby do call forth, the militia of the several States of the Union, to the aggregate number of seventy-five thousand, in order to suppress the said combination and to cause the laws to be duly executed.

I appeal to all loyal citizens to favor, facilitate and aid this effort to maintain the honor, the integrity and the existence of our National Union, and the perpetuity of the popular Government, and to redress the wrongs already long enough endured.

I deem it proper to say that the first service assigned to the forces hereby called forth will probably be to repossess the forts, places and property which have been seized from the Union.

In witness whereof, I have hereunto set my hand and caused the seal of the United States to be affixed.

Done at the city of Washington, this 15th day of April, in the year of our Lord one thousand eight hundred and sixty-one, and of the independence of the United States the eighty-fifth.

ABRAHAM   LINCOLN.

By the President,
WILLIAM H. SEWARD,
Secretary of State.

MOBILIZATION

Governor Curtin was notified by the Secretary of War that Pennsylvania was to provide 16 regiments, two within three days, due to the expected attack on Washington by Confederate forces from Virginia. In anticipation of the expected request for troops, Captain Selheimer advised Governor Curtin that the Logan Guards were ready to move and offered their services.

On the 16th, Miss Elizabeth Cogley, who was in charge of the telegraph office at Lewistown Junction, received the message:

> *Atlantic & Ohio Telegraph Lines.*
> *Harrisburg, April 16, 1861.*
>
> *To Captain Selheimer:*
>
> *If your company numbers seventy-seven men rank and file, come to-night; if not, increase number if possible and be ready to come when telegraphed for. Answer.*
>
> > *Eli Slifer,*
> > *Secretary of Commonwealth.*

Miss Cogley immediately transcribed the message on the regulation form and gave it to her brother, Elias Cogley, instructing him to deliver it, at once and in person, to Captain Selheimer.

When news of the telegram hit the streets, business in Lewistown came to a halt.

A tide of excitement swelled the number of usual town's folk to a throng, all collecting around the Square and overflowing east and west, north and south on Market and Main streets. Fathers, sons and brothers, all prepared to leave the comforts of home for an unknown future in response to President Lincoln's call to arms.

When the news *of Fort Sumter's surrender hit the streets, Lewistown and the surrounding area was thrown into a hubbub of activity...*

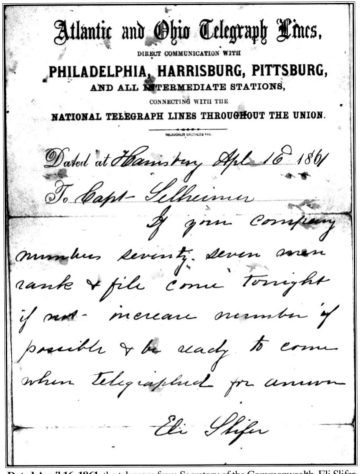

Atlantic and Ohio Telegraph Lines,

DIRECT COMMUNICATION WITH

PHILADELPHIA, HARRISBURG, PITTSBURG,

AND ALL INTERMEDIATE STATIONS,

CONNECTING WITH THE

NATIONAL TELEGRAPH LINES THROUGHOUT THE UNION.

Dated at Harrisburg Apl 16 1861

To Capt. Selheimer

If your company numbers seventy-seven men rank & file come tonight if not - increase number if possible & be ready to come when telegraphed for ammun—

Eli Slifer

Dated April 16, 1861, the telegram from Secretary of the Commonwealth, Eli Slifer to Captain John B. Selheimer, calling the Logan Guards into service. The original resides in the State Museum, Harrisburg. – Courtesy MCHS Archives.

When word quickly spread to the outlying districts of the county, farmers and laborers came by the dozens. It was electrifying and energizing in a way not seen or known before in this rural area.

Captain Selheimer had the response delivered to the telegraph office, "We are coming." He hastily opened a recruiting office in the National Hotel (next to the Embassy Theatre) on the Square and had a full company of 92 picked men within one hour. A fifteen word message was then sent to Governor Curtain at Harrisburg:

"We have the requisite number of men and will be down tonight. Have quarters ready."

The volunteers rushed to set their business affairs in order, as best they could on such short notice. Some had to simply close shop doors or leave their responsibilities in the hands of others, not completely knowing the magnitude of what was ahead. Contemporary accounts stress the fortitude each man exhibited that day. The town was a hubbub of activity, as the prominent people of the community came and mingled with those gathering to leave, assuring them of financial support for wives and children left behind. A subscription of $50 each was started earlier that day, and by the time a huge public gathering convened later that night some $3,000.00 was collect for support of the families of the departing soldiers.

Elizabeth Cogley
Her career as a railroad telegrapher began in 1855 at Lewistown Junction, the first known female in that capacity. She was promoted to the Harrisburg office in 1862 following her "expert and diligent service" at the start of the war.
– Courtesy MCHS Archives

Throughout his life, William F. McCay remembered that day and evening. It was the most significant event of his generation. He recalled his experience in later years:

The great excitement prevailed, extending to the women and children and, as the shades of night came on, the streets of Lewistown in front of the Red Lion Inn (Coleman House) *and in front of the courthouse were densely packed with men, women and children. It seemed, indeed, as if everyone had left their homes to bid us goodbye.*

It was well past dark. Flickering gas lamps illuminated Lewistown's streets, as did smoky kerosene torches of the type so common at political rallies of the era. Light from kerosene lamps in almost every window of homes and businesses in the town's center threw a soft glow upon the main streets. People walked or gathered around their loved ones to speak in hushed tones about the unthinkable, the war. How long would it last? Would there be uniforms and supplies for the men? What about ammunition?

Most questions went unanswered, as the Logan Guards began to assemble in front of the Red Lion, as the sounds of weeping and sobs now mixed with the martial music of the town's band. And then it was time. The volunteers prepared to step off to the Junction, board the train to the state capital, and from there to Washington, D.C. They wore old civilian clothes, assured of new uniforms, perhaps at Harrisburg.

THE GIRL I LEFT BEHIND ME

At 10:00 p.m. they formed up to move out smartly. The reluctant crowd parted, allowing their loved ones to advance. Captain Selheimer drew his sword and gave the order, "Company, forward – march." A fifer and two drummers led the procession, the beat of the drums echoed along Market Street, the whole scene illuminated with lamps and torches. Drummers Joseph Postlethwait and William Hooper pounded out the tempo. The hand painted silk Guards' flag, presented by the ladies of Lewistown the year before, came next. Hoisted by flag bearer William Mitchell, the image of old Chief Logan recumbent among its folds, led the way.

TELEGRAM FROM GOV. CURTAIN — This exhibit at the State Museum, Harrisburg, shows the message Captain Selheimer received calling the Logan Guards into service, April 16, 1861. Telegrapher Elizabeth "Lib" Cogley immediately transcribed the message on the regulation form (shown above) and gave it to her brother, Elias Cogley, instructing him to deliver it, at once and in person, to Captain Selheimer. Years later, the Selheimer family donated the telegram and envelope to the Commonwealth. – 1998 photograph

Guardsman William F. McCay remembered the song the fifer played as they quick marched up the street. Just as the column reached the intersection with Wayne Street, fifer Sammy McClaughlin brought the fife to his lips. Above the beat of the thundering drums pounding out the cadence behind him, the strains of "The Girl I Left Behind Me" reached out into the night. It was a common melody of the time, known to all soldiers as a marching tune,

SIGNING UP RECRUITS — This image, from Billings' 1887 *Hardtack & Coffee,* illustrates the intensity of a recruiting meeting during the Civil War, with the old timers' patriotic enthusiasm hard to restrain. On April 16, 1861, Logan Guard Captain John B. Selheimer hastily opened a recruiting office in the National Hotel (next to the Embassy Theatre) on Lewistown's Market Square and had a full company of 92 picked men within one hour. – Courtesy MCHS Archives

adopted from the British during the War of 1812. Many a Logan would recall the words as they stepped down Market Street toward Lewistown Junction:

> *I'm lonesome since I crossed the hill,*
> *And over the moor that's sedgy.*
> *Such lonely thoughts my heart do fill,*
> *Since parting with my Betsey.*
> *I seek for one as fair and gay*
> *But find none to remind me,*
> *How sweet the hours I passed away*
> *With the girl I left behind me.*

The volunteers marched the length of West Market Street, and crossed the Juniata River on the covered bridge, the pulse of their footfalls echoing through the rafters and beams of the old wooden structure. The Logan Guards were followed by their families and friends, all planning to soon watch their "boys" embark for Harrisburg. They would have a long farewell – the train was almost three hours late! This delay would allow another company of Pennsylvania volunteers to later assert the claim of being "First of the First."

The Lewistown company arrived in Harrisburg early in the morning of April 17, 1861. When they departed Lewistown, they believed Federal uniforms would be issued at the state capital or Washington, but they actually wouldn't receive regular uniforms until May 30th. Like the Minute Men of the Revolution, they were still in civilian clothes, and not their best clothes, either, figuring these would be discarded when issued new uniforms upon arrival. They were intensely aware of their "un-uniformed" appearance, as some would later write, a circumstance that caused the roving mobs in Baltimore to call them "convicts and poor-house paupers" fit only "to be food for Southern powder!" Some epithets would be far more provocative.

Weapons would be a significant problem, too. Some units that departed Pennsylvania reluctantly left their artillery behind, on orders from the War Department. So ill prepared was the Federal response to the coming war, rifles or muskets and ammunition were not readily available for the vanguard of volunteers rushing to defend the capital city. The Logan Guards brought thirty-four .58 caliber Springfield muskets, but that left some 58 men without even the appearance of a weapon. The officers of the volunteer companies, as a rule, did carry side-arms and swords.

The Springfield muskets, though few, made the men from Mifflin County the best armed of the Pennsylvania volunteers. Four other companies joined the Logan Guards at Harrisburg (date of formation): the Ringgold Light Artillery of Reading (1850); the Allen Infantry of Allentown (1859); the Washington Artillery of Pottsville (1840); and the National Light Infantry, also of Pottsville (1831). These five companies had a combined strength of 475, but with a later reorganization, 530 officers and men eventually made up the ranks of the First Defenders.

At Harrisburg, the men were mustered into Federal service for a term of three months. Captain Thomas Yeager of the Allen Infantry recalled the swearing in process through a letter to the editor of the *Lehigh Patriot* in late April 1861:

We all had to take the oath of allegiance by holding up our right hand to God and swear that we would support the Constitution of the United States and Pennsylvania, and obey the orders of our superiors.

TAKING THE OATH — The Pennsylvania volunteers took the oath en masse upon arrival at Harrisburg April 17, 1861. Captain Thomas Yeager of the Allen Infantry of Allentown, one of the First Defender companies, recalled the swearing in:

> We all had to take the oath of allegiance by holding up our right hand to God and swear that we would support the Constitution of the United States and Pennsylvania, and obey the orders of our superiors.

Volunteers in Washington, D.C. being sworn into service, above, April 1861. The oath could be administered by a judge, magistrate or any commissioned officer, according to the 1861 *Revised Regulations for the Army of the United States*. The text cites this oath to be administered verbatim to all new recruits as soon as practicable or within six days, according to the Articles of War approved that year: *I, — —, do solemnly swear or affirm that I will bear true allegiance to the United States of America; and that I will serve them honestly and faithfully against all enemies or opposers whatsoever; and that I will obey the orders of the President of the United States, and of the officers appointed over me, according to the Rules and Articles for the government of the armies of the United States.* – Courtesy MCHS Archives

The five companies of the First Defenders traveled south by rail on the line of the Northern Central Railway Company, a line that would become a major north-south supply route for the eastern United States throughout the war. The Pennsylvania Railroad absorbed the railway company in 1861. This same line would later transport Abraham Lincoln to Gettysburg in November 1863, and carry his body on the funeral train from Washington, D.C., to Springfield, Illinois in 1865.

Two Northern Central Railroad trains carried the Pennsylvania volunteers, filling a total of forty-two rail cars. The men were

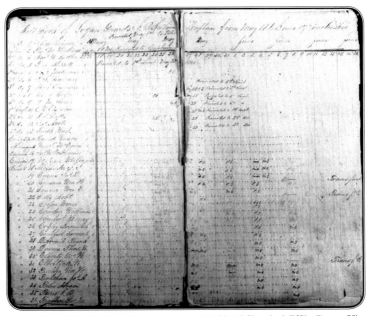

Logan Guards Roll & Day Book, copies provided in 1960 to the Mifflin County Historical Society by Joseph B. Heitman grandson of Capt. John B. Selheimer, the original roster of Logans on duty at Washington, D.C. – Courtesy MCHS Archives

generally optimistic, anxious to visit Washington, as a sort of outing. Four-dozen United States Regular troops were picked up at Carlisle, where they were stationed as part of the 4th U.S. Artillery. These armed Federals bucked up the men, if, indeed, they had worries about setting out without arms and ammunition. The U.S. regulars were under the command of Captain John C. Pemberton. In less than a week, he would resign his U.S. Army commission, and join the forces of the Confederacy. Although born in Pennsylvania, Pemberton's wife was born in Virginia and her sympathies were with the South, as were his. His nephew, also named John Pemberton and a Confederate soldier, would be credited with inventing Coca-Cola in the years after the war.

The basically unarmed volunteers would soon reach Baltimore, lacking a real grasp of what dangers awaited along the streets of the pro-Southern city. From captain to private, the two mile march would test the courage and character of each man.

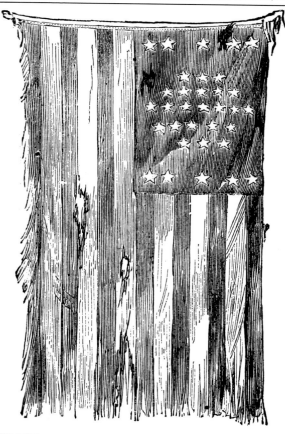

FORT SUMTER FLAG, 1861 — Fort commander Major Robert Anderson took the garrison's 33-star flag with him following Sumter's surrender. On April 20, 1861, Anderson participated in a patriotic rally at New York City's Union Square, considered the largest public gathering in North America up to that time. He then went on a highly-successful recruiting tour of the Union states, where the battle-torn banner became an icon that rallied thousands of volunteers throughout the North. The commander visited central Pennsylvania the next month.

Major Anderson arrived in Mifflin County May 15, 1861, as his train passed through Lewistown Junction during his journey to his new command of the Department of Kentucky, later Department of the Cumberland. The Slemmer Guards of the town greeted the revered commander. The unit, composed of male youth of the town, regularly acted as an honor guard for visiting dignitaries. The hero of Fort Sumter gave a brief, but stirring speech at the railroad station; accepted a bouquet of flowers from the devoted ladies of the community; and, to the rousing cheers of the crowd, mixed with the strains of patriotic music from the fifes, drums and brass of the Lewistown Band, departed the station amid swirls of smoke and steam. — Contemporary engraving of the Fort Sumter flag appeared in newspapers of the day.

- 4 -
FLOATERS, IDLERS & RED-HOT SECESSIONISTS

The Baltimore Riot - April 19, 1861 — The First Defenders marched two miles through the city the previous day, facing pro-southern citizens, incensed by their mere presence in Baltimore. The 6th Massachusetts engage the mob on the 19th, resulting in deaths on both sides. The contemporary illustration shows the "rain" of bricks and stones remembered by First Defenders the previous day. — Courtesy MCHS Archives

The First Defenders arrived in Baltimore at 1:00 p.m., April 18, 1861. Because the Northern Central Railroad had no direct line to Washington, the soldiers had to disembark, march across town, and take another train to finish the journey. During the age of steam, cities like Baltimore banned engines from passing through the town thoroughfares; the fire potential from sparks and hot cinders emitted by chugging steam engines was a real danger. Trains were pulled though the city with horses to avoid this hazard, but the volunteers opted to march rather than ride.

The men on the troop train from Harrisburg assembled near Bolton Station. They were told they had a trek of some two miles through the city to the Baltimore & Ohio Railroad's Camden Station. The intervening streets were obstructed by an intensely infuriated pro-Southern mob. The officers of the different companies held an emergency meeting in the train. It was resolved unanimously to "go through Baltimore to Washington, let the result be what it may," according to recollections of officers present.

Baltimore, a predominantly pro-secession metropolis, cast only 1,100 votes for Abraham Lincoln in the election of 1860 out of more than 30,000 votes cast for president. The First Defenders had to traverse this city, but their appearance came so quickly after Lincoln's call for volunteers, that the anti-Union elements there were too chaotic and unorganized to stop the volunteers' progress. That's not to say they didn't try.

One member of the Washington Artillery recalled:

It was also decided that we would not go to the regular depot at Baltimore to get off the train, but would get off at the upper end of the city... When the mob found we had got off at the Bolton station they came up the street like a lot of wild wolves. There were many desperate-looking characters among them, armed with clubs, stones and brick-bats, all yelling like Indians. They cheered for Jeff Davis and the Southern Confederacy, and when they reached us there were about 2,500 of them in number.

Baltimore's mayor George William Brown and 120 city police arrived at Bolton Station, to insert themselves between the mob and the troops. The companies finally "columned up," with the U.S. Regulars in the vanguard, followed by the Pennsylvania companies. The Baltimore police proceeded the soldiers and the noisy mob followed them all, determined to impede these Unionists as they progressed through their city. The troops marched down Howard Street to Camden Street, then to Eutaw Street and lastly along Pratt Street to Camden Station.

The march was accompanied by the constant jeering of the mob. Heber Thompson's 1910 *First Defenders* recounts some of the taunts the volunteers endured. "You'll never get back to Pennsylvania," "Let the police go and we will lick you," "Hurrah for Jeff Davis," and "Abolitionists, convicts, stone them, kill them!"

Mid-way on the march, the Regulars turned from the column to the garrison at Fort McHenry. At this juncture, the mob whipped into a rage, forced their way through the police, bent on breaking the volunteers' line of march. This now left the Logan Guards in the vanguard, with young William Mitchell holding the Guards' banner at the head of the company, and not a round of ammunition

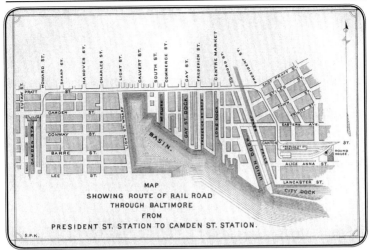

MAP
SHOWING ROUTE OF RAIL ROAD
THROUGH BALTIMORE
FROM
PRESIDENT ST. STATION TO CAMDEN ST. STATION.

Area of Baltimore Riot or Pratt Street Riot, April 19, 1861 — Map from Mayor George William Brown's 1887 *Baltimore and the 19th of April, 1861*. The book was Brown's recollections, and justification of his actions, as Baltimore's mayor during the riot. He was arrested by Federal authorities in May 1861 and imprisoned in Fort McHenry during the war. – Courtesy MCHS Archives

among them.

Samuel Bates' *History of Pennsylvania Volunteers* records the reaction of Allen Infantry historian, James Schaadt, present on the march through Baltimore:

The mob, on seeing the formation of the column, and the march begun, were driven into a frenzy. At every step its numbers increased, and when … Pemberton and his regulars left the head of the column and filed off toward Fort McHenry the mob lashed itself into a perfect fury. Roughs and toughs, longshoreman, gamblers, floaters, idlers, red-hot secessionists, as well as men ordinarily sober and steady, crowded upon, pushed and hustled the little band and made every effort to break the thin line… It was a severe trial for the volunteers with not a charge of ball or powder in their pouches.

The Logan Guards' Captain John Selheimer ordered the thirty-four armed men to carry their Springfield muskets at "support arms." A tin of percussion caps was produced and the caps were quickly distributed among the thirty-four armed soldiers of the Mifflin County company. The unloaded muskets were capped, bayonets fixed, and hammers set at half-cock. The impression was that with a single command these ranks could bring their weapons to bear. The ruse was to intimidate the mob to the extent that the column could advance to Camden Station.

Officers coolly reassured the men, calmed them, and shouted the orders to move forward. The outwardly confident column advanced. The mob may have hesitated as the troops advanced. Local historians have discussed this ruse for generations, implying the mob was sufficiently intimidated to allow the Pennsylvanians to reach the waiting boxcars two miles away at Camden Station.

When the mob saw an African American, Nicholas Biddle, marching with white comrades, howls and derogatory racial epithets were flung at the unflinching Union soldiers. So, too, were rocks, sticks, boards and bricks. A 65 year-old former slave, Biddle, company orderly with the Washington Artillery, was struck on the head by an unknown projectile. He had been part of the Pottsville unit since its formation in 1840. This assault on Biddle is considered by his unit to be the "first blood" in the Union cause, notes historian John David Hoptak in *First Defense of the Union - The Civil War History of the First Defenders*

As the troops boarded the boxcars, the mob continually showered them with all manner of stony projectiles. The Logan Guards were first to load, as each company followed in its turn. Most Mifflin County volunteers were unhurt, only a few had minor injuries according to descriptions in letters home after the event. The Allen Infantry

Support Arms — Illustration from *U.S. Infantry Tactics for the United States Infantry of the Line, Light Infantry and Riflemen* authorized and adopted May 1, 1861 by the Secretary of War. The move is part of Lesson II, Manual of Arms. The 34 armed Logan Guards were ordered to "support arms" on the streets of Baltimore by Captain John Selheimer, but lacked ammunition. After the event, Governor Curtain pledged no Pennsylvania soldier would ever leave the state again unarmed.

Insulting Pennsylvanians.

An infamous sheet published at Baltimore called the Republican, controlled by a whorehouse whelp, had the following remarks relative to the first Pennsylvania troops which passed through that city—among whom were the Logan Guards of this place :

THE PENNSYLVANIA VOLUNTEERS.—It is said the miserable creatures which passed through our city yesterday, under the name of Pennsylvania volunteers, were the emptyings of the poor houses and jails of the State; the Black Republican rulers there thus transferring the burden of their support from themselves to the Washington administration. The appearance of the ragged, filthy crew would justify the report.— If this is the character of Old Abe's volunteers, it is no wonder Pennsylvania is so ready to part with them. They are not, however, such materials as the citizen soldiery of this State can ever fraternize with.

Lewistown *Gazette* Editorial, April 1861 — Editor George Frysinger, under the headline "Insulting Pennsylvanians" took offence with the (Daily) *Baltimore Republican*. That newspaper characterized the Keystone State's volunteers on their march through the Maryland city, wondering if, "...the miserable creatures which passed through our city...under the name of Pennsylvania volunteers, were the emptyings of the poor houses and jails of the State...the appearance of the ragged, filthy crew would justify the report..."

The *Gazette* didn't mince words, lambasting the "infamous sheet," declaring the paper controlled by a "whorehouse whelp." The (Daily) *Baltimore Republican* ceased operation in June 1861. – Courtesy MCHS Archives

finally boarded, suffering the worst punishment, perhaps, considering the company's position - last in the line of march through Baltimore. Some sustained serious injuries. Bones were broken, teeth knocked out, head wounds left some unconscious. One seriously injured soldier lost his hearing for life.

THE MOB'S WORST YET TO COME

Rocks and bricks continued to rain on the boxcars at Camden Station, but the First Defenders were relatively safe inside, as the train pulled away. The incessant howling and cursing faded behind them. Comrades dispensed first aid and comforted the injured as the jostling, swaying train gained speed on the journey to the Capital city. Any idealistic thoughts of the "glory of war" quickly vanished after facing the pro-southern mob.

Bates records Governor Andrew Curtain's reaction when the news of the march reached Harrisburg, noting the governor "raised his arm, and pledged in his characteristic manner, that not another Pennsylvania soldier should leave the state unarmed."

There is no doubt at the time of the arrival of the First Defenders in Washington on April 18, the outspoken sentiment of the city was distinctly pro-secession. Any expression of Union support was dangerous. Attacks were expected nightly on the United States capital, and hundreds of barrels of flour were brought from Georgetown and used to barricade the windows of the Capitol.

EVENTS IN BALTIMORE AGITATE LOCAL NEWSPAPER — Another image of the riot, a topic that sold papers. The Lewistown *Gazette* castigated Baltimore newspapers in an editorial: "... the citizens of Baltimore suffer the gang of infamous tories who head the *Republican, Sun* and another sheet there to control their city in the work of treason and defamation ..." – Courtesy MCHS Archives

Once they arrived, the Logan Guards and the other First Defenders immediately set about their military duties. A guard routine was established and sentries posted. In the early morning hours of the 19th, First Sergeant Robert W. Patton, accompanied by Sergeants Mathews and Weber, delivered the morning report of the Logan Guards to Major McDowell and Colonel Mansfield. Historian Willis R. Copeland asserts that this was the first official volunteer report received by the Government from anywhere in the United States outside of the District of Columbia.

At this same time, two troop trains were streaming towards Baltimore from the northeast. The lead train was carrying the Sixth Massachusetts Infantry which had set out on its journey on the 16th, the same date as the departure of First Defenders for Harrisburg. The following train carried twelve companies of the Washington Brigade from Philadelphia which had left the Quaker City at 3:00 a.m. on the morning of the 19th. The latter volunteers would be forced to return to Philadelphia due to intense resistance in Baltimore.

At 11:20 a.m., the New Englanders arrived at the President Street Station, where the locomotive was uncoupled and the cars were drawn singly by horses to Camden Station. The regiment planned to embarked for Washington from there on the Baltimore and Ohio Railroad. A mob of about 2,000 rioters greeted the soldiers with groans and curses, following the cars on their passage across the city. Eight cars reached the Camden Station in safety before the mob barricaded the tracks.

The four companies in the cars behind the barricade descended and columned up in the street for the march to Camden Station. This action exposed them to the wrath of the mob. In the running street battle between the soldiers, the mob, and the Baltimore police, three of the Massachusetts volunteers were killed outright, one mortally wounded, eight seriously injured, and several slightly hurt. Nine Baltimore citizens were killed and twelve injured. The regiment was forced to abandon much of their equipment, including their marching band's instruments. The rail cars in which the soldiers sought refuge were sent off to Washington as soon as possible. At 8:00 p.m. on April 19, the 11 companies of the Sixth Massachusetts, weary and hungry and carrying their wounded on stretchers, arrived in Washington. They were welcomed and fed by the First Defenders, as other volunteers soon arrived.

In the aftermath, the mob destroyed the office of the pro-Union *Baltimore Wecker*, a German-language newspaper, and chased the publisher and editor out of town. However, by mid-May, Federal troops under General Benjamin Butler occupied Baltimore, and placed the city under martial law. Officials, including the mayor, city council and police commissioner were arrested and imprisoned at Fort McHenry.

The *Daily Intelligencer* of Washington, D.C., April 19, 1861, carried a six-line item on page 5 under "Miscellaneous News,' which read:

Seventeen car loads of troops, numbering about 600 men, arrived last evening from Harrisburg, via Baltimore, and were quartered in rooms in the Capitol. They passed through Baltimore about five o'clock without serious molestation from disorderly persons. Other bodies from the same quarter were expected to arrive during last night.

The previous day, April 18, the paper reported, quoting from the *Philadelphia Inquirer* of April 17:

Pennsylvania is thoroughly aroused. Everywhere through her borders her brave sons are gathering in defense of the Union and in indication of the insulted honor of our country's flag. The President asks this Commonwealth for 12,500 men. From present appearances there will be enrolled and ready for orders before the close of the week more than twice the number required. Already regiments and companies are on the march to Harrisburg, and some are actually in camp in that city.

LATEST NEWS.

The first volunteers from a distance arrived at Washington on Thursday evening, from Pennsylvania, consisting of the following companies:

The Ringold Light Artillery, of Reading, one hundred and eight rank and file. Capt., Jas. McKnight; First Lieutenant, Henry Nagle; Second Lieutenant, W. Graeff.

The National Light Infantry, of Pottsville, one hundred and three rank and file. Capt. E. McDonald; First Lieutenant, James Russel; Second Lieutenant, H. L. Cake, editor of the Mining Record (straight Douglas); Brevet Second Lieutenant L. J. Martin.

The Logan Guards, of Lewistown, eighty five rank and file. Capt., J. B. Selheimer; First Lieutenant, Thos. M. Hulings; Second Lieutenant, F. R. Sterrett.

The Allen Infantry, of Allentown, fifty strong, commanded by Capt. Yeager.

The Washington Artillery Company, of Pottsville, Schuylkill county. Capt. James Wren; First Lieutenant, David A. Smith; Second Lieutenant, Francis B. Wallace; Third Lieutenant, Philip Nagle; First Sergeant, Henry C. Russel.

The Secretary of War did not receive the dispatch informing him of the approach [...] on as he [...] them at [...] in the

Disgraceful Riot at Baltimore.

At three o'clock on Friday morning, the Massachusetts Volunteers and the Pennsylvania Regiment, under Col. Small, left the depot, at Broad and Prime streets, Philadelphia, in thirty-six cars, for Baltimore, at which place they arrived safely at half past ten o'clock, without any detention. A large crowd had assembled, evidently to give them an unwelcome reception. The arrangements contemplated the

THE LEWISTOWN *GAZETTE* reported on the arrival of the five companies of Pennsylvania volunteers and the Baltimore riot. – Courtesy MCHS Archives

On April 20 the *Intelligencer* devoted a half column to the report of the "Mob at Baltimore," giving an account of the attack on the Sixth Massachusetts Regiment, also reporting that later in the day, a Philadelphia regiment of 800 men was refused permission to pass through the city and returned to Philadelphia.

Benson J. Lossing's *Pictorial History of the Civil War*, published in 1866, describes the arrival of the "First Defenders" in Washington:

... the startling rumor spread over the city that 2,000 Northern troops, well armed with Minie rifles, were quartered in the capitol. The real number was 530...   It is believed by the best in-formed that these troops arrived just in time to awe the conspirators and their friends and to save the capitol from seizure. It is believed that

*if they had been delayed 24 hours — had they not been there when
on the next day a tragedy we are about to consider was performed
on the streets of Baltimore -- the President and his cabinet, with
the General-in-Chief, might have been assassinated or made prisoners, the archives and buildings of the government seized and Jefferson Davis proclaimed a dictator from the great eastern portico
of the Capitol, where Mr. Lincoln was inaugurated 45 days before.
These citizen soldiers well deserved the thanks of the Nation voted
by Congress at its called session in July following and a grateful
people will ever delight to do homage to their patriotism.*

The Logan Guards, and the other First Defenders from Pennsylvania, would bivouac throughout the halls of Congress at the end
of this harrowing day. Most men from Mifflin County appeared
safe and sound, hale and hardy, keen to begin their three months in
Federal service.

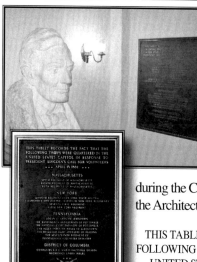

AOC Plaque Program, Washington, DC

Plaque recalling First Defenders and volunteer troops quartered in the US Capitol, April 1861 — Placed December 17, 1965, the bronze plaque can be found at the East Front Entrance, United States Capitol first floor on the House side, flanked by a bust of Lincoln. The plaque was authorized during the Civil War Centennial. The text from the Architect of the Capitol reads:

THIS TABLET RECORDS THE FACT THAT THE
FOLLOWING TROOPS WERE QUARTERED IN THE
UNITED STATES CAPITOL IN RESPONSE TO
PRESIDENT LINCOLN'S CALL FOR VOLUNTEERS
*** APRIL 15, 1861 ***

MASSACHUSETTS
Sixth Regiment Of Massachusetts
Eighth Regiment Of Massachusetts
Fifth Regiment Of Massachusetts

NEW YORK
Seventh Regiment (New York State Militia)
Ellsworth's Fire Zouaves (Eleventh New York Regiment)
Seventy-first Regiment
Fifth New York Regiment

PENNSYLVANIA
Logan Guards of Lewistown
The Washington Artillerists of Pottsville
The National Light Infantry of Pottsville
The Allen Infantry Rifles of Allentown
The Ringgold Light Artillery of Reading
The Seventeenth Regiment of
Pennsylvania Volunteer Infantry

DISTRICT OF COLUMBIA
Companies E. A. C. and F (National Guard)
Mechanics' Union Rifles

Authorized By 88th Congress Of The United States – August 17, 1964

- 5 -
ON THE SOFT SIDE OF A STONE FLOOR

BIVOUAC IN THE CAPITOL ROTUNDA — Contemporary image from *Harper's Weekly* showing some of the first volunteers to reach Washington camping in the U.S. Capitol building. A Logan Guardsman wrote, "We are quartered in the Hall of the House of Representatives and some five thousand volunteers are quartered throughout the building."
– From a letter printed in Lewistown's *True Democrat,* May 1861

The First Defenders arrived in Washington, D.C at 6:00 p.m., April 18th and were marched to the Capitol Building. The tired and hunger volunteers all agreed that they were glad to have made it and proceeded to erect barricades. William F. McCay remembered the events in the Logan's history:

> *We finally reached the Baltimore and Ohio Depot at Washington about dusk, and marched to the Capitol building, the Logans being on the right of the line and, consequently, being the first company of volunteers to enter the Capitol building for its defense. We were very tired and hungry, but immediately began to barricade all the open space and corridors in the building with barrels of cement and the iron plates which were intended for the dome, it being unfinished.*
>
> *In a short time every gas jet was lighted, and the secessionists*

down in the city (and they were legion) heard that ten thousand Yankee volunteers had just marched into the Capitol. Many believing this, did not wait for the morrow, but 'skedaddled' in hot haste across the Long Bridge and down the river to Alexandria, which was garrisoned by General Ben McCullough with eight thousand men. We got our first taste of hardtack and bacon that night, and one of our Logans absolutely shed tears because he could not get more than one teaspoonful of sugar in his coffee. This young man found afterward how to endure privations, made a good soldier, and, by his own merits, rose to the rank of captain in the Forty-Ninth Pennsylvania Volunteers. We occupied the hall of the House and, while there, we organized a Congress of our own, George W. Elberty being elected Speaker.

Later, on the evening of April 18, the Pennsylvania volunteers were quartered throughout the Capitol. The Logan Guards occupied the hall of the House of Representatives. Bates' *History of Pennsylvania Volunteers* reflects on the day's events:

At 9:00 o'clock P. M. of the day of their arrival in Washington, April 18, 1861, the five companies of the First Defenders, then quartered in the committee rooms and corridors of the Senate and the House of Representatives, were marched to the basement of the Capitol…

New Springfield rifles from the United States arsenal were distributed to the men, along with ammunition and other equipment, all packed in boxes freshly opened in the presence of the First Defenders. President Lincoln, Secretary of State William H. Seward, and Secretary of War Simon Cameron were in attendance at the distribution of these weapons. President Lincoln passed down the line of volunteers, shaking hands as each man was issued his new weapon.

Bates' narrative continues:

This visit of President Lincoln and his Secretaries of State and War most forcibly expressed the relief which the presence of these First Defenders afforded, as well as the generous purpose of Mr. Lincoln and his Cabinet to honor those who first responded to their call for volunteers.

The next day, prayers of thanks swept through many a home, and through the halls of power in the North, as the First Defenders took up their positions in and around Washington, D.C.

Governor Curtin himself gave public thanks and again vowed to never let another Pennsylvania volunteer leave the Commonwealth so ill-equipped as these men. In the area now called Camp Hill, across the Susquehanna from Harrisburg, a military training center was established at what was known as Camp Curtin. Most of the State's regiments prepared there for the conflict.

Much of the details of a soldiers daily life during the Civil War years is derived from letters to family or friends and from diaries. Correspondence was freely shared around the community, and regularly appeared in local newspapers for all to read. By the end of the first week of the Logan Guards' absence nearly 50 letters were received in one day at the Lewistown Post Office from members of the company. Letters were read by so many relatives, friends and neighbors that the paper on which they were written literally "went to pieces" by one account. In many letters home, sentences like the following can be found:

"I am proud to say that the Logan Guards were the first volunteer company to reach Washington." Another: "We were the first

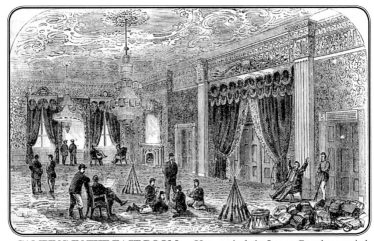

CAMPING IN THE EAST ROOM — Upon arrival, the Logan Guards occupied parts of the US Capitol. Lossing's *Pictorial History of the Civil War* illustrates Union volunteers billeted in the Presidential mansion in Washington. Here, Union soldiers are in the East Room, and had been sleeping on the carpet, prompting the president's secretary, John Nicolay, to say, "The White House has turned into a barrack." – The White House Historical Association, Teacher's Study guide for *Lincoln and the Civil War*.

company of volunteers to set foot in Washington, and were very warmly welcomed, as an attack was expected that night." Writing of the luxuries enjoyed while quartered in the House of Representatives at Washington, one soldier explained, "We sleep on the soft side of a stone floor and snore as much as we want." Another stated, "We use our big crackers for plates and then eat the plates." Another wittily thanks the donors "for the combs sent, which had been needed for several days, especially the fine ones."

A letter from soldiers in the field were eagerly awaited by those at home. Some of the Civil War's moist poignant moments have been revealed through correspondence .

This letter appeared in Lewistown's *True Democrat* on May 2, 1861, under LOCAL AFFAIRS. The preface began, *From the "Logan Guards."*

We find the following letter in Saturday's Bulletin (Philadelphia) *from a member of the "Logan Guards" at Washington, addressed to his brother "typos" at L. Johnson & Co., Philadelphia – The initials indicate the writer to be L.* (Lucien) *T. Snyder, of this place* (Lewistown) *for some time employed in the establishment referred to:*

Washington City, April 22, 1861

Dear Boys: - I do not know when this will reach you. All communication with the North has been out since Saturday. We don't know what they are thinking of doing in the North, but our determination is to stand for the Flag, and keep step to the music of the Union. We have our motto, a death's head printed on a coffin, with the cross bones, &c. Every man courts death and fear is a stranger in the minds of our volunteers. We are quartered in the Hall of the House of Representatives and some five thousand volunteers are quartered throughout the building. Our fare is of the roughest description, but entirely acceptable. Let me give you a sketch of my adventures since I left you. Left Philadelphia at

CAMP CURTAIN, TRAINING PA VOLUNTEERS — After the Baltimore Riot, Governor Andrew G. Curtin's affirmation that no Pennsylvania soldier would leave the Commonwealth so ill prepared as did the First Defenders. In the area now called Camp Hill, across the Susquehanna River from Harrisburg, a military training center was established at what was known as Camp Curtin. Most of the State's regiments prepared at this training ground during the Civil War. – Courtesy MCHS Archives

noon, reached Harrisburg at 4 O'clock, and found our company had hastily departed for Washington before I arrived. – Having received a dispatch from the Secretary of War that the Capital was in danger, and all possible dispatch was to be used, in order to reach here in time for its defense. I am proud to say that the Logan Guards was the first volunteer company from Pennsylvania to reach Washington. I found they had departed from Harrisburg, so I called on Governor Curtin and General Hale. Just as I engaged in conversation with these gentlemen, a dispatch came the Logan Boys had been mobbed in Baltimore, and that many of them were severely injured. Curtin was much affected and hardly knew what to do. He had dispatches to send there and to make a long story short, I brought them.

I am now with the boys, and would rather remain here than be in Harrisburg... And now for a description of my mode of living. My first supper here consisted of a navy biscuit and a tin-cup of water. This morning we had coffee for the first time, and plenty of beef and flitch (bacon). We live like Lords, and care but little for anything but a fight. I only wish I had a blanket and a revolver. They are indispensable to a soldier. We slept on the soft side of a stone floor and snore as much as we want. On Saturday night the

Government forces seized 1200 barrels of flour intended for the Secessionists at or near Georgetown. We now have plenty to eat and a spoiling for a fight. I have no more time to write more, and don't know when I will be able to write again. (Unreadable) *...the midst of a riot in Baltimore, but have no time to give you an account of the fearful scenes enacted.*

Yours, &c.,   L. T. S.

Another letter from a companion of Snyder's appeared in the same edition of *The True Democrat*. Sgt. Joseph S. Waream of the Logan Guards wrote to his family, and the newspaper editor was permitted to publish an extract. Waream wrote, in part:

I doubt very much if our company will be marched out of the city. I think we will be kept here with the other Pennsylvania troops to protect the Capitol. There are now 12,000 troops here and more arriving everyday... I doubt they can muster enough troops in the South now to take the Capitol now. The danger was when we first came. We were the first company of volunteers to set foot in Washington, and were very warmly welcomed... Chauncey Shull and Samuel Comfort came on the day, and were in the riot at Baltimore, but having no uniforms, escaped unscathed. When we came through the day before we were abused most foully, but no one was hurt much. Some two or three were hit with stones. I suppose Lewistown seems quiet without us, and you are all anxiously awaiting news from us. There will be many joyous countenances and light hearts when mail from the North arrives here...

You ought to see us. We are as lively as crickets. You should see how full of life the boys are - in fact they feel perfectly at home. It would amuse you to see us at table - each man has a cracker as big as a plate, and so hard that it would almost require a sledge hammer to break it. We then get a piece of

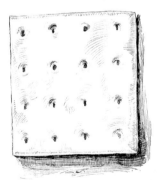

We got our first taste *of hardtack and bacon that night, and one of our Logans absolutely shed tears because he could not get more than one teaspoonful of sugar in his coffee.* – William F. McCay

Another name was skillygalee *"...soaking hardtack in cold water, then frying them brown in pork fat, salted to taste...* – John D. Billings, *Hardtack & Coffee* 1887

beef or flitch, it don't matter which, nor how it is cooked, a tin cup full of coffee with sugar... We have rice occasionally. No knives, forks or spoons. We use our cracker for plates, and then eat the plate. I got leave of absence for Saturday, and with L. T. Snyder (who came on with James Jackson) went up town and had dinner with Harry Frysinger. You may guess whether we didn't "pitch in" to the dinner we got there, and whether we enjoyed the peaches and cream that followed...

Troops made their way to the Capital from across the North to support the Pennsylvania volunteers. A soldier from New Hampshire gave the following description of his regiment upon its arrival in Washington, D.C. to reinforce the First Defenders:

We are warriors now in full feathers and trappings: ten pounds of gun: eighty rounds per man of ball cartridge, one pound of powder, five pounds of lead, heavy equipments; knapsack, haversack, three-pint canteen, all full; three days' rations; rubber blanket, woolen blanket, shelter tent, full winter clothing; tin cup, tin plate, knife, fork, spoon, spider, et cetera too numerous to mention, and too many to carry, and a pound of mud on each shoe.

HARDTACK — An example of actual Civil War hardtack is on exhibit at the McCoy House Museum, 17 N. Main Street, Lewistown, PA.

Unlike the New England soldier above, the Logan Guards arrived lacking many things. The Ladies

Volunteer Aid Association of Lewistown, later called simply "Soldiers' Aid," aimed to correct that condition as quickly as possible. The organization was formed on the evening of May 28, 1861, at a meeting held at the home of George W. Elder at which time the following officers were elected: President, Mrs. H. J. Walters; secretary, Mrs. F. J. Hoffman; treasurer, Mrs. G. W. Elder; managers, Mesdames George Frysinger, R. H. McClintic, M. M. Faxon, Jerman Jacob, J. D. Simpson, and Misses Maggie Blymer, Martha Stoner, Phoebe Weekes, Emma Milliken, Jane A. Kerr.

This group of patriotic women and girls banded together to furnish "their boys" with articles of clothing, sewing kits, soap, candies, stationery, and many other articles not ordinarily obtainable to the volunteers; especially welcome were homemade foods straight from a wife or mother. Uniforms arrived for the Logan Guards at the end of May, but one item especially requested early on... fresh underwear.

THE HAVELOCK

In two months time, Soldiers' Aid had made 625 havelocks; 425 of which were sent to Colonel Irwin for his Seventh Regiment, then encamped near Chambersburg; 100 to the Logan Guards, and 100 to Major Haskin for the Regulars under his command at Fort Washington. A box of hospital related items was also sent to Miss Dorothea Dix at Washington, D.C., also a number of pocket cases containing needles, thread, pins and buttons. These cases were assembled and sent at the suggestion of Miss Dix who was the Superintendent of Union Army Nurses.

The havelock was a white cap cover with a long tail draping over the wearer's neck and shoulders. It was considered fashionable military apparel in the late 1850s in hot climates, ostensibly to prevent sunstroke. The cap cover was made popular by Sir Henry Havelock of the British army in the Sepoy Rebellion in India in 1857.

A *Gazette* item concerning havelocks dated June 6, 1861:

Our ladies continue to devote their time and means to the manufacture of articles for the comfort of our soldiers, and on Saturday last sent off 90 havelocks for the Logan Guards, and since then, 420 for the use of Col. Wm. H. Irwin's regiment at Chambersburg. In addition to such matters many presents have been contributed, embracing choice delicacies for table use, &c. No less than three boxes were forwarded on Saturday last.

HAVELOCK IN THE FIELD
Col. Lewis Wallace of the 11th Indiana Volunteers is shown in western Virginia wearing a havelock in the August 10, 1861 issue of *Frank Leslie's Illustrated Newspaper.* He would rise to Major General, oversee the trial of infamous Andersonville Prison commandant Henry Wirz, and was author of the novel *Ben Hur.* – Courtesy MCHS Archives

Accounts attest that the havelock actually made soldiers hotter. Some contemporary reports indicate Union and Confederate soldiers alike used their havelocks not as cap covers, but as coffee strainers, dishcloths, or gun patches. One soldier from Pennsylvania reported his whole regiment received havelocks made by ladies in their home county. (The source didn't specify if it could have been Mifflin County.) "We sent home thanks and threw the head bags away." The havelock was soon eliminated from uniform requisitions when soldiers found that it cut off air circulation around the head and face. No letters from Mifflin County soldiers have been discovered to date expressing what must have been a general negative feeling about the havelock in the field. To the contrary, the following is an example of many that were published in local newspapers.

Fort Washington, MD
June 25th, l861
To MRS. H. J. Walters,
President Soldier's Aid Association
Lewistown, Penna.
Madam—Your letter accompanying the Havelocks for the use of the Regiment under my command has been received, and a pair

of slippers for myself, has been received. I truly appreciate the kindly feelings which prompted these useful gifts. For the Havelocks, the Regulars heartily thank you—and for the slippers, which are a marvelous proper fit and a "convenience" that I have for some time desired, and beg you to accept my grateful acknowledgements.

As for my "kindness and courtesy towards your volunteers," I can only say I have endeavored to do my duty, and am sincerely pleased that my manner of doing it has met the approbation of their cherished relations and friends at home.

I heartily unite with you in your sincere desire for an early termination of the unfortunate contest in which we are now engaged, and sincerely pray that, in the good providence of God, the time may soon come when Union, happiness and prosperity will again be restored to our beloved country.

I am, Madam, most respectfully, your obedient servant.

J. A. Haskins

Bvt. Maj. and Capt., 1st Art'y.

By all accounts, the Logan Guards were complete thankful for all the items sent from home. The *Gazette* published this item and letter, also dated June 1861:

The overcoats, knapsacks, canteens, haversacks, and shoes of the Logan Guards, were received on the 30th of May having it appears been stored at the Navy Yard at Washington for some time. The company also received the leather sacks forwarded by the ladies of Lewistown including many useful articles in camp life, for which, as will be seen by the following resolutions, they are duly grateful.

FORT WASHINGTON, MD
May 30. 1861.}
At a meeting of the Logan Guards at Fort Washington, the following resolutions were unanimously adopted, and the Clerk of the company instructed to forward a copy to the newspapers of Mifflin county and request their publication:

Resolved, That the Logan Guards acknowledge the receipt and tender their warmest thanks for a copy of the New Testament for

Soldiers' Aid sewing havelocks.

each member of the company from the Female Bible Society of Lewistown.

Resoled, That the cordial and unanimous thanks of the Logan Guards, be tendered to the citizens of Lewistown generally, and the ladies especially, for the many useful and handsome presents this day received from their hands.

Resolved, That we again pledge our unalterable devotion to the American Union, and promise that we will not alter should an opportunity offer to protect the flag of our country, the lives and property of our citizens, and the mothers, wives, daughters and sweet-hearts of our homes.

These resolutions were unanimously adopted when put by Capt. Hulings, and the meeting adjourned with three hearty cheers and a tiger for the ladies of Lewistown.

J. A. MATHEWS, Clerk.

LETTERS HOME

Another perspective from Washington, D.C. was sent to George R. Frysinger, and published for all to read. It remained a common method of spreading news throughout the community:

Correspondence of the Gazette
FORT WASHINGTON, MD}
Friday, June 7, 1861

Friend Frysinger —War's loud alarms have been completely drowned by the voice of the Logan Boys since the arrival here of several boxes of eatables, made up at short notice by the nimble fingers of the patriotic ladies of our town. 'Long laces grew short, smiles succeeded frowns, cheers took the place of "growls," and every one was tickled at the idea of receiving something from "home, sweet home." Nor were they disappointed in their "ideas." Flitch and mess pork have given way to tomatoes and green peas;

army crackers and navy biscuit have succumbed to pound cake and ginger snaps; and bean soup is not even looked at when the multitudinous cans of peaches, raspberries, apples, pears, plumbs, rhubarb and pickles, and the bottles of catsup are thought of without mentioning, as an Irishman might, could, or should say, the butter and molasses in many of the largest cans. Of course our men share with each other. Nothing is eaten by one man unless a-general invitation is extended to all to partake; and I really believe that not a single mouthful is eaten by any man without its being succeeded by a complimentary allusion to or remark about the Lewistown ladies—God bless them! In fact, if you were ubiquitous, or could exercise the power of an Asmodeus (a Biblical demon), and look in upon the happy hearts of our gallant boys, you would undoubtedly say that in no movement heretofore undertaken have the friends of the company, and especially the ladies, struck a cord that so tremulously vibrated to such tender touches.

Cheers, with tigers attached, went up for the donors, when the boxes were received, as well as for those gentlemen through whose energy and determination the boxes were packed and forwarded...

How many changes can be made within a little time. When first we reached the National Capitol, we received the sobriquet of the "Fan Tail Rangers,"—induced, I suppose by the open work appearance of our motley uniforms. Then all was alarm and confusion. Uncle Samuel was pronounced "defunct" but before his body had time to become cold some of his distant relatives commenced Jeffing (a traditional gambling game) for his garments, and a lady-fair sent her Beauregard upon hearing of

WRITING A LETTER HOME
Letters from soldiers to their families and friends form a unique primary source of military life during the Civil War. Image from John D. Billings' *Hardtack & Coffee*, 1887 – Courtesy MCHS Archives

his sudden death. But viola! the people placed another Link into the chain of life, and the reckless garments cannot now escape Scott free. Now, you should see us. A comfortable barrack—plenty of room—the cool river breeze on a sultry day—plenty to eat and drink—under the eye of a veteran officer— equalling the regulars in drill and manoeuvres—well armed and equipped—and better clothed than any volunteer company I have yet seen, we are indeed, more favored than the rest. Then, we were pronounced "Wild Cats," "Fan Tail Rangers." &c. Now, both State and Government authorities are denounced for "petting" the Logan boys. But, some persona will growl.

We are all in good health and perfectly contented with our positions- excepting, probably, two or three dissatisfied spirits, who would find fault with the Almighty himself, were he connected with the volunteer organization.

News also came home with soldiers on leave. This June 1861 *Gazette* item was headlined ARRIVAL of SOLDIERS, and reported:

Sergeant Jos. S. Waream and Lucien T. Snyder of the Logan Guards arrived here on Thursday last, and were heartily greeted by all classes. They represent the company in good condition, in fine spirits, and ready for a big or a little fight. On Friday evening Lieut. Col. Selheimer of the 25th Regiment, made his appearance, and also received a warm welcome. Messrs. Waream and Snyder returned on Saturday, and Lieut. Col. S. on Monday.

Sergeant Chauncey M. Shull refers to the visit of Waream and Snyder, and further describes the existing conditions in and around Fort Washington in this excerpt from a private letter home:

Fort Washington, Md.}
June 6, 1861.
We are in no danger here now. We are just as safe as if we were at home. The very devil himself could not take our fort now. We have everything in ample order for defense. Our hard work is over and we have nothing to do but drill and stand guard. Of the latter I have none to do, although I am Sergeant of the Guard today — that is, I have charge of the guard and the main entrance to the fort. No person can pass in or out without my permission. It is rather an important post. During the time I hold this position I dare not sleep

a wink under penalty of death.

We have had fine living since Waream and Snyder came back and, besides that, we have been furnished with very nice overcoats, knapsacks, canteens, etc. We have excellent quarters and, if we get a mattress or something of the kind to sleep on, we will need nothing more. We will then be as comfortable as could be expected. We received all the things the citizens of Lewistown had the kindness to send us, and it is unnecessary for me to return my thanks, as they can imagine themselves how glad we are to receive anything from home.

JOURNALS AND DIARIES

Diaries were an additional way to record events experienced by the soldiers. The following excerpts from the diary of Sergeant Valentine Stichter, of the Washington Artillerists, reveals the daily routine, the soldier's day, experienced by a First Defender:

April, 1861

21—Sunday. On guard from Saturday evening, 7:30 o'clock until Sunday evening at 8:00 o'clock. Read a chapter in the Bible to comrades in the evening. A certain attack on the Capitol last night; all prepared; squads barricading the inlets and windows with flour, which was seized at Georgetown : 6,000 barrels.

22—On guard for seven hours shift.

23—Had a dress parade in the park. Trouble about our cooking arrangements. Moved quarters.

24—More troops arrived from New York, a regiment of 1000. Numbered the muskets today. On 24 hours shift guard at upper door. Flour seized by the U. S. Government, amounting to 7000 barrels, making in all 13,000 barrels, with rice, coffee and sugar.

25—Paid a visit to patent office and post office. Park parade; cheers given for our company. Gave Massachusetts regiment a serenade with the comb band. Longed to see friends at home.

Constant drilling turned the First Defenders into well oiled military units. Image from *Hardtack & Coffee*, 1887. – Courtesy MCHS Archives

26—Had dress parade in park for three hours. Downtown and bought wearing apparel. Rhode Island and Massachusetts troops arrived. All well today. Seen President Lincoln and lady in park. New York regiment sworn in.

27—In park, 1600 Pennsylvania troops arrived. Received shoes, blankets, etc.

28—Sunday. Chapter road out of Bible by Captain Wren. Prayer by Frank Myers. President Lincoln visited all the volunteers. Shook hands with him and Secretary Seward. Visited Long Bridge. On guard from 7:00 o'clock last evening. Twenty-four hours shift. Preaching in the Senate Chamber T. Wrote letter home.

29—Parade in park three and a half hours. Squad went downtown to exchange shoes. Another Massachusetts regiment arrived.

30—Drill in the park. Orders at 1:00 o'clock to proceed to Fort Washington; in half an hour all prepared for the march and on our way; 1:30 o'clock arrived at Navy Yard; boarded the steamer Philadelphia seized by the government; passed Alexandria, Palmetto flag floating over the city; the dock was commanded by rebels with two brass six-pounders; prepared for an attack with 32-pound shells on steamer; arrived at Fort Washington at 6:30 o'clock; packed in a small house with the Logan Guards.

DUTY AT FORT WASHINGTON

On April 30th, First Defender companies, including the Logan Guards, were moved to Fort Washington. The fortification was located a few miles below Mt. Vernon, approximately 15 miles south of the Capital on the Maryland side of the Potomac River. Except for a few guns at the Washington Arsenal, Fort Washington was the only defense for the Capital, until a circle of temporary forts was completed around the city after the Civil War began. The Logan Guards worked to put the fort in order for what some considered an attack on the arsenal and Navy Yard nearby. The original roster of volunteers was significantly altered by this time due to promotions and transfers.

In a letter home from Fort Washington, the writer states that they are on guard for 24 hours; two hours on and four hours off around the clock. Their day began at sunrise, breakfast 10 minutes later, a meal at 12 noon, and if their rations were not completely eaten, supper at 6 p.m. Fisheries located along the river provided alternative fare, prompting many volunteers to trade their Army pork for shad, herring and other local fish.

A letter from Lucien T. Snyder appeared in the *Gazette*, dated May 6, 1861, pointed out the activities in preparing the fort, as well as some of the hardships, endured there too, writing:

Dear Boys: Received your letter Saturday evening. We received our orders on Tuesday for this place. The Secessionist scamps were going to take this night before last, but failed to attempt it. We work night and day, cutting trees, digging trenches, mounting guns, &c. We have but two batteries casemented (ready for action), *but they are grape and canister, and can sweep into eternity any storming party that can be sent to take us.... Major Haskins, the commander, says he never saw one company do as much work in as short a time as ours has done. He says, "If you can fight as well as you work, boys, I am perfectly satisfied." We have no paper, pen, or ink here for our own use. There is a store here from which we could get the necessities of life, if we had the means. If any one around the firm has a gold dollar, or two, they would be welcome visitors here. Pennsylvania bank notes are not saleable here. We eat pork and crackers still, and never get sight of a plate, knife or fork. Are not allowed to go to Washington (16 miles from here) not even the officers. Expect an attack tonight, but I believe the cowardly whelps will not undertake to storm us. Eleven thou-*

UNION FORT ca 1861

Mr. Elder, of this place, whose departure we noticed last week, informs us that the clothing for the Logan Guards was at the Washington Navy Yard on Monday a week awaiting a requisition, and that the U. S. Government would also issue a requisition for another set, so that the Guards would be amply provided. If therefore the clothing has not been received the fault does not lie with the State authorities.

The Lewistown *Gazette* reported on attorney George W. Elder's mission to Harrisburg and Washington to secure supplies for the Logan Guards. – Courtesy MCHS Archives

sand Secessionists are encamped about nine miles from here. We may have a fight; if so, you will hear from me or about me. I send this enclosed in another letter, as I have no stamps - neither have I the means to procure one. We are all in good health, and waiting to see them take down our glorious flag. They must first annihilate our company... We are not yet supplied with our clothing or blankets, and still sleep on the floor. Our supplies have not yet reached us, but whether they reach us or not, we will still "keep step to the music of the Union."

By mid-May, the promised uniforms and supplies for the Logan Guards had still not been supplied. Local newspapers editorialized on the deplorable plight of "our boys" not yet provided with necessities, including under clothing. In the May 16th edition, the *Gazette* lambasted the "powers that be" for the delay, decrying "although it was said every day that they (supplies and uniforms) were expected, up to last week had not arrived." A delegation of prominent local citizens, headed by attorney George W. Elder, Esq., left for Harrisburg and then Washington to probe the delay. The *Gazette* declared, "...if it can be shown that the neglect was either wilful or premeditated, the officeholder had better prepare to make tracks for the dominion of Old Nick, alias Jef. Davis."

Apparently finding no fault with the quarter mastering process at the State Capital, Mr. Elder's investigation revealed that the clothing for the Logan Guards was at the Washington Navy Yard awaiting Army requisition. Eventually, supplies for the men arrived on May 30th, including: overcoats, knapsacks, canteens, haversacks and shoes. Other necessary materials followed in short order.

A private letter published in the *Gazette*, dated June 6, 1861 tells of another type of experience at Fort Washington, explaining:

Four slaves came to the fort yesterday from Sewell's Point.

They said they had to fight till they fell down exhausted. When they got up again, nobody was about, so they took their master's boat, worth about $50, and came here in it. They were sent to Washington City. I suppose according to the Dred Scott decision they will be confiscated property...

Most of the chores securing Fort Washington and making it fit as a defensive location were completed, as the men settled into a routine that was described by some as endless drill. It was here that the Logan Guards learned to be soldiers, their basic training, as it were. One soldier recalled in a somewhat typical letter home, "We awake each morning for drill. Then breakfast and some more drill. A break for lunch, followed by afternoon drill, and after the evening meal we have more drill until bedtime."

Some of the boredom was mitigated when parcels arrived from home. The folks back in Mifflin County developed a well-oiled system of sending packages of necessities, and delicacies, to the men in the field. This "service" was deeply appreciated by the men, usually scarce of cash to buy those little niceties not provided by the army. Occasionally, a donor of a hometown parcel would smuggle a little "bark juice" or "apple lady," as the men might call cherished alcoholic liquid. Such goodies must have gotten through, as this somewhat incensed editorial in the *Gazette* of June 20, 1861 attests:

Considerable feeling has been created among the Ladies Association as well as others, by an apparently well-founded report that advantage was taken by some persons to forward liquor in cans, etc., with false labels in the boxes which were forwarded to our soldiers.

A brief memorandum in First Sergeant Mathews' morning report notes that some "liquid contraband" must have reached its

Liquid Contraband? Smuggled in a tin can? Pshaw! — It vexed the editor of the Lewistown *Gazette* that someone would send spirits to the "boys" in D.C.

desired recipient, as he wrote: *Private _____, To one Kettle Drum. Broke when drunk. $1.75.*

Pay was an issue and was not always forthcoming. Willis Copeland wrote that the Logan Guards would not be paid for their three month service until their term ended. The general rule was to be paid every two months in the Union Army, however it often stretched to every four months.

Volunteer army troops, when brought into Federal service were to follow a set pay scale. *The Civil War Dictionary* explains that privates received $13 to start, with pay raises up to $16 per month by 1864. Infantry officers at the start of the war: colonels, $212; lieutenant colonels, $181; majors, $169; captains, $115.50; first lieutenants, $105.50; and second lieutenants, $105.50. Other line and staff officers drew an average of about $15 per month more. One, two, and three star generals received $315, $457, and $758 respectively.

The Logan Guards term of service went two weeks beyond their three month enlistments. In a letter published that June in the *Gazette*, a writer explained:

ARRIVAL OF PARCELS & LETTERS FROM HOME — One letter to the *Gazette* editor cheered, *"... every one was tickled at the idea of receiving something from "home, sweet home."* Image from *Hardtack & Coffee*, 1887 – Courtesy MCHS Archives

CIVIL WAR-ERA ENVELOPES often bore patriotic illustrations, like this example sent to Capt. John B. Selheimer while he was stationed at Fort Washington, Maryland. The original is in the State Museum, Harrisburg, donated by his family after his death in 1893. – Courtesy MCHS Archives

Our hard work is finished. We have little or nothing to do than drill; and when we return home you will see a company of perfectly-drilled and thoroughly disciplined soldiers. Brevet Major Haskins, the commander of the post, informed me the day after my arrival here, that from the tenor of the dispatches he had that moment received, he inferred that we would remain here until the expiration of our time...

Days and weeks of boredom, interspersed with intense activity is the soldiers lot. Years later, some of the Logan Guards at the fort recalled July 21, 1861, as an oppressively hot. The Battle of Bull Run was fought across the Potomac River that day, well within earshot of the men manning Fort Washington. When word came that Federal troops were routed, Fort Washington was alerted to expect an attack that night. The guns were trained on the opposite shore and loaded, some double loaded with canister shot, in anticipation of the Confederate assault. None came.

During down time at Fort Washington, the Logan Guards showed themselves resourceful in what might be called camp amusements, as stories of their off duty activities made it home via letters, visitors' tales or men on leave. The company held cotillions on the fort green and, in the absence of ladies, the dancers were kept busy to know who was "it," leading to awkward moments followed by gales of laughter, and much knee-slapping.

John D. Billings wrote in his 1887 memoir of a soldier's life, *Hardtack and Coffee*, about entertainment among the enlisted men in the typical Civil War camp:

There was probably not a regiment in the service that did not boast at least one violinist, one banjoist, and a bone player in its ranks... and one or all of them could be heard in operation... most of a pleasant evening... However unskilled the artist, they were sure to be the centre of an interested audience...

Among the Logan Guards at Fort Washington, Augustus "Gus" Smith played the fiddle, while Private Chauncey Shull called the dances. Another diversion was the theatrical-like performances in regularly organized "soldiers' shows." One published letter sent home recalled Elias Eisenbise, nicknamed "Lide" by his comrades, sang the lead in one particular show. "The Rock Beside the Sea" – acclaimed by the men as Eisenbise's most memorably delivered presentation – was a romantic ballad accompanied by piano, or in this case, by violin. A popular mid-19th century "romanza," the piece was composed by Charles C. Converse in 1852, dedicated to Mrs. M. A. Ralston of the Oakland Female Institute of Norristown, Pa. Those who heard Eisenbise attested in letters sent home, or by word-of-mouth when on leave, that he "left nothing to be desired."

This and myriad other stories entertained the veterans in later years at the annual reunions. Yet one place was always fondly reserved in the memory for the gifts and letters that arrived from home. Comfort for the men from the folks back in Mifflin County came in many guises.

CHARLES CROZAT CONVERSE , (Oct. 7, 1832 - Oct. 18, 1918) was an attorney in Erie, PA, also composed church songs. Born in Warren, Massachusetts, perhaps his most notable song today is the hymn "What a Friend We Have in Jesus." However, his 1852 romanza, "The Rock Beside the Sea" was popular with the Logan Guards while encamped at Fort Washington. Imagine Private Elias Eisenbise, in feminine guise, rendering these lines during a "soldiers' show" to the raucous enjoyment of his all-male audience:

> *Unto my watching heart are more*
> *Than all earth's melodies.*
> *Come back, my ocean rover, come!*
> *There's but one place for me,*
> *Till I can greet thy swift sail home --*
> *My lone rock by the sea!*

– Author's collection

[83]

- 6 -
EVEN THE LITTLE FOLKS HELPED

U.S. Army Regular
Dress Uniform

A wave of patriotic fervor swept Mifflin County in these early days of the Civil War, enlivened by the responsive action of the Logan Guards in April. As the momentum of the war increased, men from across Mifflin County joined dozens of military units around the state. Lewistown's patriotic zeal in 1861 was also duplicated around Mifflin County. In McVeytown, Newton Hamilton, Belleville, Reedsville, Milroy, and in some of the townships, large and enthusiastic meetings were held at which the citizens pledged their hearty support to the Union government. Thousands of dollars would also be pledged for the support of families of volunteers already in service.

New military companies were forming monthly, including the Mifflin County Zouaves under Capt. Jacob Linthurst. This company, numbering 42 men, took part in the Fourth of July ceremonies in 1861 at Milroy by performing the "Ellsworth Drill," a series of intricate and precise close-order infantry maneuvers executed in quick time, using drum taps as signals. The drill takes its name from Col. Elmer Ephraim Ellsworth of Illinois, considered the first Union martyr, and founder of the U.S. Zouave movement so popular at the time. The units possessed a unique esprit-de-corps, and the exotic uniforms were inspired by the French Zouaves of North Africa.

The Slemmer Guards were drilling every evening in the Brick Pond School yard (along West Third Street). Most of these young men later served the Union during the war.

Zouave Uniform

[84]

The Belleville Fencibles were engaged in drilling and in building the company up to maximum strength. They were to become Company C of the 45th Pennsylvania Volunteer Infantry on September 25, Captain William G. Bigelow commanding.

It became common place to see advertisements in the newspapers notifying men to be ready to leave with their units on short notice. The following appeared in a July issue of the Lewistown *Gazette*:

*Mifflin County Dragoons —
Attention!*

By authority of the War Department I hereby call upon the Mifflin County Dragoons to be ready to muster into service at the earliest notice, and to report themselves with their horses at my office immediately for the regular service of the United States in the present war. They will receive 40 cents per day for their horses, and if disabled, will be paid for in full, as directed by the Secretary of War. Arms and equipments to be furnished in full by the U. S.

*By order of
G. V. MITCHELL
Captain*

The Dragoons left Lewistown on August 7, and were mustered into the First Pennsylvania Volunteer Cavalry as Company C, Captain John P. Taylor commanding, on August 10.

Adam J. Slemmer, namesake of Lewistown's Slemmer Guards. The male youth of the town who made up this unique uniformed unit, took the hero of Fort Pickens as their role model. The Slemmers were not intended for military service due to their age, but served as an honor guard for the arrival and departure of local units and famous persons. They made for a sharp, martial appearance in their uniforms of cadet gray. *Harper's Weekly* described their namesake in February 1861:

Lieutenant Slemmer, is a native of Pennsylvania, where he was born about 1828. He entered West Point in 1814, and graduated as second lieutenant of artillery in 1850. He was ordered to Florida... he assumed the command of Pensacola harbor, where he still remains. When the Florida troops seized the Pensacola Navy-yard, he followed the example of Major Anderson and seized Fort Pickens as the strongest work in the harbor. At latest dates he was still in possession, and said he could hold it. Lieutenant Slemmer enjoys the reputation of a cool, brave soldier, worthy of the important trust now committed to him.

The Burns Infantry, under Captain Henry A. Zollinger, was the second military organization to leave Mifflin County, departing April 20, just four days after the Logan Guards marched to the rail station. This unit became Company I, Seventh Pennsylvania Volunteer Infantry, Colonel Irwin's regiment.

Two companies of "Home Guard" were formed in May 1861. One was composed of men 45 years of age and older, known appropriately as the Silver Grays. About 70 members organized and elected Dr. Joseph Henderson as Captain. Another company with 87 members under the age of 45 organized, with Joseph W. Parker elected captain. The *Gazette* carried an announcement addressed to "the young men of Lewistown" requesting them to gather at the Apprentices' Hall on Third Street to form a Junior Home Guard. Applicants for this group were to be advised that a height requirement was in effect, specifying five feet four inches tall, plus members must not be under 16 or over 21 years of age.

HELP FROM THE HOME FRONT

Local citizens continued to make donations for the benefit of the soldiers' families. A committee of professional gentlemen, George W. Elder, William Willis, Andrew Reed, Esq., David Mutthersbaugh and Dr. R. Martin, pledged to collect at least six thousand dollars in as short a time as possible for relief purposes.

Judging by weekly newspaper reports, necessities were sent to soldiers throughout the war. For example, a news item in 1862 described that the ladies of Wayne, Oliver and Bratton townships forwarded provisions to the United States Christian Commission (formed in the fall of 1861) for the soldiers and the wounded. In one shipment they sent: 50 shirts, 18 pairs of drawers, 10 wrappers, 10 slings, 45 bandages, 13 pairs pillow slips, 17 towels, 31 pocket handkerchiefs, 4 pillows, 8 pairs of socks, 3 cans of fruit, 3 1/2 bushels of apples, 1 1/2 bushels of dried cherries, 1 peck of dried peaches, a lot of hand bandages and some lint (cotton swabbing).

The *Gazette* reported that even the children took part in war-related activities in support the troops, laboring along side the ladies. Under the headline, "The Little Folks," a brief report told that local boys and girls sent a lot of what were called "housewives" to the sick and wounded soldiers in a Philadelphia hospital in 1863. The newspaper was pleased to announce that the children had a great reward for their kindness, explaining:

...last week their little hearts were made glad and exultation of the most buoyant kind exhibited, by the reception of quite a number of letters, returning thanks for the gifts. Many of them were written in eloquent and feeling language, others with a Christian fervor that showed the disciples of Jesus were not so rare in the army as many supposed...

What is a "housewife"? John D. Billings explained its function in his 1887 memoir. He remembered a soldier's domestic chores, and described this necessary item, writing, "Every man had a "housewife" or its equivalent, containing the necessary needles, yarn, thimble, etc., furnished him by some mother, sister, sweetheart, or Soldiers' Aid Society, and from this came his materials to mend or darn with."

Local newspapers frequently published sentiments like this that accompanied the "Little Folks" article mentioned above:

Truly we cannot do too much for our soldiers, and if all at home would but contribute towards cheering them, whether in the tented field or in hospital, how many carry reminiscences of acts of kindness, no matter how little...

A "HOUSEWIFE" OR "THE SOLDIER'S FRIEND"– After use, the enlisted man's necessities were rolled up in this cloth kit for easy field storage.

Train loads of soldiers passed through Lewistown Junction on a regular basis. Locals would gather at the station or along the rail line to cheer the passing troops. Many county soldiers had their pay sent to their relatives back home. During the month of November 1861, over eight thousand dollars was sent to Mifflin County family members by loved ones in military service. Large amounts of money would often be given to trusted relatives or friends to be safely hand delivered home.

With the increased number of men leaving for longer enlistments, and as the conflict intensified, major and minor battles resulted in published casualty lists. The names of those killed, wounded, or paroled prisoners of war, became a daily part of life back home, as readers eagerly anticipated news reports. Casualties rapidly increased, pushing authorities in Harrisburg to ask counties to help take care of their own sick and wounded. Mifflin County was able to provide hospital beds for 200 possible patients.

SENDING MONEY HOME — In one month of 1861 alone, over $8,000 was sent home to families in Mifflin County from local soldiers in service.

In addition to the published casualty lists, letters describing harrowing events and incidents surrounding the real dangers of conflict were also published. A typical example from early in the war, the *Gazette* told of a "close call" involving William T. McEwen serving in the 1st Pennsylvania Cavalry dated December 1861. The newspaper extolled that McEwen, who served five years before the war with the regular army in Texas, is "an efficient and highly esteemed officer" who was fired upon while riding with his Colonel near Drainesville, Virginia. Describing the event, the *Gazette* took a swipe at the Confederate persona of the Old South, reporting that McEwen captured a rebel lieutenant from the South Carolina "chivalry," in other words, cavalry. A letter from McEwen to his parents was published following this lead-in story. Note the specific military details he men-

Southern "Chivalry"

tions, and realize the letter was published in the newspaper; military censors in later wars would readily redact such comments. The letter appeared, in part:

Wesson's Breech-Loading Rifle.

Length of Barrel, 24 inches; Diameter of Bore, 32-100 of an inch; weight only 6 pounds.
This is the best Rifle yet invented, its great superiority consisting of rapidity and facility of loading, and being used with a metallic Cartridge, there is no escape at the breech, and cannot possibly be loaded improperly; shoots with perfect accuracy; can be used all day without cleaning, and will not heat with the most rapid firing.
J. W. STORRS,
Sole Agent, 256 Broadway.
Also Agent for Smith & Wesson's Revolvers and Cartridges.
313-380

Capt. McEwen wrote home about using the Sharps breech loading carbine. The Sharps and Spencer were the most popular brand during the Civil War, but others were produced, as this 1862 ad attests. From *Frank Leslie's Illustrated Magazine* – Courtesy MCHS Archives

Dear Father and Mother:

I received your letter but one hour since....Our men are in good health. Capt. Taylor is mending; Lieutenant Mann is very improved; he left here on Friday night with the remains of our much loved and much lamented young Surgeon, Dr. Alexander of Milroy. Poor fellow! He was shot in the abdomen by the same rebels who fired at me. I made a very narrow escape, indeed. I was riding, at the time in advance, of the Colonel of our regiment, whose horse was shot out from under him, being pierced by eleven bullets. Col. Bayard was slightly wounded in two places... One of our young townsmen, A.B. Selheimer, captured Capt. Farley, one of the South Carolina chivalry, with his own hands.

Our Colonel has confided in me the command of one hundred picked men of our regiment, who are armed with Sharpe's breech loading carbines. I am to employ them as skirmishers.

My love to our relatives and friends. I will write as my duties permit. It is snowing a little now...Our friends would do us a great kindness if they would forward us the Lewistown papers occasionally.

Your affectionate son,
William T. McEwen

AFRICAN AMERICANS JOIN

Mifflin County's free black community tendered their enthusiastic help as the war began. Parts of the county, specifically Armagh Township, held an abolitionist stance for decades prior to the Civil War. Milroy residents, like crusading anti-slavery Presbyterian minister Rev. James Nourse, and ardent abolitionist Dr. Samuel Mc-

United States Colored Troops or USCT, about 1863 — After President Lincoln signed and issued the Emancipation Proclamation on January 1, 1863, and the U.S. Army implemented General Order 143 on May 22, 1863 which established the United States Colored Troops, men of color by the tens of thousands enlisted. — Courtesy Dover Civil War Photos Collection

Clay, were prominent in the cause. McClay reputedly maintained a stop on the Underground Railway located in his Milroy home, just a few doors from Rev. Nourse's church, where the minister is interred in the churchyard.

Slavery in the United States: A Narrative of the Life and Adventures of Charles Ball was published in Lewistown in 1836 by John Shugart of the Lewistown *Republican*; later editions went under the title *Fifty Years in Chains*. It is believed Ball, an escaped slave, settled in Lewistown, where his story was transcribed by local attorney Isaac Fisher. This book predated Harriet Beecher Stowe's *Uncle Tom's Cabin* and helped explain the plight of slaves in America, invigorating local abolitionist factions.

In addition, the African Methodist Episcopal Church of Lewistown was well supported by its membership and influential in the greater community. So it came as no surprise when the Lewistown *Gazette* reported in the May 5, 1861 edition:

A meeting of the colored citizens of the community was held with Samuel Molson presiding, when it was resolved by those attending to offer their services to the State "to be used in any capacity; whether to build breastworks, dig entrenchments, or march to battle." About this time, a number of runaway slaves from Maryland and Virginia made their way through the mountains of Central Pennsylvania and were humanely treated by the citizens; a station of the "underground" being located in Mifflin County.

After President Lincoln signed and issued the Emancipation Proclamation on January 1, 1863, and the U.S. Army implemented General Order 143 on May 22, 1863 which established the United States Colored Troops, men of color by the tens of thousands enlisted.

Genealogist Jeannette L. Molson, great-great-granddaughter of Samuel Molson mentioned in the news item above, found that members of her family from Mifflin County joined the Union cause as the war progressed. Molson family members with Mifflin County connections who joined the USCT and regular army units

Avoid the Draft.
BY ENLISTING IN THE
FIRST
PA. RESERVE CAVALRY,
Or any other Pennsylvania Regiment or Battery now in Service.

$400 Bounty---$73 in Advance, will be paid to all men who re enlist, provided they have served nine months and have been honorably discharged.

$300 Bounty---$73 in Advance, will be paid to men who enlist for the first time.

Payment will be made as follows:—At the Principal Depot after being mustered into service, veterans, $60.00; new recruits $60.00; also, one month's pay in advance, $13.00—total to each, $73.00.

The remainder of the bounty will be paid in six equal instalments. Persons enlisting at the present time can have themselves credited to any Ward, Township or County in the State, and will thereby receive a Local Bounty of from one hundred and thirty to two hundred dollars, in addition to the United States Bounty.

☞ Pay and subsistence from date of enlistment. WM. H. PATTERSON.
Cap't. 1st Pa. Cavalry, Recruiting Officer, Feb. 17, 1864.3t. Lewistown Hotel.

Draft bounties equal to a laborers annual wage enticed Union enlistees, as this Lewistown *Gazette* advertisement attests. — Courtesy MCHS Archives

included: David W. Molson, PA 48th Reg't., Co. B; James S. Molson, NY 107th Reg't., Co. F; William Nelson Molson, USCT 43rd Reg't., Co. B; and Samuel B. Molson, USCT 43rd Reg't., Co. D.

The *Gazette* continued to report on the war efforts among Mifflin County's black citizens through the war years. An item appeared in the March 4, 1863 edition, after the Emancipation Proclamation was enacted:

A meeting of our colored citizens was held at the A.M.E. Church on February 10 - Samuel Molson President; Jas. Richardson, Cyrus Morrison and Isaiah Thompson Vice Presidents; H. C. Molson, William Hollins and Benj. Slater Secretaries. John L. Griffith, H. C. Molson and Wm. Palmer were appointed a committee on resolutions. H. C. Molson offered resolutions hailing the 1st of January as a new era in our county's history - offering their service to sustain the government even to the sacrifice of life - sympathizing with it in its troubles, and imploring the protection of

God on the President and friends of freedom everywhere. Resolutions somewhat similar in spirit, though different in language, were reported by John L. Griffith, when, after some patriotic remarks by the latter, both sets were unanimously adopted. The meeting passed off with good feelings throughout, and quite a number we understand are ready to take the field if wanted.

The military draft effected the community, too, as quotas were established by the Federal authorities for each county, and lists of draftees appeared in local newspapers. The Draft Law of 1863 stipulated, in part:

The Governors of the States are ordered forthwith, to proceed to furnish their respective quotas of the 300,000 militia called for by the President... They are also ordered to cause an enrollment to be made forthwith, by the Assessors of the several counties. When the enrollment is completed, it is to be filed in the offices of the Sheriffs of the several counties. The Governor is then to appoint a Commissioner for each county to superintend the draft and decide upon exemptions. Exemptions for physical disability will not be allowed, unless it unfits the claimant for service for a period of more than thirty days, and it must be certified by a Surgeon to be appointed in each county for the purpose. Within ten days ...the Sheriff of the county, who is to publicly place in a Jury wheel a separately folded ballot for each name on the list; and when they are all in, a person to be appointed by the Commissioners is to draw, blindfolded, a number of ballots, equal to the quota for the county.

Draft wheel was used to select eligible men, then lists of draftees were published in the county newspapers.
— Courtesy MCHS Archives

In that first year, for example, Mifflin County needed to provide 450 men for military service. Each volunteer credited to Mifflin County subtracted one less man from the draft. Bounties of $400 were offered by the government to re-enlist, and $300 to those enlisting for the first time. A borough or township could add $50 or $100 to this,

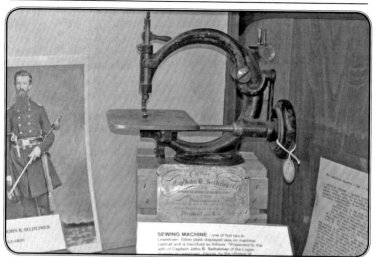

A SURPRISE PRESENT — The Lewistown *Gazette* announced in the May 9, 1861 edition, that: *Captain Selheimer's lady was not a little surprised as well as gratified on Monday evening last, on returning home from a visit, to find an elegant sewing machine in her house, bearing the following inscription: PRESENTED TO the wife of CAPTAIN JOHN B. SELHEIMER of the LOGAN GUARDS, LEWISTOWN, PA., by the citizens of PHILADELPHIA, As a token of their respect for him and his Company for their prompt respond To the call of the President of the U. S. April 15, 1861.* – Sewing machine exhibit located in the MCHS museum, McCoy House, 17 N. Main St, Lewistown, PA.

and the option to enlist was more rewarding to volunteers. Several of the townships offered a bounty of $200 to get volunteers to sign up. Under certain conditions, men could excuse themselves from the draft by paying a $300 commutation fee to the government, an amount equal to about a year's salary for an unskilled worker. This fee was used by the government to pay the bounties given to volunteer soldiers. A part of this fee was also returned to the local communities to cover part of the bounties which they paid volunteers. However, this situation contributed to the idea that the conflict was a "rich man's war and a poor man's fight," as Southern newspapers offered scathing criticism of the practice.

As for the Logan Guards, their period of enlistment had expired by the end of July 1861. The men were ready to come home, but many would re-enlist in other units almost immediately. For the First Defenders, this first phase of the war was over.

- 7 -
THREE CHEERS AND A TIGER!

Having **voluntarily served** about two weeks beyond their three month term of enlistment, the Logan Guards prepared to leave for home. Though nominally the color company of the 25th Regiment, which was called the Advance or Cameron Regiment, they never saw the regimental colors until after the end of the war when the colors were displayed at veteran reunions. It had been the intention, at the formation of the regiment, to concentrate all its companies, but, on reconsideration, it was thought unwise to move the companies on duty at Fort Washington and at the Washington Arsenal. The Logan Guards never did a day's duty with the regiment, but remained at the post to which they had been assigned. Willis Copeland notes:

Major Haskin, and the efficient officers under him at the fort, had worked kindly and zealously with the volunteers in perfecting them in their duties as soldiers, and had won the unqualified respect and esteem of the men serving under him in the three companies of First Defenders.

On Monday, July 29, 1861, the Logan Guards were mustered out of the Federal service at Harrisburg, being paid in gold, the first pay they had received for military services since leaving home. Anticipating their boys' return, the citizens of Lewistown made preparations for the homecoming of the Logan Guards.

A meeting for the purpose of formulating plans for their reception had been held in the Town Hall on July 16, with the following committee officers present: James McCord, president; George W. Stewart, William Shimp, H. Zerbe, E. Banks, George W. Patton, and John Davis, vice presidents. On motion, Joseph Alexander, N. J. Rudisill, George Frysinger, S. Belford, D. W. Woods, Amos Hoot, Alfred Marks, John Hamilton, and H. J. Walters were appointed a

Committee of Arrangements and, after a brief discussion of the mode and manner, were invested with discretionary power. Secretaries at this meeting were L. J. Elberty and George Frysinger.

The Ellsworth Cadets, a company of small boys under the command of Captain Louis Rudisill, were making plans for their participation in the reception for the Logan Guards. The cadets' uniform consisted of red pants and cap, white shirt and a blue coat.

A meeting of the Town Council was held on July 3 to consider the propriety of granting $50 for providing a supper for the Logan Guards, where the following resolution was unanimously adopted:

Resolved: That $50 be appropriated towards furnishing a supper for the Logan Guards; provided that the Chief Burgess ascertain, before making out said order, that the Town Council has power to grant money for such purposes.

THE BOYS RETURN
After patiently waiting for several days, information was finally received on Monday evening (July 29) that the Logan Guards would return by early train on Thursday, and the town at once became energized by the news while elaborate preparations were made for their reception.

At three o'clock in the morning bells across

The Logan Guards were given "three cheers and a tiger," warmly greeted, and escorted into town from the station...

Lewistown were rung and, in a short time, the Lewistown Band, the Slemmer Guards, most of the citizens, and hundreds of children, gathered on the public square and proceeded to the railway station at the Junction to meet the returning company.

On the arrival of the train, the Guards were warmly greeted, and escorted into town by Chief Marshal Joseph W. Parker, assisted by Charles S. McCoy and John Swan, the Lewistown Band, Committee of Arrangements, the Orator and Clergy, Slemmer Guards, 34 young ladies, dressed in white with tri-color rosettes, representing the 34 States in the Union. The procession was proceeded by a young lady dressed in red, white and blue, representing the Goddess of Liberty welcoming her "boys" home.

The assemblage paraded through a portion of town, then returned to the courthouse and formed on the Square. The soldiers were welcomed by the Rev. Mr. McMurray's animated address delivered in dramatically style, orating, in part:

On behalf of the citizens of Lewistown, I bid you welcome — a welcome, though expressed in words, no words are adequate to express — a welcome of hands and a welcome of hearts — welcome to our midst — welcome to our homes — to your own homes, and to the embrace of loved ones who long to greet you as they cannot here in public. While we thus bid you welcome, it is in the expectation that, as our country still bleeds, and your companions are yet in the field and the danger more imminent —

with the same heroism, the same bravery of soul, the same patriotic fires burning, and with an acquired discipline for effective service; many, if not most of you will return to the field of action, and that you will go multiplied in numbers. Foremost to the rescue at the outbreak of hostilities, stand by your country's flag and your country's cause to the last! Honored members of the Logan Guards! Soldiers of the Republic ' Again, we bid you welcome!

A Soldier's heart-felt welcome home

Mr. Parker then announced that arrangements had been made for a dinner at the Mifflin County Courthouse on Friday afternoon at three o'clock, for the Logan Guards and the Burns Infantry, and also that the latter company would be received in the same manner as the Guards had been. "Three cheers and a tiger" were then given by the crowd for the company and country. The Logan Guards were again extended profuse

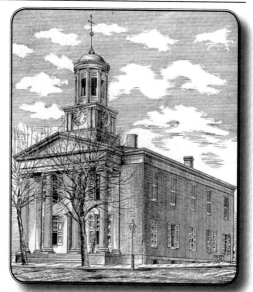

Mifflin County's 1843 Courthouse, setting for the Logan Guards welcome home banquet. From *History of Pennsylvania* by Egle, 1876 – Courtesy MCHS Archives

praise by Rev. McMurray. Private David Wertz, in was announced, age 41, did not return with the Logan Guards, being hospitalized with a rheumatic condition, not specified in the contemporary press reports.

George Frysinger, treasurer of the Logan Guard Relief Fund, reported contributions in Lewistown amounted to $561.03, not including other "patriotic" pledges which were made but no payments were yet received. Including contributions collected and distributed by the McVeytown Relief Committee, the total expended was $1,140. The families of 57 Logan Guardsmen were granted financial relief from this fund.

THE BANQUET & ACCOLADES
The editor of the *Gazette* relates this account of the dinner served in honor of the Logan Guards on August 2, 1861:

In pursuance of arrangements made with Major Daniel Eisenbise to provide dinner for our returned soldiers, tables were set in the hall of the Court House on Friday afternoon, where the Logan

Guards, under command of First Lieutenant F. R. Sterrett (Captain Hulings being absent), Captain Zollinger and such of the Burns Infantry as were in town, and a few soldiers from other counties, sat down to one of those sumptuous entertainments which the Major and his lady are proverbial for providing.

Among others present were Colonel William H. Irwin of the Seventh and Lieutenant Colonel John B. Selheimer of the 25th Regiment. A large number of citizens also partook of the dinner, both at the Court House and at the hotel, making the total number who dined at least 300. The Lewistown Band gave our citizens some music during the afternoon, and the Newton Hamilton Band, which came down to escort three of its members home who had returned from the war, discoursed some excellent music on the streets during the afternoon and, in the evening, under the guidance of Charles Caughling, Jr., serenaded many of our citizens.

The Congressional Globe published the "Thanks of the House" resolution to the First Defenders, July 1861.

On Friday morning the same program as that accorded to the Logan Guards was given to Captain Zollinger and his men here or in the vicinity. The Logan Guards were added to the escort, so that with the Slemmer Guards, the Burns Infantry and Captain McFarlane's company from Boalsburg, Centre County, which also arrived that morning, made a fine military display, according to the local newspapers. The word of welcome home was given to all by George W. Elder, Esq., in a brief address.

The *Gazette*, August 7, 1861 included:

Social Note: Lieutenant F. R. Sterrett, having testified his love for the Union by taking into his care and keeping one of the daughters of Kishacoquillas Valley, left with his bride on Tuesday evening for Lake City, Minnesota. The party were escorted into town by the Logan Guards, who were determined to give him a last testimonial for his kindness and care while in the service.

This news item lends credence that the Logan Guards, though no longer officially existing as an organization, were continuing to function as a group, apparently bound by the ties of comradeship. Historians suggest this comradeship prevailed among the former members of the five companies of First Defenders to the end of their days. They were forever proud of the fact that they were the vanguard of the millions of men and boys in blue who followed them into the army of the United States for the preservation of the Union.

The *Congressional Globe*, predecessor of the *Congressional Record* chronicled a resolution of gratitude, introduced by Rep. James Hepburn Campbell of Pennsylvania's 11th Congressional District. The resolution passed on July 22, 1861 by the House of Representatives states:

THANKS TO PENNSYLVANIA SOLDIERS.

Mr. CAMPBELL offered the following resolution; and demanded the previous question on its adoption:

Resolved, that the thanks of this House are due and are hereby tendered, to the five hundred and thirty soldiers from Pennsylvania, who passed through the mob at Baltimore and reached Washington on the 18th day of April last for the defense of the National Capital.

The previous question was seconded, and the main question ordered; and under its operation the resolution was agreed to.

The ink on the discharge certificates of the Logan Guards was scarcely dry when recruiting was begun for a new company, appropriately called the "Second Logan Guards," many of its men having been members of the original Logan Guards, as were also all the commissioned officers of the new company: Captain Joseph Ard

Mathews, First Lieutenant Henry A. Eisenbise, Second Lieutenant William B. Weber. Each of these lieutenants, in turn, afterwards received promotion to the captaincy, as did John M. Nolte, who had been a corporal in the original Logan Guard, and was made first sergeant of the Second Logans on the formation of the company. In the organization of the 46th Pennsylvania Volunteer Infantry (three years service), the Second Logan Guards was designated Company A. Upon the death of Major A. C. Lewis (September 22, 1861), Captain Mathews was promoted to major of the regiment, placing Henry A. Eisenbise in command of the company.

The Second Logan Guards, over 100 strong, left Lewistown on the night of August 26, 1861, escorted to the station by the ubiquitous Slemmer Guards and a crowds of friends and relatives.

Mifflin County was sending her sons to the war as the tempo of the conflict increased. A typical report in the Lewistown *Gazette* extolled local volunteers, like this September 4, 1861 item:

On Thursday last, Captain Linthurst's Milroy company arrived in town and, in the afternoon, took the cars for Harrisburg, being escorted to the station by Colonel Irwin's regimental band under the leadership of Charles Caughlin, Jr., of Newton Hamilton, and

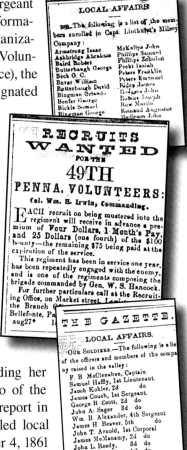

Volunteers signed up for local units as the call for more soldiers went out. The Lewistown *Gazette* listed the men who volunteered.

the Slemmer Guards, who now parade with the Minnie muskets lately held by the Logan Guards, Captain Zollinger's company left yesterday afternoon, being escorted to the station by the Slemmer Guards and a large number of citizens. We have now in service Captain Taylor's Cavalry Company, the Logan Guards, the Milroy company and the Burns Infantry, and Captain Neice of McVey-town is rapidly filling up the fifth, Captain Bigelow of Belleville, the sixth, and recruiting has commenced for the Teacher's Company. The greater portion of Colonel Irwin's regimental band is also from this county.

The story of the Logan Guards is brief, compared to the staggering magnitude of the Civil War's cost in lives and treasure. Perhaps some considered the Logan Guards mere footnote material. Bearing in mind, their chief claim to fame is being part of those first volunteer companies to arrive in response to Lincoln's call for volunteers in April 1861. It is one of the "what ifs" of history. If those five companies of Pennsylvania volunteers had not arrived when they did, would Southern sympathizers have seized the capital city? When their three month stint concluded, the service rendered by the first volunteers faded fast from the collective memory.

• 8 •
FORGOTTEN SOLDIERS, HONORED HEROES

Almost ninety years to the day after Mifflin County's first Civil War volunteers set foot in the nation's Capital, General Douglas MacArthur addressed a joint session of the U.S. Congress at the time of his retirement from the Army. In the closing lines of his April 19, 1951 remarks, he opined, "The world has turned over many times since I took the oath on the plain at West Point, and the hopes and dreams have long since vanished, but I still remember the refrain of one of the most popular barracks ballads of that day which proclaimed most proudly that old soldiers never die; they just fade away..."

Those words nearly mirrored the fate of the first volunteers from Pennsylvania. The Logan Guards and the other First Defender companies did not always hold a secure place in American history. Almost as soon as the war was over, the acts of the First Defenders faded away, as General MacArthur later proclaimed, and those men were not yet old soldiers. Perhaps the colossal nature of the Civil War itself, the unprecedented casualties, the national tumult, culminating in Lincoln's death, overshadowed their accomplishments. In his monumental history of the Civil War, Samuel P. Bates wrote in 1869:

> *In the progress of the gigantic struggle which ensued, of which the most farsighted had then no conception, so many and such brilliant services have been rendered by the soldiers of the National armies, that the timely march of these companies (the First Defenders) had been little noted.*

Their remarkable sense of volunteerism undoubtedly brought hundreds of others to the Union cause locally. After the company was mustered out, 71 of the original Logan Guards re-enlisted and saw service in battles, including: Antietam, Chancellorsville, Gettysburg, The

Wilderness, Spotsylvania and Petersburg. Of the unit's original strength, perhaps fifty percent would go on to receive commissions as officers during the war — a remarkable average rarely duplicated. Just one of many examples is William Mitchell, who carried the Logan Guards flag on the march through Baltimore. After his service in the Guards, he was a brevet brigadier general at Gettysburg and eventually served as assistant adjutant-general to President Garfield in the 1880s.

HEBER S. THOMPSON (1840 - 1911) — Author of *The First Defenders*, 1910, was a private in the Washington Artillerists when he arrived in Washington, D. C. with the other volunteer units in April 1861. He rose to Captain, Co. I, 7th Pennsylvania Veteran Volunteer Cavalry, July 1, 1863. He credits sixty-eight Logan Guardsmen with receiving commissions, from lieutenant to brigadier general. – Courtesy MCHS Archives

Heber S. Thompson asserts in *The First Defenders* that 68 of the Logan Guards received commissions during the course of the war, including: four of the number being brevet brigadier generals (one posthumously), four colonels, four lieutenant colonels, six majors, eighteen captains and thirty-two lieutenants. Thompson enumerated the brigadiers:

> Among the privates in the ranks of this company, in their march through Baltimore, was Brigadier General William H. Irwin, who commanded a brigade of General Franklin's corps at Antietam; Brevet Brigadier General William G. Mitchell, chief of General Hancock's staff; Brevet Brigadier General J. A. Matthews [sic], who commanded the Second Brigade of General Hartranft's division in the Ninth Corps; and Brigadier General Thomas Mr. Hulings, who was killed while gallantly leading his regiment into the thickest of the Wilderness fight.

Most of the Logan Guards served two, three or four enlistments for various periods and in various organizations, as if the spirit of camaraderie impelled them to join a new unit in groups or at least in

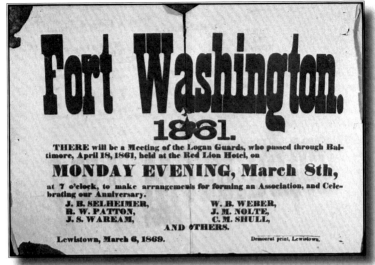

Fort Washington.

1861.

THERE will be a Meeting of the Logan Guards, who passed through Baltimore, April 18, 1861, held at the Red Lion Hotel, on

MONDAY EVENING, March 8th,

at 7 o'clock, to make arrangements for forming an Association, and Celebrating our Anniversary.

J. B. SELHEIMER,	W. B. WEBER,
R. W. PATTON,	J. M. NOLTE,
J. S. WAREAM,	C. M. SHULL,

AND OTHERS.

Lewistown, March 6, 1869.

Democrat print, Lewistown.

FIRST REUNION OF THE LOGAN GUARDS — This fragile, thin paper broadside printed by the *Democrat* announced a meeting to prepare for the Lewistown company's first reunion. It was after the close of the war that the surviving members living in Mifflin County, and others who moved away, gathered to observe the anniversary of their departure for the war. The gathering was held in the county courthouse April 16, 1869. – Courtesy MCHS Archives

pairs; rarely, according to Copeland, did a "loner" re-enlist.

The reorganization of the 78th Pennsylvania Volunteer Infantry (an old line regiment) in March 1865, a newly organized company from Lewistown, under the command of Captain A. B. Selheimer, was assigned to the regiment as Company C. Joseph S. Waream and David B. Weber, who had been captain and first lieutenant respectively of Company K, 131st P.V.I., and who had served with this company until it was mustered out in 1863, seized upon the opportunity to go soldiering once more and enlisted in the new company as Sergeant Waream and Corporal Weber -- taking ten of their old Logan comrades with them. These twelve men remained with the company until it was mustered out of the service September 11, 1865. The twelve had the distinction of being among the first troops to enter the war and of being among the last to return home at its conclusion.

One case of enduring comradeship and devotion to duty is that of James N. Rager, who fought with the Juniata Guards (Co. D, 11th U. S. Infantry) under the command of Captain William H. Irwin in the

Mexican-American War in 1847. At the "ripe old age" of 40, Rager marched away to the Civil War with the Logan Guards, his old company commander beside him in the ranks, and who later enlisted in the 49th Pennsylvania Volunteer Infantry, in which Irwin was the regimental commander. Having served as a private during his entire army career, he died at Fort Delaware in 1864.

From the day of their return from their three months service until the close of the war in 1865, so many of the Logan Guards enlisted with other military units in the field, that the few remaining at home were not held together as a distinct organization. It was after the close of the war that the surviving members living in Mifflin County, and a few who had moved away, gathered to observe the anniversary of the Logan Guards departure for the war at a public meeting held in the county courthouse on April 16, 1869. The Lewistown *Gazette* report on the event included the varied introductions, a keynote address, and a musical program, concluding with a supper for themselves and their ladies at the Red Lion Hotel.

The keynote address was delivered by Thomas M. Uttley, an original Logan Guard. Uttley recounted the Guards' history to a large, attentive audience thoroughly amused by his account of the way the "originals" deceived Major Daniel "Uncle Dan" Eisenbise at the time of the company's organization, which the speaker related in these words:

This company was organized in June, 1858, by Major Daniel Eisenbise, brigade inspector for Mifflin County. The militia law of 1858 required that thirty-two members should be enrolled and uniformed before an organization could be effected and the necessary arms and equipment drawn from the State Armory. Uniforms,

"First in Defense of the Capitol, April 18, 1861," inscription on the front or obverse of the medal presented in 1891 to members of the five companies. On the reverse side is the name of the First Defender, his company, and a list of the other four companies. – Courtesy MCHS Archives

in those days, were almost as expensive as they have been during the war, and many of us were not provided with the necessary funds to procure an outfit on short notice. To obviate this difficulty and get the company organized, some dozen or more appeared at the polls in rotation, to vote for officers, clad in the same regimentals, and the good old Major was thus deceived into organizing a military company in violation of the law.

MEDAL OF HONOR depicted in *Four Firsts from Berks* by Dr. Arthur D. Graeff. Medal historian Anthony R. Margrave suggests this may be the design to which Col. John B. Selheimer objected, or it may represent a patriotic event medal design, or reunion piece. – Courtesy MCHS Archives

Copeland is skeptical that Major Eisenbise was actually hoodwinked by the ruse. After all, "Uncle Dan" was present to muster in a company of militia in which he had a deep personal interest, and knowledge of the men. It's doubtful he would not have questioned the ownership of so many fresh uniforms, notes Copeland. Regardless, it makes for a good story, and likely brought gales of laughter from the old troop when retold, time and again, at the annual reunions.

THE FIRST DEFENDER MEDALS OF HONOR

The year 1869 marked the organization of the survivors into "The Logan Guards Association", with their old captain, John B. Selheimer as president; Lieutenant (Major) Patton, vice president; Sergeant (Captain) Weber, treasurer, and Sergeant (Captain) Waream, secretary. This organization kept the survivors in touch with one another, though widely scattered in various parts of the country. It rekindled their patriotic zeal and enlivened recollections of the experiences of the great conflict. They gathered annually (with a few exceptions) and ceremoniously called the company roll — a moment's silence following the name of each deceased comrade. Intoxicating liquors were banned at these meetings.

At this same time, The First Defenders Association was formed

through the impetus of the
two Pottsville companies, and
a constitution was formulated.
Article I of that document
states:

    *This Association shall be
known as "The First Defenders
of the National Capitol April
18, 1861" and is organized for
the express purpose of building
together in a social league, the
members of the said five companies and for the purpose of
celebrating in a becoming man-*

**MEDAL (REVERSE SIDE) PRESENTED
TO C. M. SHULL**, a sergeant in the Logan
Guards. – Courtesy MCHS Archives

*ner, on the eighteenth day of April of each year... and to attend the
funerals of deceased members and to wear a suitable medal on each
such occasion.*

    The "suitable medal" became an object of ongoing discussion for
the better part of twenty-five years. After the Civil War, other types of
veteran societies were formed, from memberships of whole armies to
individual companies, like the Logan Guards organization, each produced their own lodge or society medal to be worn on special occasions. The Grand Army of the Republic medal of honor resembled the
original Congressional Medal of Honor so closely, that in 1904 an act
of Congress changed the design of the latter so the two would not be
confused. It is possible, according to medal historian and writer Anthony R. Margrave of Sussex, England, that the "suitable medal" may
be the one he described in a 1974 monograph. He notes this medal is
of aluminium or white metal, 1 1/2 inches in diameter, and quite thin.

    That medal, Margrave states, is widely regarded as a reunion piece,
however, he contends that it could be a Federal medal, or even a special
piece for a specific First Defenders Association gathering. It does not
appear to be a State authorized medal, as that was struck in the 1890s.

    On April 5, 1882, a special meeting of the state Association was
held to discuss a suggestion by the Logan Guards. Specifically, the
Lewistown company wanted to secure some recognition from the U.S.
Congress, and a committee was formed to accomplish the task. At

Gen. David M. Gregg (1833-1916), born in Huntingdon, PA, accepted the First Defenders medals from the Commonwealth during the Oct. 1, 1891 Medal of Honor ceremony in Pottsville, PA. Gregg was the first cousin of Pennsylvania's Civil War Governor Andrew Gregg Curtin, and was one of the oldest surviving Union generals at the time of his death in Reading, PA. – Courtesy LOC Prints and Photographs Division Washington, D.C.

the April 18, 1884 annual meeting, Lt. Col. Oliver C. Bosbyshell of the Washington Artillerists, chairman of the Medal Committee, offered a design, and plans were made to secure Congressional legislation to authorize a medal for the five companies. Unfortunately, the committee was unable to move Congress, but a promise was extracted from Pennsylvania's governor to use his influence to garner a medal from the Commonwealth. After a number of fits and starts, a State Medal of Honor was finally achieved. On May 26, 1891, the Pennsylvania General Assembly made an appropriation of five thousand dollars for medals of honor to be presented to the First Defenders. The medals authorised by this Act were prepared and struck in the United States Mint at Philadelphia, of bronze, in the shape of a Maltese cross with a centerpiece showing the Capitol of the United States Government. (Lt. Col. Bosbyshell was Director of the Mint at the time.) Each was marked "First in Defense of the Capitol, April 18, 1861," and on the reverse side with the name of the First Defender, his company, and a list of the other four companies.

This process was not without controversy. An original plan was to list the five companies on the reverse, in the order of which they reported for duty in Harrisburg, as determined by the Medal Committee. Col. John B. Selheimer took vehement exception to this suggestion, insisting the Logan Guards should be listed first. In a letter to the pertinent officials, and submitted to the *Philadelphia Times,* he wrote, in part:

> *In the first place we did not approve the law as introduced... We object to the inscription adopted for the reverse side of the medal. The Logan Guards should be the first company named on the medal...*

This medal business has all been fixed up to suit the other companies without consulting the Logan Guards. The only notice we received of the preparation of the medals was a few weeks ago, when we received a communication from the committee on medals asking us to authorize them to select a design. We did so, and at the same time passed a resolution that before the design was adopted it should be submitted to us for our approval. The design had not been submitted to us, nor did we know about it until we read the article in The Times... We are not satisfied with the design and never will be until we are allowed full justice...

A MEDAL OF HONOR, which was awarded to Chauncey M. Shull, a First Defender of the Civil War, is presented by his grandson Chauncey E. Shull, Jr. to Willis R. Copeland of the Mifflin County Historical Society in 1961. The "minie ball" musket in the photograph was used by the elder Shull during his later service with Company I, 83rd Pennsylvania Volunteer Infantry. – Courtesy MCHS Archives

Other members of the First Defenders Association were becoming concerned about the medal, to the extent that Bosbyshell wrote a letter to the *Pottsville Republican* July 31, 1891, attempting to still some of the controversy, stating, in part:

So much misapprehension and unnecessary alarm seems to exist among the "First Defenders" relative to the medal of honor the State of Pennsylvania intends to bestow on them... the medal named was not so much to glorify a certain set of volunteers above another set, but to emphasize the fact that 530 Pennsylvanians were the first volunteers to President Lincoln's call for 75,000 and to set at rest Massachusetts bogus claim...

Anthony R. Margrave compiled an exhaustive study of the First Defenders Medal of Honor in 1974. As a member of the Orders and

Medals Society of America, Margrave authored an article on the First Defenders' medal and its design, published in *The Medal Collector.* Correspondence in the early 1970s between Margrave and J. Martin Stroup, Mifflin County Historical Society's Corresponding Secretary and Society past president, reveals the existence of an earlier medal design, and its possible intended use.

Four First for Berks, Dr. Arthur D. Graeff's 1961 book published by the Berks County Historical Society, profiles the Ringgold Light Artillery and other "firsts" in that county's local history. This Civil War centennial publication illustrated what is believed to be the initial medal design for the First Defenders, speculates Margrave, the design opposed by Col. Selheimer. On the front, a central panel features an infantryman, flanked by Lincoln's profile and a Union shield. The reverse featured five entwined rings, each bearing names of the First Defender companies. Selheimer's objection may have centered on the use of the linked "gold rings" an illusion, perhaps favoring the Ringgold company over the others. Whether this is an element for the objection, is not known, as additional issues are posed in Selheimer's letter.

Eventually, a compromise was crafted so that the company name from each town should head the list on the medals going to that particular place. The result was that all medals going to Lewistown, for example, had the recipient's name engraved above "Logan Guards" in larger lettering, with the other companies listed below. The medals were proudly worn by recipients throughout their lives at subsequent reunions and patriotic gathering.

The actual presentation occurred in Pottsville on October 1 1891, when the Schuylkill County Civil War memorial was unveiled. The Association Medal Committee invited Pennsylvania Governor Robert E. Pattison to participate, and asked him to bestow the medals on the attending veterans. Following ceremonies and speeches, the medals were accepted from Governor Pattison by General David McMurtrie Gregg, Commander of the Pennsylvania Commandery of the Military Order of the Loyal Legion of the United States. The First Defenders marched to near the old Pennsylvania Railroad depot in Pottsville, where the medals were distributed to attendees.

In 1892, the surviving members of the five companies formed an organization, "The Pennsylvania First Defenders." This veteran group held annual meetings on April 18 alternating in the towns from which

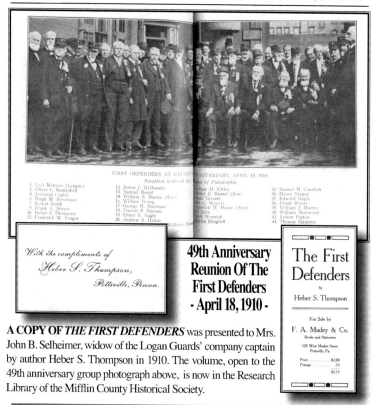

FIRST DEFENDERS AT REUNION ANNIVERSARY, APRIL 18, 1910.
Reception tendered by City of Philadelphia.

1. Levi Mattson (League)
2. Oliver C. Boslyshell
4. Jeremiah Cogley
6. Hugh M. Stevenson
7. Robert Smith
9. Frank A. Stitzer
10. Heber S. Thompson
11. Frederick M. Yeager

12. James J. McDonald
13. Samuel Beard
14. William S. Sheetz (Son)
16. William Irving
17. George H. Hartman
18. Francis B. Bannan
19. Elmer E. Nagle
20. Andrew S. Helms

Thomas M. Uttley
Daniel R. Russel (Son)
Louis Gresser
James C. Weaver
Frederick H. Hause (Son)
David Betz
Frank Wetrich
Charles Slingluff
William Aum...

33. Samuel M. Comfort
34. Henry Yerger
35. Edward Nagle
36. Frank Wentz
38. William J. Martin
39. William Sherwood
42. Robert Patton
44. Thomas Hammer

With the compliments of Heber S. Thompson, Pottsville, Penna.

49th Anniversary Reunion Of The First Defenders - April 18, 1910 -

The First Defenders
by
Heber S. Thompson

For Sale by
F. A. Mudey & Co.
Books and Stationery

103 West Market Street
Pottsville, Pa.

Price $2.00
Postage .... .13
$2.13

A COPY OF *THE FIRST DEFENDERS* was presented to Mrs. John B. Selheimer, widow of the Logan Guards' company captain by author Heber S. Thompson in 1910. The volume, open to the 49th anniversary group photograph above, is now in the Research Library of the Mifflin County Historical Society.

the companies originated.

The First Defenders observed the 35th anniversary of their departure for the war by staging a re-enactment of the journey on April 15, 1896, with 14 surviving members of the Logan Guards participating. It was a grand event, a journey back in time, as it were, all the way to Washington, D.C.

At noon, church bells and the courthouse bell in Lewistown were rung and whistles sounded. The Logan Guards assembled on the public square and, preceded by the Lewistown Band, marched to the railway station. Captain L. N. Slagle, commanding Company G, Fifth Infantry, National Guard of Pennsylvania, officiated as marshal. The escort was composed of members of Colonel Hulings Post No. 176, Grand Army of the Republic and the Lewistown camp of the Patriotic Order Sons of America. Rev. M. S. Cressman, pastor of St. John's Lutheran Church, Lewistown, delivered a patriotic address at the station, as reported in

FIRST DEFENDER CAP worn at Civil War reunions and other Veterans' affairs. This cap, once belonged to Captain Robert W. Patton, is among the Mifflin County Historical Society exhibits at McCoy House Museum, 17 N. Main Street, Lewistown

the Lewistown *Gazette*.

Upon their arrival at Harrisburg, the veterans were joined by the survivors of the other four companies, and all attended a reception held in their honor at the Executive Mansion on Front Street. They spent the night at the Bolton Hotel, a popular destinations for noted individuals and politicians of the era, once located on 2nd Street. On April 16, led by the Ringgold Band of Reading (this had been the regimental band of the 25th), they marched to the Harrisburg station and entrained.

In Baltimore, they were met and greeted by a committee of the City Council. The veterans then retraced the route they trod in April 1861, menaced so many years before by the angry mob. Marching with them were the Fourth Infantry Regiment, Maryland National Guard, and several hundred members of the Maryland Division, Grand Army of the Republic. After passing in review at City Hall, the Pennsylvanians were the guests of honor at a banquet where they were addressed by both Maryland Governor Lloyd Lowndes, Jr. and Governor Daniel H. Hastings of Pennsylvania.

The editor of the Lewistown *Gazette* reported:

The reception was hearty and kind and went far to wipe out the ill usage received by the same men 35 years ago. The veterans left for Washington on the evening of April 16 and received a royal welcome in the national capital. They were cheered as they marched into the House of Representatives, where they were greeted by President Grover Cleveland.

They later visited Fort Washington where the Logan Guards and the Washington Artillerists had been stationed during their service with the 25th Infantry.

Fourteen years later, at the 49th Anniversary Reunion of the First

Defenders, Heber Thompson recalled details of the event in *The First Defenders*. Forty-seven surviving veterans and the sons of seven others gathered in Philadelphia on the afternoon of April 18, 1910 in the club house of the Union League on Broad Street. Thompson noted that proper ceremonies and welcoming speeches were delivered by the dignitaries.

Thompson's 1910 roll of 23 living Logan Guards, and place of residence, if known, for the 49th Anniversary Reunion included:

Betz, Robert
Butts, P. P.
Burns, James D., National Military Home, Dayton, Ohio
Cogley, Jeremiah, 430 W. Lemon St., Lancaster, Pa.
Comfort, Henry
Comfort, Samuel M., 128 S. 15th St., Philadelphia, Pa.
Eckebarger, James B., Lewistown, Pa.
Eisenbise, E. W., 811 Barclay St., Chester, Pa.
Fichthorn, Joseph A., Market St., Lewistown, Pa.
Henry, James W.
Miller, Joseph A., Lewistown, Pa.
McLaughlin, S. G., Beltzhoover, Allegheny Co., Pa.
Patton, Robert W., 23 W. 12th St., New York City
Postlethwait, Joseph W., Petrolia, Pa.
Postlethwait, John M., National Military Home, Dayton, Ohio
Rothrock, Bronson, National Military Home, Dayton, Ohio
Sherwood, William, Lewistown, Pa.
Snyder, Lucien T., 202 N. 12th St., Philadelphia, Pa.
(National Military Home, Hampton, Va.)
Snyder, Joseph A., Lewistown, Pa.
Uttley, Thomas M., 29 N. Main St., Lewistown, Pa.
Wentz, Franklin H., 124 W. 3rd St., Lewistown, Pa
Walters, Henry A., 100 3rd St., Lewistown, Pa.
Zeigler, Edwin E., Duquesne Station, Harrisburg, Pa.

Thompson described the banquet:
The table was handsomely decorated with sweet peas, honeysuckle, daffodils, lilacs, lilies of the valley, brilliant colored tulips, and roses. The menu was excellent and delicious.

The event included many formal toasts and extended responses. Thompson, President of the First Defenders Association, wrote:

After the dessert, and with the coffee and cigars, the President of the Union League, Mr. James F. Hope, made an admirable address full of patriotic sentiment and most complimentary to the members of the First Defenders' Association. To the toast "The Commonwealth of Pennsylvania," His Excellency Governor Edwin S. Stuart responded in an inspiring speech, speaking for the State and for the Union, and in earnest and impressive manner extolling the virtues of patriotism and public duty. Inspiring and patriotic addresses were delivered also by Hon. W. W. Porter, Hon. W. T. Tilden and General Louis Wagner. The President of the First Defenders, Heber S. Thompson, responded to the toast "The First Defenders."

First Defender Thomas M. Uttley, of Lewistown made an extempore address recalling the stirring days at the beginning of the war, at Lewistown, Penna., and gave some accounts of the brilliant records made by the members of the Logan Guards, of Lewistown, in the subsequent history of the War of the Rebellion; recalling the fact that from this company alone there rose ...68 officers, who served during the four years of the war.

Special mention was made by First Defender Uttley of Brigadier General Thomas M. Hulings, who was killed in the Battle of the Wilderness while gallantly leading his Brigade; of Brigadier General J. A. Matthews [sic], commanding the 2nd Brigade, Hartranft's Division, 9th Corps; of Brigadier General William H. Irwin, commanding a brigade of General Franklin's corps, at Antietam; Sergeant Frederick Hart, killed in the first day's fight at Gettysburg; Sergeant William Hopper, who died of wounds received at Fredericksburg; of Captain William Butler Freeburn, who died of wounds received at Fredericksburg; of Sergeant Robert D. Morton, killed in the Shenandoah Valley; of Corporal Thomas D. Nurse, who was killed at Antietam; of Corporal John E. Nail, killed at South Mountain; of Lieutenant Gilbert Waters, who was killed at Winchester, Va.; also of General William Galbraith Mitchell, whose gallant conduct at Gettysburg and later service as chief of staff of General Hancock have given him fame and honor.

It would be obvious to the aging veterans that their ranks were dwindling, and an emotional poem written and delivered by First Defender Oliver C. Bosbyshell for the occasion expressed how many a comrade felt that day. Bosbyshell would be remembered for his service as a private in the Washington Artillerists in 1861, and for rising to major in the 48th Pennsylvania Volunteer Infantry Regiment. He later served in the Pennsylvania National Guard for decades, attaining colonel of the 19th Regiment in 1898. His dramatic reading moved many First Defenders attending the 49th reunion, according to Thompson. The last four stanzas follow:

46th Reunion ribbon of Joseph A. Fichthorn, Logan Guards, Lewistown.
– Courtesy MCHS Archives

The Union League now welcomes you
Within its loyal halls,
And bids you know, it's honored, too,
To have you in these walls—
Old Pennsylvania is proud
Of each and every one,
For having honor'd her so much
As FIRST in sixty-one.

Of all the many thousand troops
Who sprang to Freedom's call—
The FIRST of all the mighty host
To haste the rebels' fall.
A glorious note in Hist'ry's page
Your action well displays—
The youth who reads will prompted be
In Patriotism's ways.

A strain of sadness comes o'er all,
In gathering here today—
The vacant places in the ranks
Are more than one dare say.
Of five hundred thirty youngsters
So blithe in sixty-one,
The numbers now are quickly told—
Soon answer will be "none!"

As long as any shall be left
To welcome Eighteenth day,
The mem'ries of the past will come
To cheer all on the way
To the blest and happy Country
Coming so very near,
Where, as the Sergeant calls the roll,

Five hundred thirty "here!"

In 1912, the Logan Guards gathered in Lewistown for the 51st re-union of the company with other members of the local G.A.R. Post. This would be one of the last gatherings of the "Boys of '61," their number then at fourteen. Nine attended, while health, distance or both prevented the other five from meeting with their comrades one last time. The May entry in the Meeting Book of the G.A.R. Post reflected the 1912 reunion, mentioning, in part:

There being no further business the Post closed to attend the ban-quet at the Nichols' Cafe...The Post formed in line and marched to the office of Com. Uttley where they were joined by nine of the old Logan Guards...

The Lewistown *Daily Sentinel* recorded the event held at the Crys-tal Café of W. W. Nichols at 34 W. Market Street, in its April 17, 1912 edition:

One of the most pleasant social events in the annals of Col. Hul-ings Post, No. 176, G. A. R. was enjoyed last evening when the sur-viving veterans of the post held a banquet in the café of W. W. Nich-ols on West Market Street, forty-six veterans, including nine First Defenders, sat down around the banquet tables surrounded by the star-spangled banner. The excellent menu served and patriotic deco-rations received commen-dation from everybody. The menu consisted of breaded veal, peas, mashed potatoes, lobster salad, ice-cream, pie, coffee, and cigars. The old soldiers made a charge upon the eats with as much vigor as they did upon the rebel forces in the sixties and the grub dis-appeared in a hurry. While the hoary-headed survivors of the Civil War ate and chatted and listened to several addresses, they all wondered who the big-hearted and generous man was who furnished the banquet. His name has not yet been revealed but the secret only increases the

GRAND ARMY MEN BANQUET

Col. Hulings Post Guest at Feast Provided by Friend

SPEAKERS REVIEW WAR DAYS

Veterans from Other Cities Join in Making Occasion Happy

One the most pleasant social events in the annals of Col. Hul-ings Post, No. 176, G. A. R., was en-joyed last evening when the surviv-

Lewistown *Daily Sentinel*, April 17, 1912

THE LOGAN GUARDS, 1912 — Nine original Logan Guards sat for their portrait by Lewistown photographer John C. Nolte at the 51st reunion of the company. In attendance were, front row from left, William Sherwood, Joseph A. Miller, Lucien Snyder (Philadelphia), Thomas M. Uttley, Edwin E. Zeigler (Pittsburgh); standing, Joseph Fichthorn, Jeremiah Cogley (Lancaster), Franklin H. Wentz and Elias W. H. Eisenbise, all of Lewistown at the time. – Courtesy MCHS Archives

appetites and relishing of the grand old men.

After the meal, Thomas M. Uttley, on behalf of the First Defenders, thanked the unknown gentleman, who anonymously donated the banquet, for his generosity. In his address, Mr. Uttley paid tribute to the survivors of Col. Hulings Post and the Logan Guards. He extolled the broad range of "illustrious patriots... who later won distinction as lawyers, statesmen, merchants, poets and philosophers." Uttley pointed out that there were seventy-three Democrats among the Logan Guards "who buried their political prejudices to fight for the Stars and Stripes." Where the other nineteen Lincoln Republicans? That can only be speculated.

The 51st banquet and gathering was dedicated to the memory of Capt. Charles Selin Davis who died, the *Daily Sentinel* reported, while fighting at the head of his command at Lookout Mountain in 1863. Lucien T. Snyder, a First Defender who made the journey to Lewistown from his Philadelphia home, prepared a poetic reading which, due to frail health, Mr. Uttley read aloud on his behalf.

My Dear Brother Logans and Boyhood Friends:

With much happiness, not unalloyed with pain, we assemble here today to recall old times and the names of our many dear associates who have passed through the Valley of the Shadow into the Great Beyond, and to unite in mourning their absence and in honoring their memories. Let the few of us remaining continue to cherish the acts and deeds of our dead, and let us endeavor to instill in the minds of our children and of our children's children that love of liberty and justice that will ever assure the perpetuity of our now vast country...

The noble monument erected here in remembrance of the sufferings and sacrifices of our Boys in Blue exhibits the love and reverence of this community for them, and a Grand Army Post does honor to itself in perpetuating the name of one who, in life, was gentle as a child, and whose brotherly love was so great that, had each of his kind acts been repaid with a single bud, his grave would have been covered with a wilderness of flowers...

... the grand mountain-tops surrounding this beautiful Valley of the Blue Juniata – first to receive the kiss of the morning sun and last to throw their shadows across the swelling turf above the sleeping comrades – seem like watch-towers of angels and the moonlight like the shadow of God.

And now, brother soldiers and friends, "Hail and Farewell." The strings of our hearts vibrate to the notes of the last call and the New Song.

> *But, singing the New Song,*
> *Where tears and heart-ache shall have pass'd away,*
> *Where hills glimmer with immortal day,*
> *I would not all Life's lesser loves forget!*
> *Leave me, Great Father, some sweet memories yet*
> *Of those dear friends on Earth whom I have met*
> *And loved so long!*

Dr. W. H. Parcels, one of the guiding spirits behind the planning, construction and dedication of the Soldiers' and Sailors' Monument in 1906 mentioned by Lucien T. Snyder, also addressed the veterans. He gave a brief history of the Logan Guards, and of their exploits during the journey through Baltimore in April 1861. Dr. Parcels referred touchingly, according to the newspaper, to the mere dozen Logan

THE 51ST GATHERING OF THE LOGAN GUARDS, 1912 — Logan Guards and other Civil War veterans of the G.A.R. gathered at the Crystal Café of W. W. Nichols at 34 W. Market Street. Nine original Logan Guards attended, with five absent. The photograph was taken using the new " electric flash-light" equipment of local photographer John C. Nolte, son of a Logan Guard. – Courtesy MCHS Archives

Guards in attendance at the monument dedication, noting their ranks had diminished even further, so that only nine could make the 51st reunion. He concluded by saying:

Comrades you have reached the eventide of your life and the most consoling thought of your declining years is that you have fought the good fight.

The old soldiers did indeed fade away, with several passing in the year 1912 alone. Joseph A. Fichthorn would be the last Logan Guard residing in Mifflin County when he died in 1925. Elias W. H. Eisenbise, former county resident from Lewistown, would be the last survivor of the Logan Guards. He died in Delaware County, Pennsylvania in 1929, sixty-eight years after he and his comrades marched off to defend the U.S. Capital. Only two of the original 530 First Defenders were able to attend the annual gathering in 1929. The Lewistown, Allentown and Reading companies were gone by then; the remaining ten survivors were from the two Pottsville companies.

▪ 9 ▪
FIRST OF THE FIRST?

SAMUEL P. BATES, LL.D.
(1827 - 1902) — Pennsylvania State Historian, appointed by Governor Andrew G. Curtin in 1866. His *History of the Pennsylvania Volunteers in 5 volumes* remains a preeminent Civil War research tool. Bates credits the Ringgold Light Artillery of Reading with the honor of being the First of the First, a position disputed by Logan Guards during their lifetimes.
– Courtesy MCHS Archives

State historian Samuel P. Bates labored for years on his Civil War tome, five volumes of over 1,400 pages each, entitled *History of the Pennsylvania Volunteers.* Published by the Commonwealth at an expense of nearly a quarter of a million of dollars, it is said to form an enduring monument to the patriotism of Pennsylvania. Recorded in the years immediately following the war, much of the history could be gathered while memories were fresh. In the early pages of this history, Bates commented on the companies of First Defenders, in part:

In the progress of this gigantic struggle which ensued... the timely march of these companies has been little noted. But the value of their presence in the Capital at this critical juncture, can not be overlooked, in any fair estimate of the causes which led to our triumph; and it must ever be regarded as one of the links in that chain of great events, seemingly planned by Providence... at the head of the grand column of the two million men, who afterwards... marched in their footprints.

In his 1910 book, *The First Defenders,* author and First Defender veteran Heber S. Thompson lauded them, too, saying:

Hardly a single great battle was fought in the four years of the war—from Bull Run, Antietam, Fredericksburg, Chancellorsville, Gettysburg, Wilderness, Five Forks to Appomattox in the East, and from Shiloh to Stone's River, Mufreesboro, Chickamauga, Resaca and Atlanta in the Middle West—in which the First Defenders were not repre-

sented. Their individual war records would fill volumes of history.

Aside from the honor of priority awarded the five companies as a whole — the first troops to reach Washington for its defense, April 18, 1861 — which the Congress of the United States was called upon on two occasions to confirm as a matter of history, there is the question of which company of the five reached Harrisburg first in response to the call of the Governor. Was it the Logan Guards of Lewistown; Ringgold Light Artillery of Reading; Allen Infantry of Allentown; Washington Artillery of Pottsville; or the National Light Infantry, also of Pottsville?

RINGGOLD LIGHT ARTILLERY NATIONAL COLORS — "First Flag of the War" shown in a flag case, Pennsylvania Capitol Rotunda, cited by Berks County historian John E. Strohecker. This flag was the first National Colors, Stars and Stripes, to enter Washington, as noted on the attached sign. – From *Four Firsts in Berks*, Historical Society of Berks County, 1961; MCHS Archives.

There was considerable discussion and supportive material put forth by several of the companies on the point of which group was the "First of the First." In Mifflin County, this was not considered debatable ground before the appearance in the late 1860s of Bates' *History*, which gives credit to another company as first to arrive at the state capital – the Ringgold Light Artillery.

Mifflin County Civil War historian Willis R. Copeland lays out the case for the Logan Guards being "First of the First." His analysis makes several points:

According to contemporary accounts, members of the Logan Guards stated at the time, and held to the statement, that they were the first troops to arrive in Harrisburg in 1861.

They neither saw nor heard of any organized force there until after their arrival.

A few men of their own company, and perhaps of companies from other places, had gone to Harrisburg in advance, on the afternoon of

the 16th or the evening of that day, to get some knowledge of the situa-
tion and, in the case of the Logan Guards, to ascertain why transporta-
tion was not furnished at Lewistown when the company was at the sta-
tion, ready to go, which was the only cause of the company not reaching
Harrisburg until the next morning.

Shortly after the outbreak of the war the Harrisburg *Patriot* edi-
torially called on newspapers in different parts of the country to cease
making the claim that the Sixth Massachusetts Infantry, mobbed at Baltimore, April 19, 1861, was the first body of soldiers to pass through Baltimore and reach Washington at the opening of hostilities. The *Patriot*
editorialized:

> *On the afternoon of the 16th of April the National Light Infantry of*
> *Pottsville, Captain E. McDonald; the Washington Artillerists of Potts-*
> *ville, Captain James Wren; the Ringgold Light Artillery of Reading,*
> *Captain McKnight; the Logan Guards of Lewistown, Captain J. B. Sel-*
> *heimer; and the Allen Infantry of Allentown. Captain Yeager, left their*
> *respective homes in answer to the President's call and went to Harris-*
> *burg. The Logan Guards were the first to arrive early on the morning*
> *of the 17th. The assertion frequently made by the Boston and New York*
> *papers that the Massachusetts regiment was the first to pass through*
> *Baltimore is not true. On the morning of the 18th the above named com-*
> *panies were ordered off to Washington, and started about seven o'clock,*
> *numbering five hundred and five men. About one o'clock they arrived in*
> *Baltimore — the first that had up to that time passed through.*
>
> *This number of men (five hundred and five) were sufficient to have*
> *formed seven companies, but the State Government could not recognize*
> *them as a regiment. But for this the Logan Guards would have been*
> *Company A in the First Regiment.*

Again, based upon accounts of the volunteers themselves, Copeland
asserts that the Logan Guards were placed at the head of the five companies when they left Harrisburg for Washington, held that position in
the passage through Baltimore and also when they marched from the
train to the Capitol building at Washington, which while not to be taken
as a proof of first place from a military point of view, was at the time
regarded as a mark of honor, recognized by the authorities of the state.

Being the "First of the First" remained an issue, one that was stirred
at recurring commemorative events over the years. The Civil War flag

ceremony in 1866 was one such example. A joint resolution of the Pennsylvania Legislature, approved May 16, 1861, provided:

That the Governor procure regimental standards for all the regiments formed or to be formed in Pennsylvania, upon which shall be inscribed the number of the regiment and painted the arms of this commonwealth, and that all these standards, after the rebellion is ended, shall be returned to the Governor that they may be carefully preserved by the state.

After the war, Pennsylvania's regimental flags were collected by the State's military department, though many were returned as the regiments mustered out of service. On July 4, 1866, a state ceremony was

JOHN B. SELHEIMER, Captain of the Logan Guards, later Lt. Col. 25th Pennsylvania Infantry, was adamant throughout his life that the Logan Guards were the "First of the First." He declared about his unit:

It was the first company to report to Governor Curtin in Harrisburg. Early on the morning of April 17, 1861, I called on Governor Curtin and reported my company, and at the same time asked the Governor if any other companies were in, to which he replied that no other companies had as yet arrived, that mine was first.

From a letter published in the *Philadelphia Times*, July 1891, at the time of the authorization of the First Defenders Medal of Honor. – Courtesy MCHS Archives

held at Independence Hall, Philadelphia, when all the regimental organizations returned their battle flags to Governor Curtin, on behalf of the Commonwealth. A massive, and impressive, parade of veterans carrying the venerable banners ensued. In Richard Sauers' *Advance the Colors*, the author notes that a controversy broke out between Reading's Ringgold Artillery and the National Light Infantry of Pottsville, citing the *Philadelphia Press* and the *Inquirer* as sources, about which company should be first in line. Logan Guardsmen present recall a different argument, specifically between their company and the Ringgold Artillery.

The parade marshal intervened to restore order. After some discussion as to place, the Logan Guards were assigned the right of the line by Major General Winfield Scott Hancock, chief marshal. Willis Copeland recounts in *The Logan Guards* that Hancock's decision in the Lewistown company's favor was based on the fact that the Logan Guards were the first company to report to Governor Curtin in 1861, and were therefore assigned the right of the line, the position they held from Harrisburg to Washington and therefor were entitled to at Philadelphia in 1866.

This decision was bitterly contested and vehemently rejected by the veterans of the Ringgold Light Artillery, a large contingent being present at the event, and accompanied by their famous brass band. Rejecting their assigned position of rear guard by General Hancock, the Ringgolds refused to participate in the parade and returned home. That company always asserted that they were the first of the five companies to arrive in Harrisburg and that the right-of-the-line position of the Logan Guards was open to question. The Philadelphia papers published the order of march, as best as the reporters covering the event could ascertain. The vanguard was called "Mounted Police Officers" that included the Liberty Cornet Band, and Major General Hancock and his staff, followed by the First Division, listed as:

Major-General James S. Negley & Staff, Logan Guards, National Light Artillery, Washington Artillery, Allen Light Infantry

---

WHO WERE FIRST DEFENDERS?

Pennsylvania to Investigate Claims of Civil War Organizations.

HARRISBURG, Penn., May 3.—A resolution was adopted by the House of Representatives to-day directing the Adjutant General of the National Guard to make an investigation, with a view of having the credit of being the first defenders in the civil war conferred upon the military body in this State now known as the "First Defenders."

The resolution states that the credit has wrongly been given to the Sixth Massachusetts Regiment and goes on to say that the Washington Artillery and National Light Infantry, of Pottsville; Ringgold Artillery, Reading; Allen Infantry, Allentown, and Logan Guards, Lewistown, were the first defenders, having responded immediately to the calls of President Lincoln and Gov. Curtin on April 16 and 17, 1861, and having been the first troops to reach Washington to defend the National property.

THE FIRST? — In May 1907, a news item states the Pennsylvania Legislature refuted the idea that the 6th Massachusetts was the first to defend Washington, D.C. In this era, the 6th was accorded that honor, including shedding "first blood" in the fight to preserve the Union. Since then, the Pennsylvania companies of First Defenders garner that mantle, and first blood shed points to Nicholas Biddle, officer's aide, Washington Artillery of Pottsville, injured during the march through Baltimore April 18, 1861.
– Courtesy MCHS Archives

Apparently, the mounted police had a difficult time keeping the street clear of the throngs, as troops marching eight abreast had to squeeze through the jammed boulevards.

This recurring question of who was first arose four years later. In

1870 the following resolution was offered in the U.S. House of Representatives: *Resolved by the House (the Senate concurring) that a suitable medal be ordered for each member of the battalion first to arrive at Washington from Pennsylvania on the 18th of April, 1861.*

During debate in April 1870, Rep. Henry Lutz Cake, member of the U.S. House from Pennsylvania's 10th District, discussed this resolution on the House floor. A First Defender himself, and later colonel of the 96th Pennsylvania Infantry, Rep. Cake answered some inquiries by giving a brief history of each First Defender company. He credited the Logan Guards with the "first" honor as to arrival in Harrisburg, and stated that the Ringgolds of Reading arrived there the evening of the 16th and the Lewistown company the same day. However, even the Logan Guards did not make that im-

WINFIELD SCOTT HANCOCK (1824 - 1886) — Born in Montgomeryville, Pennsylvania, Hancock rose to major general in the Union Army. He was the Democratic candidate for President in 1880. On July 4, 1866, an impressive state ceremony was held at Independence Hall, Philadelphia, where all the Pennsylvania regimental organizations returned their battle flags to the Commonwealth. General Hancock was the parade marshal who placed the Logan Guards in the line of march over the objection of another First Defender company, after a dispute arose over who should be first. – PD image courtesy LOC Prints and Photographs Division Brady-Handy Collection

possible claim. They marched through Lewistown to the railroad station on the evening of the 16th, but due to the trains running late, did not see Harrisburg until the early morning of April 17th.

However, Cake's own company, National Light Infantry, has its own claim to be first. On the evening of April 11, 1861, hours before that initial shots were fired at Fort Sumter, the officers of the National Light Infantry met in Pottsville. The meeting produced several resolutions, including one offered by then Corporal Henry Lutz Cake, stating:

On motion of Corporal H. L. Cake that the services of this company be tendered to the Secretary of War and the Governor of Pennsylvania in defense of the Union, and that the company be ready to march at six hours' notice.

The resolution adopted, a telegram was sent to Governor Curtin and Secretary of War Simon Cameron, announcing the National Light Infantry's willingness to serve, if needed. Given the early date, the National Light Infantry became the first company to offer its services to the government at the start of the Civil War.

Secretary of War Cameron issued a statement on the subject at the July 4, 1866 regimental flag event at Philadelphia. The handwritten certificate states:

> *I certify that the Pottsville National Light Infantry was the first company of volunteers whose services were offered for the defense of the Capital. A telegram reached the War Department on the 13th making the tender. It was immediately accepted. The company reached Washington on the 18th of April, 1861, with four additional companies from Pennsylvania, and these were the first troops to reach the seat of Government at the beginning of the war of the rebellion.*

The letter appears in Thompson's *The First Defenders*, and in *Schuylkill County in the Civil War,* a 1961 Civil War centennial publication of the Schuylkill County Historical Society. However, Thompson essentially disproves that official acceptance, stating:

I certify that the Pottsville National Light Infantry was the first company of volunteers whose services were offered for the defense of the Capital... – Simon Cameron, Secretary of War, July 4, 1866, from a handwritten certificate.

> *No authority existed on the part of the Secretary of War by any law or provision of the Constitution of the United States to accept the offer of troops 'til the Proclamation of President Lincoln on April 15.*

When the 1870 resolution finally moved to the U.S. Senate, the Massachusetts Sixth was also included and a discussion developed as to who were the first troops to enter Washington during the war. Pennsylvania Senators Simon Cameron and John Scott defended their state's claim to that honor and proved that Pennsylvania furnished the first soldiers to defend the nation's capital in 1861. The *Philadelphia Inquirer* reported in April 1870:

... *Therefor there need be no objection to the Resolution proposed by a Senator on Tuesday, recognizing service done to the country by the volunteers that first reached Washington, upon the idea that some invidious distinction is to be made. His resolution suggests nothing more than that recognition should be made of the merits of those military organizations which were best prepared to act in immediate response.*

There had been considerable interest in a national silver medal for the 530 rank and file First Defenders. A bill was introduced in the House of Representatives by Rep. Constantine Jacob Erdman (1846-1911), Pennsylvania's 9th Congressional District, from Lehigh County, for that purpose in the 1890s. An article appeared in the Jan. 20, 1896 edition of the *New York Evening Post*, under the heading, "Special Dispatch from Washington, City." It implied animus existed between the Massachusetts 6th Regiment and Pennsylvania's First Defender companies, over which could claim the honor of "first."

Maj. William F. McCay, Logan Guard and company historian, took exception to the newspaper's tone, in part, writing in response:

The Mass. Boys never did claim to be the first troops to reach Washington. They do claim that they were the first full regiment to arrive there. No one can question their right to this great distinction... the First Defenders... claim for themselves the great honor of being the first volunteers not only to encounter the blood thirsty mob at Baltimore... just 24 hours preceding the attack on the 6th Mass. and the first to reach

Secretary of War Certificate.

HAND-WRITTEN CERTIFICATE provided by Simon Cameron, Secretary of War, July 4, 1866. – Thompson's *The First Defenders*, 1910.

the Capital the same evening... When the 6th reached Washington, they found the First Companies of Pennsylvania... occupying the Capitol... They never had any dispute in regard to these facts... when the Grand Encampment of the Grand Army of the Republic was held at Washington, The First Defenders and the 6th Mass. held the Post of Honor in the Grand Review and at the head of the mighty Army of veterans... marched side by side in fraternal honor...

An earlier report from the Lewistown *Gazette,* dated April 7, 1876:

The Legislature has given the Logan Guards the precedence to which they are entitled, of being placed at the head of the roll of military organizations who responded to the call for volunteers at the outbreak of the Rebellion in 1861.

The 30th anniversary of the start of the Civil War, again brought up the "First of the First" question. An act of the General Assembly dated May 26, 1891 established that the Commonwealth of Pennsylvania would have medals of honor struck for each of the living First Defenders. In the lengthy letter to the *Philadelphia Times,* referred to in the previous chapter, Logan Guards' Colonel John B. Selheimer complained that an injustice had been done his company in that the design for the medal had not been submitted to them for approval, nor had they been consulted in regard to the position assigned his company on it. An excerpt follows from his letter dated July 27, 1891:

The Logan Guards should be the first company on the medal. It was the first company to report to Governor Curtin in Harrisburg. Early on the morning of April 17, 1861, I called on Governor Curtin and reported my company, and at the same time asked the Governor if any other companies were in, to which he replied that no other companies had as yet arrived, that mine was first.

Oliver C. Bosbyshell, a First Defender from the Washington Artillerists of Pottsville, was director of the Philadelphia mint at the time the medals were struck. He had considerable correspondence concerning the matter, and received a letter from then ex-Governor Curtin residing in Bellefonte, in which the former governor wrote:

I have been called upon repeatedly to know which company reported to me first, and I have answered according to the truth, the Logan Guards did report first ... I have had to answer this question before, and took pains to examine and found that the fact was as I now state to you to be correct.

The Ringgolds have excellent documentary evidence to bolster their claim of being "the first of the first." In his 1961 *Four Firsts in Berks — 1861*, Dr. Arthur D. Graeff, then president of the Pennsylvania First Defenders Association, cites an excerpt from a news item which appeared in a Harrisburg newspaper under the dateline April 17, 1861:

Last night about eight o'clock the Ringgold Artillery, Captain James McKnight, numbering 100 men arrived. They took up quarters at Herr's Hotel . . Our citizens welcome them with cheers.

Historian John E. Strohecker, Berks County Historical Society, argued that an item in the *Pennsylvania Daily Telegraph* of Harrisburg, dated April 18, 1861 proves the Ringgold's case. The newspaper states:

We give below a list of the companies that arrived last night:
Washington Artillery—Pottsville, Captain Wren, 110 men.
National Light Artillery—Pottsville, Captain McDonald, 104 men.
Allen Infantry Allentown, Captain Yeager, 64 men.

Strohecker concludes, "The Ringgold Company is not mentioned, for it had arrived the day before, the 16th." Strohecker further asserts that the flag of the Ringgold Light Artillery, now preserved by the Capitol Preservation Committee near the State Capitol, bears the date April 16, 1861.

As to the Logan Guards' case, Copeland asserted:

After exhausting all available sources of information pertaining to first honors, it would seem as if both claims (Ringgolds and Logans) are not without reasonable support — the break in the matter being expressed in provincial phrase that neither company "got there with both feet." The Reading company may have got there first, but the Lewistown company reported first.

John Strohecker further declared in 1961:

But the significance of which one of these five gallant companies was first—by a few hours—diminishes when we consider the colossal issues involved... let us dismiss this century-old controversy and rather rejoice in the fact that five companies of southeastern Pennsylvania were first to respond to President Lincoln's call for the defense of Washington in a crisis that divided not only the States, but the sympathy and loyalty of people within each of those States.

In the final analysis, Willis Copeland concluded, "...there was glory enough for all concerned.

- 10 -
LOGAN'S BANNER ENSHRINED

The fringed white, satin flag, handsomely designed and suitably inscribed, which the ladies of Lewistown presented to the Logan Guards in September 1859, was carried through Baltimore in April 1861. Whether the flag saw the battlefield after that is another matter. The War Department discouraged the use of company flags as the war proceeded, however the flag's condition suggests the banner must have been conserved early in its existence. The flag owes its preservation in great part to the thoughtful action of several of the Logan Guardsmen during and following the war.

Flag Day, 1914 — Front page image of Civil War veterans at State capital battle flag ceremony. – The Harrisburg *Patriot*, June 15, 1914, Historical Society of Dauphin County

John B. Selheimer, Logan Guards company commander, had possession of the flag until sometime between 1909 and 1914. During this period, former Logan Guard Edwin E. Zeigler acquired the flag, and had it placed between panes of glass held together with a heavy wooden box frame to prevent further deterioration. He eventually donated the relic to the Commonwealth, accompanied by Logan Guards, Frank H. Wentz and William B. Weber. The two were selected for the purpose by the surviving members of the Guards. In 1914, the flag was transferred to the Pennsylvania Historical and Museum Commission, displayed during the Civil War centennial in the former State Museum (renamed the Speaker Matthew J. Ryan Legislative Office Building in 1999). Today, it is on occasional exhibit in the military section at the present State Museum on the corner of Third and North streets in the Harrisburg capital complex. Now classified as a "banner" by the state, the original Logan Guards' silk flag cannot be taken from its casing

LOGAN GUARDS FLAG IN 1961 — Garver M. McNitt, at right, president of the Mifflin County Historical Society, and board member W. Randall Leopold, look at the Logan Guard flag in what was the War Trophies Room of the old State Museum, Harrisburg. The card at the center of the flag (concealing a missing section) stated: "Logan Guard Flag. The first flag carried through Baltimore and into Washington, D.C. in defense of the Union, April 18, 1861." The flag remains part of the State Museum's military collections. – Courtesy MCHS Archives, J. Martin Stroup photograph

without causing serious damage to the frail textile.

During repairs made in the Capitol building in 1895, the other state Civil War flags or national colors, were providentially moved to the State Library and Museum thus saved for posterity when the Capitol fire of February 2, 1897 completely gutted the brick structure.

On June 14, 1914, these state issued flags – generally with thirteen stripes in the field and a blue canton with the Pennsylvania coat of arms nestled among the national stars – were transferred to the 1906 Capitol building and placed in the rotunda during "inspiring and patriotic ceremonies." These old ensigns and standards, many showing evidence of having been in battle, were carried in procession through the streets of Harrisburg. The day included ceremonies of transfer, and as the pro-

JOHN P. TAYLOR (1827 - 1914)
The Reedsville, PA veteran, who had just passed his 87th birthday on June 5, 1914, carried the regimental flag of the First Pennsylvania Cavalry, which he had commanded during the Civil War. The Harrisburg march was on June 14th, Brigadier General Taylor died less than two weeks later, on June 27th. A soldier to the end, he made provisions to be buried in a coffin made from a recast bronze cannon. Local lore states it was a captured Confederate field piece used for the purpose, but prior to his death he denied that assertion in the county press. He insisted he acquired a decommissioned cannon tube through his contacts in the War Department. Yet the story persists. Taylor did serve as president of the Gettysburg Battlefield Monument Commission charged with placing monuments and cannons on that hallowed ground. Taylor's grave is in the Church Hill Cemetery, Reedsville, PA, marked by a large granite monument bearing his bearded profile in bronze.
– Courtesy MCHS Archives

gram culminated just before evening, the bearers marched past Governor John K. Tener, and entered the massive bronze doorway of the Capitol. The procession of veterans was led by survivors of the First Defenders, while the flag assigned the Logan Guards was carried on the occasion by Frank H. Wentz. This was not the original Logans' company flag, notes Willis Copeland, but a national flag bearing the name of the "Logan Guards." Copeland, however, does not mention the mystery surrounding this particular flag. Richard A. Sauers explains in *Advance the Colors!*, Vol. II, that in 1905 the War Department returned flags captured during the war, this one being a thirty-two star national color, delivered to Pennsylvania. The canton included a crouching Federal eagle on a shield, amid the stars, and a scroll inscribed "Logan Guards." A notation sent along stated: "U.S. Flag. Probably belongs to the State of Illinois, Inscribed 'Logan Guards,' no history." Sauers further notes that it was assumed by the War Department that it belonged to Pennsylvania because Company A, 46th Pennsylvania, was the old Logan Guards. At the time, Pennsylvania Adjutant-General Thomas J. Stewart sent a letter to the First Defenders Association inquiring about the flag. Henry A. Eisenbise, original Logan Guard of Lewistown, replied that the company survivors could not recall ever having this particular flag during their service. Nothing further is know about it, according to Sauers, and thus its provenance remains suspect.

IMPRESSIVE SCENES AS VETERANS CARRY COLORS FOR THE LAST TIME

SCENES DURING BATTLE FLAG TRANSFER — Harrisburg newspapers – *Patriot, Telegraph* and *Star-Independent* – reported that spectators wept, and applauded the aged soldiers, carrying the battle tattered flags to the Capitol building. At right above, are First Defenders Capt. Frank H. Wentz, Logan Guards, and Capt. Frederick M. Yeager, Ringgold Light Artillery. – *Harrisburg Telegraph*, Tuesday evening, June 16, 1914, Historical Society of Dauphin County

Nevertheless, this is the flag carried by Wentz during the 1914 ceremonies, along with fellow aged Civil War veterans, who formed up bearing their respective flags. Next to Wentz, carrying the Ringgold Light Artillery's flag, first U.S. colors to enter Washington, D.C., was Capt. Frederick M. Yeager, both men proudly wearing their First Defenders caps and association medals.

A total of 322 Civil War ensigns, standards and guidons were on parade, together with 22 flags from the Spanish - American War and one from the War of 1812, combining to make a massing of colors that had never been seen in Harrisburg. Several Mifflin Countians took part in the ceremonies, each designated to carry the flags of the regiments in which he had served.

Brevet Brigadier General John P. Taylor of Reedsville, who had just passed his 87th birthday (June 5), bore the regimental flag of the First Pennsylvania Cavalry, which he had commanded during the war. The elderly old war horse, despite his advanced years and infirmities, insisted on participating. (In fact, just weeks before, he offered his service to the United States in the event of war with Mexico during the 1914 incursion into US territory by Poncho Villa's forces.) Taylor persisted throughout the entire march on June 15, but required assistance

FIRST DEFENDERS LEAD 1914 PARADE — First Defender Frank H. Wentz, Lewistown, PA (second from right), with Frederick M. Yeager, Ringgold Light Artillery, Reading, PA (third from right), head the veterans' line of march during the 1914 transfer of the national flags in Harrisburg. – Courtesy MCHS Archives; PHMC Division Archives & Manuscripts

at several turns, the Lewistown *Gazette* reported. He died one week later at his family home, passing, some suggested, from the strain of this last march, a soldier to the end.

Other Mifflin Countians carried flags in the march. Joseph M. Owens, who as a schoolboy left the McAlisterville Academy to join the ranks, enlisting first in the 151st and later in the 205th Pennsylvania Volunteer Infantry, carried the flag of the 205th.

Lewis H. Ruble carried the colors of the 46th Infantry, having been a member of Company A, which was locally known as the Second Logan Guards, when they left for war in the fall of 1861.

Byron Carpenter, of Company F, 107th Infantry, which was commanded by Colonel Thomas F. McCoy of Lewistown, was appointed to carry the flag of his old regiment.

Isaiah Leightly, of Yeagertown, carried the colors of the 148th Infantry, led by General James A. Beaver.

W. H. Bratton carried the flag of the 112th, with some determination, since he lost an arm on the battlefield.

Among other Mifflin County veterans present were William B. Weber and Joseph A. Fichthorn (both old Logan Guards), Richard Shatzer, John Martin, S. B. Weber, John Garrett, John Davis and Joseph Hughes.

Thousands of Harrisburg residents and other Pennsylvanians gathered to see the parade, as the flag-bearers marched between lines of bareheaded men standing with their families to watch the flags go by. Capital city newspapers covered the event. Headlines in the June 16, 1914 edition of the Harrisburg *Patriot* announced, "Hearts Throb as Battle Scarred Flags Pass By," while the Harrisburg *Telegraph* heralded, "Impressive Scenes as Veterans Carry Colors for the Last Time." The *Telegraph* filmed the entire proceedings, and later screened the moving pictures in a local theatre. During the 1915 San Francisco Panama Exposition, visitors could view the *Telegraph* movie of the flag procession at the Pennsylvania Pavilion, where the film ran continuously, according to Richard A. Sauers, in *Advance the Colors*.

The Lewistown *Gazette* commented on the event, June 18, 1914, where the editor wrote:

Mifflin County bore a conspicuous part in the impressive proceedings. The procession was led by survivors of the First Defenders, the flag of the Logan Guards of Lewistown, carried on this occasion by Captain Frank H. Wentz, being the first called into line, four other color bearers of the First Defender companies lining up with him in bearing their respective flags. This was in keeping with the order placing the Logan Guards at the head of the column in Philadelphia many years ago when the flags of the Civil War were handed over to the state and General Hancock, then in charge, designated as "the right of the line."

THE LEWISTOWN GAZETTE

LEWISTOWN, PA., JUNE 18, 1914

Flag Transfer Ceremonies. .

Flags which led Pennsylvania soldiers in the war for the suppression of the rebellion and the Spanish war were moved from the state museum to the rotund t of the new state house Monday after being carried in procession through streets of Harrisburg. Many of the men who bore the 351 standards and guidons were the color bearers of the regiments in the wars, and their escorts were veterans of 1861–'65 and of 1898–'99, and militiamen.

The day was given up to the ceremonies attending the transfer, and the program culminated in the bearers marching by the governor in single file and entering the bronze doorway of the capitol, just before evening. Thousands of residents of Harrisburg and of other places in Pennsylvania gathered to see the parade, and the division flag bearers marched between lines of bare-

1914 PARADE MADE NEWS — First Defender Frank H. Wentz and Col. John P. Taylor, 1st PVC, marched in the 1914 event in Harrisburg. – Courtesy MCHS Archives

- II -
FIRST DEFENDERS REMEMBERED - 1961 CENTENNIAL

During the closing months of 1960, the Board of Directors of the Mifflin County Historical Society moved to recognize the 100th anniversary of the Civil War. Garver M. McNitt, president of the Society, appointed the following members to serve as a Civil War Centennial Committee: Willis R. Copeland, chairman; C. Roy Long, co-chairman: J. Martin Stroup, W. Randall Leopold, James F. Morgan, Harry W. Price, Jr. and George A. Ross. This committee was authorized to proceed with plans for a memorial in honor of the Logan Guards — a bronze plaque inscribed with the names of the company's members according

MARCH OF THE LOGAN GUARDS —Reenactors carry the Logan Guards' flag, at far right, in the April 16, 1961 Centennial Parade, shown on 3rd Street, Harrisburg, PA. – Courtesy MCHS Archives

to the muster-in roll, and to be placed at a suitable location in Lewistown, ultimately on the Third Street side of the Municipal Building.

Community groups in Reading, Allentown and Pottsville were busily engaged in laying the groundwork for a 1961 centennial ceremony commemorating the arrival of the five companies of First Defenders in Harrisburg. The historical society represented Mifflin County in a series of meetings held in Pottsville and Harrisburg during the winter of 1960-61, resulting in the formation of the Pennsylvania First Defenders Association. The group formulated the plans for the First Defenders' centennial commemorative ceremony.

Civil War Centennial:
Historical Society Plans to Honor 'First Defenders'

A permanent organization was later created at a meeting in Pottsville on December 17, 1960, at which the following officers were elected: Dr. Arthur D. Graeff, president; Leo L. Ward, first vice president; Willis R. Copeland, second vice president; W. Reese Super, secretary, and James F. Haas, treasurer. Walter S. Farquhar of Pottsville was named as chairman of publicity. It was also decided that the members of the Association should consist of the officers and three men representing each of the five companies of the First Defenders. This organization was instituted with the Logan Guards being represented by J. Martin Stroup, W. Randall Leopold and Rep. Harry W. Price, Jr.

Colonel Daniel Rogers, commanding the 213th Artillery Group (Air Defense) and Lieutenant Colonel Merril W. Goss, commanding the Third Squadron, 104th Armored Cavalry Regiment, Pennsylvania National Guard, made it possible for the Association to successfully carry out their most ambitious project — of having each company of First Defenders represented at the ceremony by the guard unit that was its lineal descendant.

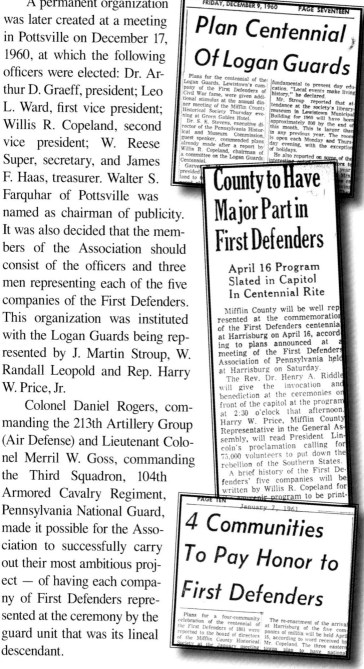

FRIDAY, DECEMBER 9, 1960   PAGE SEVENTEEN

Plan Centennial Of Logan Guards

Plans for the centennial of the Logan Guards, Lewistown's company of the First Defenders of Civil War fame, were given additional stimulus at the annual dinner meeting of the Mifflin County Historical Society Thursday evening at Green Gables Hotel.

Dr. S. K. Stevens, executive director of the Pennsylvania Historical and Museum Commission, guest speaker, commended plans already made after a report by Willis R. Copeland, chairman of a committee on the Logan Guards Centennial.

Garver presided and to

fundamental to present day education. "Local events make living history," he declared.

Mr. Stroup reported that attendance at the society's library museum in Lewistown Municipal Building for 1960 will have been approximately 800 by the end of this month. This is larger than in any previous year. The rooms is open each Monday and Thursday evening, with the exception of holidays.

He also reported on some of the interesting

County to Have Major Part in First Defenders

April 16 Program Slated in Capitol In Centennial Rite

Mifflin County will be well represented at the commemoration of the First Defenders centennial at Harrisburg on April 16, according to plans announced at a meeting of the First Defenders Association of Pennsylvania held at Harrisburg on Saturday.

The Rev. Dr. Henry A. Riddle will give the invocation and benediction at the ceremonies on front of the capitol at the program at 2:30 o'clock that afternoon. Harry W. Price, Mifflin County Representative in the General Assembly, will read President Lincoln's proclamation calling for 75,000 volunteers to put down the rebellion of the Southern States.

A brief history of the First Defenders' five companies will be written by Willis R. Copeland for souvenir program to be print-

PAGE TEN   January 7, 1961

4 Communities To Pay Honor to First Defenders

Plans for a four-community celebration of the centennial of the First Defenders of 1861 were reported to the board of directors of the Mifflin County Historical Society at the January meeting

The re-enactment of the arrival at Harrisburg of the five companies of militia will be held April 16, according to word received by Mr. Copeland. The three eastern towns plan to have nation-

MARCH OF THE LOGAN GUARDS — Members of the 104th Armored Regiment, PA National Guard and Civil War re-enactors represent the Logan Guards, April 16, 1961 march near the Capitol Building, Harrisburg, PA. – Courtesy MCHS Archives

It was a complex operation. These officers assigned line officers from their commands to serve with the five sub-committees as military consultants and liaison officers, the members of the Lewistown group were highly supportive of the selection of Captain Milton K. Brandt, Jr., commanding Headquarters Troop, Third Squadron, 104th Armored Cavalry, as their military representative. Willis Copeland commented on Brandt's selection:

Captain Brandt's keen personal interest in the project was the equal of that of any member of the Association and contributed largely toward the ultimate success of the venture.

The Mifflin Countians decided their military unit would march behind a replica of the old Logan Guard

flag. Mr. and Mrs. J. Martin Stroup made a detailed examination of the original banner at the Capitol and returned with a set of specifications which enabled work on the banner to begin at once.

The replica, of white taffeta with matching fringe, was sewn by Mrs. William R. Weyman of Lewistown, while the oil portrait of Chief Logan in repose, encircled by a wreath and by the motto, "Heroic Acts Win Immortality," is a tribute to the artistry of Mr. and Mrs. Kenneth T. Wilson, Jr. of Strodes Mills.

It was impossible to observe one side of the original flag in 1961 because of its

CIVIL WAR LINEAGE: Gov. David L. Lawrence shows the "First Defenders Centennial Week" proclamation to Willis R. Copeland, president of the Mifflin County Historical Society, and Capt. Milton K. Brandt Jr., of The Governor's Troop, Pennsylvania Army National Guard. The centennial honors the first Volunteer Militia units to report to President Abraham Lincoln for Civil War service. Among the units were the Logan Guards of Lewistown, now Headquarters and Headquarters Troop, Third Reconnaissance Squadron, 104th Armored Cavalry (The Governor's Troop).

★   ★   ★

3rd Recon Squadron Has 'Unlicked' Heritage:

Governor Proclaims
First Defenders Week

GOVERNOR'S PROCLAMATION — Willis R. Copeland, Mifflin County Historical Society; Pennsylvania Governor David Lawrence; and Capt. Milton K. Brandt, Jr., PNG, look at the "First Defenders Centennial Week" document in Harrisburg. – Courtesy MCHS Archives

extreme fragility, and with no records to guide them, the Flag Committee had appliquéed on the reverse side the legend, "Logan Guards — 1858 — Lewistown, Pa.," in blue block letters and numerals (see p. 27). Since then, the original Logan Guards' flag has occasionally been displayed in the Civil War hall at the State Museum. *Advance the Colors! Pennsylvania Civil War Battle Flags, Vol. I* by Richard A. Sauers describes the Logan's flag in some detail. The actual reverse depicts an American Eagle with the details of the presentation inscribed in a circle around the bird (see p. 28).

The official governmental portion of the First Defenders' centennial ceremony resulted through the efforts of Mifflin County's representative in the General Assembly. Rep. Harry W. Price, Jr. proposed to his colleagues from Berks, Lehigh and Schuylkill Counties that, as representatives of the counties that produced the five companies of First Defenders, they should collectively draw up and present a bill to the Legislature declaring the week of April 16-22, 1961, officially designated as "The First Defenders Centennial Week." This bi-partisan piece of legislation passed handily and was enacted into law when Governor David L. Lawrence signed the proclamation in the presence of members of the five sub-committees, with Logan Guards representatives Willis R. Copeland and Captain Milton K. Brandt, Jr. in attendance.

Governor Lawrence proclaimed:

With the designation of this centennial, we are commemorating a most important event in Pennsylvania history. Historically, in times of crisis, Pennsylvania and its people have responded quickly to the nation's needs. In no other incident is this type of responsibility more dramatically illustrated than in the response to the call for volunteers by President Lincoln.

The action is a significant landmark in the history of Pennsylvania's military establishment, the Pennsylvania National Guard, successors to the Pennsylvania Militia.

Copeland attended the First Defenders' centennial event in the state capital. Here follows his narrative:

The
Pennsylvania First Defenders
1861-1961

Centennial
Commemorative Ceremonies

STATE CAPITOL GROUNDS
Harrisburg, Pennsylvania

SUNDAY, APRIL 16, 1961
2:30 P. M.

PROGRAM, FIRST DEFENDERS CENTENNIAL CEREMONY — Groups from Lewistown, Pottsville, Reading and Allentown participated in the Civil War centennial event, April 16, 1961. – Courtesy MCHS Archives

In Harrisburg, Sunday morning, April 16, 1961, an overcast sky with more than a hint of rain, caused Major John H. Runkle to most seriously deliberate as to whether the ceremonies should be held on the steps of the Capitol, where a reviewing stand had been set up by the Pennsylvania Historical and Museum Commission, or whether they should be transferred to the security and shelter of the Capitol's rotunda.

Major Runkle, who at one time had held the office of National Commander of the Sons of Union Veterans of the Civil War and who was still an ar-

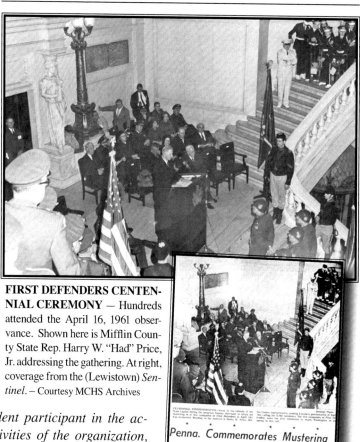

FIRST DEFENDERS CENTENNIAL CEREMONY — Hundreds attended the April 16, 1961 observance. Shown here is Mifflin County State Rep. Harry W. "Had" Price, Jr. addressing the gathering. At right, coverage from the (Lewistown) *Sentinel*. – Courtesy MCHS Archives

dent participant in the activities of the organization, had long been preparing for this day and was keenly feeling his responsibility for the success, or failure, of the ceremony. He had labored long and faithfully to set up the mechanics of the event, working mostly behind the scenes, and he was determined that the weather should not divert him from the successful completion of his mission.

As he was pondering the situation, the sound of music caused the crowd, which had been milling about the Capitol grounds, to rush to view the parade which was coming up Third Street in strict military formation with the bands playing in regulation cadence.

Units of the Sons of Union Veterans Reserves and of the North-

LOGAN GUARD REPLICA FLAG — Mifflin County participants in the First Defenders centennial at Harrisburg on Sunday afternoon, April 16, 1961 are grouped under a replica of the flag carried by the Logan Guards from Harrisburg through Baltimore to Washington in April 1861. On the other side of the flag is a image of Chief Logan. Identification with the photograph, include: Holding the flag is at left Lt. Melvin Hughes, and at right, Captain Milton K. Brandt, Jr., both of the local unit of the Pennsylvania National Guard. Others, left to right, are Willis R. Copeland, Lewistown Mayor John J. Lawler, J. Martin Stroup, Rep. Harry W. Price, Jr. and Rev. Dr. Henry A. Riddle. The little "miss" is Susan Wray, grand-daughter of Dr. Riddle. – Courtesy MCHS Archives

South Skirmishers Association, clad in blue uniforms of Civil War type, marched as escort and honor guards for the long column of steel-helmeted guardsmen which filled the street for nearly as far as the eye could see, and once again, after the lapse of a century, the flag of the Logan Guards passed in review. With bearers and guards uniformed in Union blue, a 34-star national ensign and the white standard of the Logans waved at the head of the long column of troops, in which the leading unit was the lineal descendant

[142]

CROWDS FILL THE CAPITOL ROTUNDA — Representatives from the five First Defender companies - Allen Infantry, National Light Infantry, Washington Artillerists, Logan Guards, Ringgold Light Artillery - attend the April 16, 1961 centennial ceremony. – Courtesy MCHS Archives

of the Logan Guards, Headquarters Troop of the Third Squadron, 104th Armored Cavalry commanded by Captain Milton K. Brandt, Jr. and Lieutenant Melvin Hughes. At the risk of being deemed repetitious, we would once again inform our readers that the Logan Guards held "the right of the line."

Following the cavalrymen came: the Headquarters Battery, 51st Artillery Brigade and Headquarters Battery, 213th Artillery Group, representing the Allen Infantry; Battery B, Second Gun Battalion, 213th Artillery Group, representing the National Light Infantry; the 408th Ordnance Detachment and Battery D, Second Gun Battalion, 213th Artillery Group, representing the Washington Artillerists and Headquarters Battery, Second Gun Battalion, 213th Artillery Group, representing the Ringgold Light Artillery.

The entire event, with its exhaustive planning and preparations, was a tribute to the memory of the First Defenders, and to the dedication of their descendants and to the communities that sent their young men to war in 1861. Time would work its will with the passing years, yet in 1961 there were those still living who knew some of the long lived Logan Guards.

CENTENNIAL PLAQUE
During the Civil War cen-
tennial years, the Mifflin County Historical Society moved forward with plans for a permanent memorial to the First Defenders. This effort took shape in the form of a bronze plaque enumerating the volunteers on the Muster-In Roll from April 1861.

It was decided to place the memorial on the Third Street side of the Lewistown Municipal Building. The site was the former location of Lewistown's Town Hall, a two story brick building that not only housed the borough offices, but the second floor was the location of the Col. Thomas M. Hulings Post No. 176, Grand Army of the Republic. The Post was chartered in 1868 and disbanded in 1929. The veteran's hall acted as the Borough Council meeting room, while the lock-up, and the few municipal offices were on the ground floor.

LOGAN GUARDS HONORED: A plaque honoring the role played by the Logan Guards during the Civil War is admired by officers of the Historical Society. Erected on the Municipal Building, it lists the members of the famed Guards. Chauncey E. Shull, director of the project, points to the name of his grandfather, Chauncey M. Shull, on the list. Left to right are J. Martin Stroup, secretary of the society, Shull and Garver McNitt, president.

LOGAN GUARDS COMMEMORAT-
ED — The plaque placed on the Lewistown Municipal Building's Third Street side is admired by Mifflin County Historical Society board members. Left to right, J. Martin Stroup, secretary; Chauncey E. Shull, plaque committee chair; Garver M. McNitt, president. – Courtesy MCHS Archives

Chauncey E. Shull chaired the historical society's plaque committee through the planning stages to dedication. Shull's grandfather, Chauncey M. Shull was a private in the Logan Guards when the company left for Washington in April 1861. The plaque served a duel purpose, according to a January 11, 1966 news report in the Lewistown *Sentinel*, noting, "Thus the plaque commemorates the famous Logan Guards and marks the site of the meeting hall of the Civil War veterans' organization of 1868 - 1929."

Logan Guards Plaque — Erected in 1965 by the Mifflin County Historical Society on the site of the meeting hall of Col. Thomas M. Hulings Post, No. 176, Grand Army of the Republic; chartered 1868, disbanded 1929. It can be seen on the Third Street side of the Lewistown Municipal Building, Lewistown, PA. Today, Logan Guard Post No. 90 of the American Legion, is the descendant organization of the old Logan post. Originally located in the Ahren's Building, corner of West Market and Juniata Streets according to newspaper reports in 1920 and 1921, Logan Guard Post No. 90 is today located at 100 Valley Street, Lewistown, PA. The post continues its mission to area service personnel and veterans, advocating patriotism and honor, and is affiliated with the nation's largest veterans' service organization.

- 12 -
2011 LOGAN GUARDS SESQUICENTENNIAL

Chris Walters, of Burnham, awaits the march of the company to Lewistown Junction.

Ladies and Gentlemen, we are going back in time to April 1861. The news has just reached the community of Mifflin County that General P. G. T. Beauregard, commanding the Confederate forces in Charleston, S.C. has demanded the surrender of Fort Sumter by the United States to the Confederate States.

Major Anderson, commander of Fort Sumter, refused and the Confederate Floating Battery began firing on Fort Sumter.

The next morning, April 12, 1861, the Governor of Pennsylvania received a telegram explaining what had occurred. Three days later on the 15th Abraham Lincoln issued his proclamation calling out the militia of several states to the number of 75,000 men. Governor Curtin received a telegraph from the Secretary of War that a call had been made on Pennsylvania for 16 regiments. Two regiments were wanted within three days, as a sudden dash upon the Capital was already strongly threatened.

On April 16th Governor Curtin sent out a telegraph to the commanding officer of the one militia that had already tendered its services to him.

Thus began the narrative of the sesquicentennial remembrance when Lewistown's Logan Guards mustered into service at the start of the Civil War. The narration, written by Crystal Jost of Lewistown, was delivered from the front steps of the Historic 1843 Mifflin County Courthouse on

Logan Guard March

Saturday, May 7, 2011
at 1pm in *Lewistown, PA*

This year marks the 150th anniversary of Mifflin County's own Logan Guard of Lewistown answering Lincoln's call for volunteers at the start of the Civil War. On April 16, 1861, the Guard marched from the Town Square to Lewistown Junction, entrained to Harrisburg, then on to Washington, DC. This unit was part of the First Defenders of the Union cause.

Event Program
May 7, 2011

Dan McClenahen, historian and MCHS President, offers historical perspective on the life and times of the Lewistown company in the second floor courtroom of the Historic Mifflin County Courthouse. The 1961 Civil War centennial Logan Guards' flag commissioned by the Mifflin County Historical Society can be seen behind the judge's bench.

Saturday, May 7, 2011. These words prepped those gathered around Monument Square for the reenactment of the Logan Guard March, recreating events that occurred on the very spot 150 years ago. The event was co-sponsored by the 148th Field Hospital & Venture Crew, Mifflin County Historical Society, and the Juniata River Valley Chamber of Commerce & Visitor's Bureau.

The ceremonies began in the second floor courtroom at 1 p.m., with remarks by Daniel M. McClenahen, county historian and Mifflin County Historical Society president. Flanked on either side by the National colors and the State flag, the Logan Guards' 1961 Civil War centennial flag graced the prominent position on the wall behind the judges' bench.

With this backdrop, McClenahen set the stage

Townsfolk gather outside the Historic Mifflin County Courthouse, May 7, 2011. – Author's photos in this chapter

Brandon Folk, of McClure, portrays Capt. Selheimer as he instructs young Elias Cogley (portrayed by Seth Snyder, of Lewistown) to send a telegraph back to Gov. Curtin stating the Logan Guard is ready.

for the afternoon events, speaking to the families, friends and interested citizens filling the seats in the courtroom. The presentation illuminated the historical setting that led to the formation of the Lewistown company, as well as the many other volunteer militia companies across Mifflin County. McClenahen's narrative led the gathering through the early local militia traditions to Mifflin County's anti-slave sentiment in the antebellum years of the 19th century. He described the very room in which the gathering assembled, a gas-lit courtroom in the 1850s and 1860s, the actual scene where local citizens debated the troubled times at many assemblies and meetings in the days leading up to the war.

At approximately 2 p.m., the attendees and Civil War reenactors moved to the area in front of the courthouse steps, with streets blocked off by the local fire police. Tom Sheeder, of Mount Union, narrator for the outdoor portion of the program, continued the time line of events from that April day in 1861. Characters in period costume enacted the narrative. The dialogue representing the essence of the historical events between Elias Cogley, assistant telegraph operator at Lewistown Junction, Captain John B. Selheimer, Sergeant Rob-

Narrator Tom Sheeder, of Mount Union, at the Historic Courthouse, and later concludes at Lewistown Junction.

Civilians join the ranks for the march to the Junction, assembling along North Main Street.

ert W. Patton, and Mrs. George Elder, spokesperson for the ladies of Lewistown.

Lewistown ladies offer their help on the home front, while the Logan Guards prepare to march to the Junction. Brandon Folk, McClure, portraying Capt. Selheimer; Andre Wagner, McClure; Seth Snyder, Lewistown (boy behind A. Wagner, portrayed Elias Cogley); Nathan Jost, Lewistown (obscured by tree); Crystal Jost, Lewistown; David Eward, Lewistown (black hat); Maria Maneval, Richfield; Sarah Jost, Lewistown (small girl). Far right is Rachel Jost, Lewistown; the girl looking at her from behind, Bekah Platzer, of Burnham; behind Bekah is Nathaniel Weaver, Lewistown (wearing glasses).

Elias: "Captain Selheimer! Captain Selheimer! This just came for you! It's from the Secretary of the Commonwealth!"

Captain: "Thank you Elias." (Reading): "If your company numbers seventy-seven men rank and file come tonight – stop – If not, increase number if possible and be ready to come when telegraphed for – stop – Answer." (Look around for Sergeant Patton) "Patton! Patton!"

Patton: "Yes Captain. What is it?"

Captain: "The Governor has called upon the Logan Guard to muster in. Do we take a day to get our affairs in order or do we go now? What say you?"

Patton: "The Union needs us. We must go."

Captain: "Elias. Telegraph the Governor's office and tell him we are coming!"

Elias: "Yes Sir!"

David Eward, of Lewistown, signs the volunteer book in front of the Historic Mifflin County Courthouse.

[149]

Marching past the location of the former Red Lion Inn, now the Coleman House, where the Logan Guards and citizens gathered in April 1861, hosted by Col. Daniel Eisenbise, owner of the Red Lion and local community and militia leader.

Ladies from the community approach.

Mrs. Elder: "Captain Selheimer? We would like a moment."

Captain: "Yes, Mrs. Elder?"

Mrs. Elder: "Captain, some of us ladies met together last night and we want to let you know that we will support you and our men through our Country's present crisis. We pledge to unite our labors here at home in behalf of the health and comfort of our men in the field."

Captain: "Thank you, Mrs. Elder. Rest assured we will put to use all that you might send us." And then ordered, "Logan Guard! Muster in!"

The Civil War reenactors assembled, forming up on N. Main St., facing east, toward what is now the Juniata Valley Bank. While the Guards were reenacting the mustering in, a folding table was set up by the courthouse steps, with the sign-up book, fountain pens and an original ink well from the Historic Courthouse, (now part of the Mifflin County Historical Society collections). Citizens of Mifflin County were invited to join. Citing the imperiled Union and that the call to action has come, Capt. Selheimer announced they needed men to fill the company.

Captain: "If you are willing to defend the Union, come sign up. We leave as soon as our company is full."

At this point, after the "volunteers" signed the book, everyday citizens could become part of the march, and were given the opportunity to actually "sign up," just like volunteers of yore. Soon the participants were finally assembled, and the Captain signaled, "Company, Forward – March!"

1st Sgt. Michael Alan Walters, of Burnham, proudly walked in the footsteps of his 3rd great grandfather, Henry Augustus Walters, private in the Logan Guards, April 1861.

Many members of the public, young and old alike, followed along behind the soldiers, replicating in spirit, if not in numbers, the events of 1861. The line marched west on Market Street to a steady, military cadence, tapped out to the rhythm of a drum, across the Juniata River Memorial Bridge to Lewistown Junction, where the remembrance concluded. An ambulance from United EMS followed the line, and marked the end of the parade. All along, modern traffic was stopped in both directions on old US 22/322 on West Fourth Street at the river bridge, and on PA Route 103 descending from Juniata Terrace. Traffic was held up for miles in all directions, a problem not even contemplated one hundred fifty years ago.

A rain squall swept over the gathering at the railroad station, scattering some in the crowd. Once the procession was in the parking lot at the depot, the company moved on the grassy area adjacent to the station.

Captain: "Alright men. There seems to be a bit of a problem. The train will not be here for another three hours. Fall out until the train arrives."

Sgt. Frank Jost of the 148th Field Hospital, leads a section of the civilian volunteers on the march to the Junction. Center is Thomas Maduzia, US Army Ret., Logan Guard Post 90, American Legion, Lewistown, PA.

The narrator revealed to the crowd and civilian marchers, that the train was late that day, explaining:

Most of the men remained at the train station until the train arrived. They did not want to go through the pain of parting from their loved ones again. The Logan Guard arrived in Harrisburg early the morning of the April 17th and was joined by four other units that day.

At dawn the morning of the 18th all five companies were assembled at the railway station, mustered in and sworn by the uplifted hand into the service of the United States. They were informed to leave their firearms there because they were to be issued new firearms once they reach the Capital. However, the Logan Guard did not comply with this order. Even though they had no powder, they brought their Springfield rifles anyway.

Once the units reached Baltimore, they had to march two miles across the city to catch their next train to the Capital. Baltimore was a deeply south-

The company assembles at Lewistown Junction, and receives the news that the train is late. Historically, the Logans waited hours for the train to Harrisburg.

ern sympathizing city. Sensing the mood of the crowd gathered to watch the soldiers march, one of the members of the Logan Guard passed out percussion caps to his fellows. They placed the caps on their weapons and left them half-cocked to give the appearance of being armed and ready to fire. This is believed to have kept them from being mobbed.

But because the Logan Guard was at the front of the ranks, the units at the rear were not quite so lucky. As they arrived at the Camden Station and were boarding the train of box cars, the crowd began to throw bricks with the insults they had been throwing

Crystal Jost, of Lewistown, and Sally Walters, of Burnham, ready to send off the volunteers. In the background, Sgt. Andrew Benner, of McClure, confers with Sgt. Frank Jost..

during the whole march. Several men from the other units were hurts. And thus they earned the title of having spilled "first blood" of the Civil War.

The Logan Guard reached Washington DC at 6 p.m. on the 18th of April. Less than 48 hours after the call was received. They occupied the Capital Building and began at once to strengthen it with barricades. The Guards enlistment was for 90 days because everyone believed it

Before the march — From left, Donald E. "Red" Husler Jr. of Mifflintown; Andre Wagner, McClure (back to camera); Brandon Folk, McClure (all the way in the back); and James Kenneth Platzer III. — **Capt. Lamar Richard**, at right, of the 148th Field Hospital, sets up his "medical wares" demonstrating the state of Civil War medicine.

would be over quickly. Once the 90 day enlistment was over, the members returned home. No one had to fire a shot.

Many in the Logan Guard re-enlisted not just once but several times throughout the course of the war. You may find that your ancestors were in several different units. You can check out your family history at the Mifflin County Historical Society. This concludes today's remembrance.

Sgt. Frank Jost, center, discusses the finer points of the day's march with Donald E. "Red" Husler Jr., back to camera, and Sgt. Andrew Benner, of McClure.

It was an historic day for reenactors, both soldiers and citizens, the supporting participants, the townsfolk and those walking in the footsteps of the Logan Guards. The following were involved in the program and march:

Logan Guard march participants, May 7, 2011

From the 148th PA Regt. Field Hospital, Lewistown:
David Eward, Lewistown
Bryant Hostetler, Milroy
Crystal Jost, Lewistown
Frank Jost, Lewistown
Nathan Jost, Lewistown
Rachel Jost, Lewistown
Sarah Jost, Lewistown
Zachary Jost, Lewistown
Maria Maneval, Richfield
David Monsell, Lewistown
Lamar Richard, Lewistown
Melanie Smith, Lewistown
Sue Smith, Lewistown
Seth Snyder, Lewistown
Nathaniel "George" Weaver, Lewistown

From the 147th PA Volunteer Infantry Regiment, McClure:
Andrew Benner, McClure
Brandon Folk, McClure
Andre Wagner, McClure

From the 149th "Bucktails" PA Volunteer Infantry Regiment, Lewistown:
Mike Walters, Burnham
Chris Walters, Burnham
Sally Walters, Burnham

Additional reenactors:
Brandon Benner, Thompsontown
Chase Hornberger, Mifflinburg
Donald E. "Red" Husler Jr., Mifflintown
James Kenneth Platzer III, Burnham
Bekah Platzer, Burnham
Dale Wilburne, of Lewistown (drummer for the march)

Supporting participants:
Tom Sheeder, Mount Union (narrator)
Messenger (the band), of Lewistown (sound system)
Lewistown Police Dept.
Granville Twp. Police Dept.
Lewistown Fire Police
Yoder Tourways, McVeytown (transportation support)
Mifflin County Historical Society
Juniata River Valley Chamber of Commerce

LOGAN GUARDS HONORED WITH JULY CONCERT

The 2011 Friends of the Embassy Theatre "Let Freedom Ring" concert honored the memory of the Logan Guards. A crowd numbering in the hundreds gathered on South Main Street, Lewistown, Friday, July 2, 2011. The Lewistown Community Band and Chorus filled the summer evening with the sounds of patriotic music.

The band, under the direction of Peter Marsh, included a special tribute to the Lewistown company. Marjorie Davidson, the band's narrator for the evening, shared background information on the musical selections, including: "Washington Post March", "American Patrol", "Glen Miller In Concert", "American Salute" and "Semper Fidelis."

As the story of the Lewistown company was told, Civil War-era tunes on fife and drums softly accompanied the spoken history of the Logan Guards. The narrator told of the Guards' mustering in the town square in April 1861, as the strains of "The Girl I Left Behind Me" swelled to fill the street, much as the same tune was played 150 years

July 2, 2011 — Lewistown Community Band concert remembering the events of April 1861, when the Logan Guards marched from Lewistown as First Defenders of the Union cause. Hundreds brought lawn chairs for the event. The crowd waves US flags during the finale, "Stars and Stripes Forever."

earlier, when the company stepped off toward a departure from Lewistown Junction.

The community chorus, under the direction of Terri Limes, sang "Song for the Unsung Hero," by Pamela and Joseph Martin. This was written in honor of those whose "love of freedom found power stronger than their fears" and who lost their lives on Sept. 11, 2001. The "Battle

LOGAN GUARDS REMEMBERED — Director Peter Marsh leads the Lewistown Community Band, under the marquee of the Embassy Theatre during the July 2, 2011 "Let Freedom Ring" concert. Hundreds of Mifflin Countians filled South Main Street during the commemorative event. – Courtesy Lewistown *Sentinel*

Hymn of the Republic" was a highlight by band and chorus later in the concert.

Students from Miss Stephanie's School of Dance also performed to Meredith Wilson's "Seventy-Six Trombones". The dancers include: Finnian Saylor, Mariah Stimely, Kaitlin Bell, Katherine Crowder, Megan Ingram and Olivia Runk.

The Honor Guard of Central Pennsylvania Chapter 791, Vietnam Veterans of America participated in the event, and took part in the "Armed Forces Salute" utilizing service flags from five branches of the armed forces. Chaplain Brad Williams presented a tribute to Prisoners of War and those Missing in Action. John Philip Sousa's "Stars and Stripes Forever" was the closing selection.

In a letter published in the Lewistown *Sentinel* the following week, writer and concert attendee Sis Norton of McVeytown, PA commented:

Thanks for a wonderful evening of music, dance and remembering and thanks to all who brought their chairs and themselves to be a part of this marvelous concert.

The Lewistown Community Band is shown at Monument Square, assembled days prior to the annual "Let Freedom Ring" concert held July 2, 2011. The organization continues the local tradition of celebrating a notable occasion with music, reminiscent of the send off the Logan Guards' received in 1861. Band members shown, from left, front, Marjorie Davidson and Peter Marsh; second row, Nate Peachey, Jerry Stone, John Penland, Chris Maugans, Terri Limes, Heidi Traxler, Kathy Hartley, Art Belfiore, Fred Richard, Tracy Loucks, Josie Baughman, Dave Switzer, Nancy Machmer, Gene Hoffmaster and Josh Berkey; third row, Nick Cummings, Stephanie Diehl, Kathy Carter, Joan Loewen, Sharon Marsh, Ellen Miller, Trisha Farleman, Bob Davidson, Neta Hoffmaster, Amanda Richtscheit and Dave McCachren; fourth row, Kara Kavala, Freda Richard, Carol Mater, Joy Horning, Connie Reese, Beth Myers, Pauli Belfoire, Marilyn Erb, Margie Krebs and Susan Ferguson. – Courtesy Fred & Freda Richard, Lewistown Community Band

What a nice way to start the 4th of July weekend by sitting under a sky of blue in South Main Street, Lewistown, PA. God bless America!

- 13 -
EPILOGUE - MEN OF THE LOGAN GUARDS

Throughout their lives, the men of the Logan Guards remained a close-knit group. Attendance at annual First Defender gatherings and local reunions was recorded in the minute books of the local G.A.R. post, and in the local press. Even as their ranks swiftly dwindled in the 20th century, local newspapers reported the attendance of loyal company members at each passing.

In April 1861, ninety-two men left for war from Lewistown Junction as members of the Logan Guards. Eighty-seven returned with their company at the expiration of their three month enlistments. The five men not present with their returning brethren comprise a disparate, yet intriguing group. They include:

* A militia captain who, unexpectedly and virtually overnight, became second in command of a regiment of infantry.
* A veteran of the Mexican American War who had commanded a company of U. S. Regulars in that war, and who took his place in the ranks of the Logan Guards as a private. He later attained the rank of brigadier-general. He was also the step-father of a fellow Logan, and once served as Adjutant-General of Pennsylvania.
* A young Logan Guards' standard bearer who would wear silver stars on his shoulders before war's end, and became a close aide to a future candidate for U.S. President, as well as a future president. He was also the step-son of another member of the company.
* A crippled musician who did his best to stay in the service, but who was overruled by higher authority and eventually honorably discharged due to his physical disability.
* A deserter.

John B. Selheimer was the militia captain. Lieutenant-colonel, 25th Pennsylvania Volunteer Infantry, and former captain of the Logan Guards. Colonel Selheimer was a member of one of the old military families of Central Pennsylvania. He was a great-grandson of Nicholas Selheimer who, for eight years, served as a soldier with the American forces in the War of Independence. Two of Nicholas' five sons, John and Jacob, served in the War of 1812. John was killed on the US flagship *Niagara* under the command of Commodore Oliver Hazard Perry at the battle

Capt. John Beale Selheimer, 1861
Aug. 18, 1826 - Dec. 16, 1893

of Lake Erie. The *Niagara* was designed and built by Daniel Dobbins, whose home was on the south shore of the Juniata, opposite Lewistown.

Selheimer's Hardware Store, founded in 1848 by the Logan Guards' captain, was a fixture on Market Square for over sixty years. His revered status in the community was due, in no small part, to his Logan Guard leadership. Selheimer's image in this advertisement appeared in the 1894 *Lewistown, Penna., As It Is* by H.J. Fosnot. It was published the year after his death by the *Democrat and Sentinel*.
– Courtesy MCHS Archives

John B. Selheimer's father was William Selheimer, born in 1776 in Franklin County; his father was Absalom B. Selheimer, also born in Franklin County. Colonel Selheimer was born on August 18, 1826, in Milford Township, Juniata County, where he spent his boyhood. He attended the common schools until age of sixteen, then traveled to Lewistown to became a tinsmith's apprentice, later continuing the trade in Philadelphia. Returning to Lewistown in 1848, he opened a successful hardware business, that prospered on Market Square. In 1858, the Logan

Selheimer Family Monument — St. Mark's Cemetery, Lewistown, PA. John B. Selheimer's individual marker, lower right.

Guards organized and elected him as their captain. Four of his brothers — Napoleon, David, Absalom and Oliver — served in the Union army during the Civil War. Brother David was a businessman in South Carolina, who left for the north immediately after the attack on Fort Sumter.

After the war, Selheimer maintained the family hardware business until his death, and had interests in the Lewistown Gas Company, Lewistown Electric, Light, Heat and Power Company, and the Mann Edge Tool Company. Col. Selheimer would "fight" in another sense, for the honor of his company being the "First of the First", when the Commonwealth prepared to strike Medals of Honor for all First Defenders in 1891.

He died at age 67 December 16, 1893, and is buried in St. Mark's Cemetery, Lewistown, PA. An item in the Mount Union, PA newspaper, the *Mount Union Times,* dated Friday, January 11, 1895 notes:

> *The largest monument in Mifflin county now stands in the Episcopal* (St. Mark's) *cemetery at Lewistown. It marks the last resting-place of Colonel John B. Selheimer, one of the first brace of men who reached Washington at the outbreak of the Civil Rebellion. The monument is over thirty-five feet high, and was put up by Chas Stratford.*

William Howard Irwin
1819 - 1886

William H. Irwin was a veteran of the Mexican-American War. A native of Mifflin County, Irwin had been prominently identified with the militia of the county for years prior to the Mexican War. In 1847, the Juniata Guards, of which he was company commander, was incorporated into the newly organized 11th U. S. Infantry Regiment as Company D, and was ordered to Mexico, where Captain Irwin was wounded at the battle of Molino del Rey. Returning to his home, he resumed his law practice and later was appointed by the Governor as Adjutant- General of Pennsylvania.

Enlisting in the Logan Guards as a private, he was elected brevet second lieutenant while in the Capitol, April 20, 1861, and, a few days later, was commissioned by Governor Curtin as commander of the Seventh Pennsylvania Volunteer Infantry, a three months regiment. At the end of this term of service, he received his commission as colonel of the 49th Regiment, a three years organization. He was wounded while his regiment was crossing the Rappahannock at Fredericksburg, April 29, 1863. In October 1863, he resigned his commission and retired from service With his declining health listed as "exhaustion" and disabilities from wounds, the Army concluded he was unsuited for the rigors of service. (Irwin suffered serious wounds in the Mexican-American War, as well.) He afterwards received the brevet of brigadier-general of volunteers, for gallant and meritorious services.

Irwin's official report of September 22, 1862 on Crampton's Gap and Antietam, stated, in part:

This brigade charged the enemy at 10 a.m. on the 17th, drove them from their ground, which before had been severely contested, occupied and held it for twenty-six hours until relieved at noon the next day by General Couch's division. It was under fire constantly during this time in a most exposed position, lost 311 in killed and wounded, yet neither officers nor men fell back or gave the slightest evidence of any desire to do so. My line was immovable, only anxious to be launched against the enemy. I forbear comment on such conduct. It will commend itself to the heart and mind of every true soldier.

Several officers under his command early in the war filed charges and he was tried under court martial early in 1862 for drunkenness and "conduct prejudicial to good order and military discipline." He was acquitted of the first charge but convicted of the latter, which drew an inconsequential suspended punishment. His 3rd Brigade fought well during Antietam, and Irwin was commended. Following the war, he was named as a brevet brigadier general for his service and his conduct at Antietam.

After the war, when General Hancock was in command of the Southern Department, General Irwin was on his staff as legal adviser. Irwin remained in Lewistown, engaged in business pursuits for several years after the war, and then moved to Indiana, and later to the city of Louisville, Kentucky. His health deteriorated, and was hospitalized for what today would be described as dependence on pain killers. Medically, he suffered the adverse effects of the severe wound to his foot, which caused constant pain. Laudanum was the standard prescriptive to alleviate pain in the 1880s. One laudanum dose of the period would approximate 1200 grains of opium combined with 20 fluid ounces of seventy-six percent alcohol. His complicated condition of physical pain and addiction to laudanum was recognized then as signs of insanity. Irwin was committed to what was called Central Kentucky Lunatic Asylum in 1885. He died less than three months later on January 17, 1886 from "exhaustion."

Brig. Gen. Irwin's grave marker at Cave Hill Cemetery, Louisville, Jefferson County, Kentucky, 2008. – Courtesy Mike Dover, US Army, Ret.

The undertone of alcohol use persisted. In the early 1990s, C. Eugene Miller, Ph.D., Professor Emeritus at the University of Louisville, asserted in an essay, "An Exoneration of a Gentleman from Pennsylvania," that some later historians question his sobriety at the Battle of Antietam, reporting he was under the influence of "John Barleycorn" while delivering orders during that battle. Through exhaustive research, in part completed at the Mifflin County Historical Society aided extensively by Research Librarian Jean Aurand Laughlin, Dr. Miller defended General Irwin's war record by refuting the accusations of alcoholism, pointing rather to the influence of the standard laudanum treatment of the era, among other points. Irwin's remains were placed in an unmarked grave after his death at the asylum. Dr. Miller was instrumental in having Irwin receive overdue recognition, and a proper monument was erected during an impressive ceremony in 1993 at Cave Hill Cemetery, Louisville, Jefferson County, Kentucky. A floral wreath was sent in memory of Gen. Irwin by the Mifflin County Historical Society.

William Howard Irwin was the step-father of a fellow Logan Guardsman, William G. Mitchell.

William Galbraith Mitchell 1836 - 1883

William G. Mitchell was the young standard bearer, who carried the Logan Guards' flag through Baltimore at the head of the column of the First Defenders. He left the Guards at the same time as the departure of Colonel Irwin, receiving an appointment as adjutant in Col. Irwin's regiment, the 7th. He was mustered in as first lieutenant of Company H, 49th Pennsylvania Volunteer Infantry, a three years regiment, on August 15, 1861; his regimental commander being his old comrade, William H. Irwin. Lieutenant Mitchell was promoted to the rank of major, June 25, 1863, and appointed aide-de-camp on the staff of General Hancock. His gentlemanly deportment and gallant bearing brought him rapid promotion, finally as chief-of-staff to General Hancock.

Mitchell Family Monument — St. Mark's Cemetery, Lewistown, PA. William G. Mitchell's individual marker, at left.

After the war, he was commissioned as captain in the 37th U. S. Infantry, July 28, 1866, subsequently being transferred to the Fifth U.

S. Infantry. He was promoted to major, July 1, 1881. Upon the election of President Garfield, he was appointed assistant adjutant- general at the request of General Hancock, the first appointment made by President Garfield. After a sudden and brief illness he died at Governor's Island, May 29,1883. His remains were brought back to Lewistown and surviving comrades of the Logan Guards served as escort to Mitchell's last resting place in St. Mark's Cemetery, Lewistown, PA. He was the step-son of Brevet Brigadier General William Howard Irwin and the son-in-law of Brevet Brigadier General Madison Mills of New York, Army surgeon and Medical Inspector General.

Samuel G. McLaughlin was the company fifer. McLaughlin made every effort to keep up with his unit, but was discharged due to a physical disability, believed to originate at birth, upon the official certification by his regimental surgeon, Dr. Joshua Owen. He was an excellent fifer and musician, according to contemporary reports in the Lewistown *Gazette*. Willis Copeland noted that after his discharge, McLaughlin moved to Fowler, Michigan.

Emanuel Cole, Private, was the deserter. "Deserted, April 19th, 1861" was the notation taken directly from the Morning Report of the Logan Guard's First Sergeant. Willis Copeland contends:

It would be illogical to attribute this man's desertion to cowardice. Cowards do not voluntarily join military organizations. Perhaps his defection was due to some slight, real or fancied, from an officer or non- commissioned officer; or for any one of a score of other reasons — none of them valid, of course. After all, this incident occurred a long, long time ago ...Emanuel Cole should be remembered only as being one of that gallant band of First Defenders.

LOGAN GUARDS — MUSTER-OUT ROLL BIOGRAPHIES

In the early 1960s, Joseph B. Heitman, of Tacoma, Washington, grandson of Captain John B. Selheimer, provided the Mifflin County Historical Society with copies of the pages of First Sergeant J. A. Mathews' Logan Guards morning report and muster book for May, June and July of 1861.

"Written in Sergeant Mathews' beautiful copper-plate handwriting," according to Willis R. Copeland, "the information on these pages proved of inestimable value, particularly in the correct spelling of names and in determining the rank of officers and non-commissioned officers of the Logan Guards."

In addition, Copeland noted in his 1962 history of the Logan Guards, that obvious errors and discrepancies appear in the old histories (Bates, for example) and have been copied and perpetuated by later writers. Copeland both added and deleted, basing these corrections on information "obtained by diligent research and by new evidence provided by the Patton papers and the Logan Guards' roster and morning report." Copeland believed the following muster-out roll to be as accurate as possible, and that all available information is listed with each name. Some names elicit extensive biographical sketches, others are simply names. Additional information, from local news accounts and county histories, has also been added to the list of biographies, forming an epilogue to the Logan Guards' story.

 Omissions are unintentional. Corrections and further additions are welcome for future revisions.

Thomas Marcus Hulings, Captain
(Feb. 7, 1835 - May 10, 1864)

Born in Lewistown, February 6, 1835. Attorney, served as District Attorney for Mifflin County, Pennsylvania prior to Civil War. Married Mary B. Thomas daughter of General Lorenzo Thomas and Elizabeth Brindley Colesberry. Children include Thomas Marcus Hulings (1864-1913) and Elizabeth Hulings (1862-1956) who married Nicholas Dorsey Offutt (1859-1906). Colonel Hulings sister, Maria Patton Hulings (1824-1893) married Lloyd William Williams (1815-1893).

Thomas M. Hulings

Appointed major of the 49th Penna. Vol. Inf., September 14, 1861. He took part in the Peninsula campaign under General McClellan, where his regiment was a part of General Hancock's brigade of General W. F. Smith's division. Major Hulings was first under fire at Young's Mill, Va., in April, 1862. In the battle of Williamsburg, he, with his regiment, participated in the charge on the right, which was the beginning of Hancock's fame. In the "Seven Days Fight" Major Hulings took a gallant part in the actions at Golding's Farm, Savage Station and White Oak Swamp. In August, 1862, he served with his regiment, under General Pope, in the campaign of Cedar Mountain and Second Bull Run, afterwards rejoining the Army of the Potomac. He fought at Crompton's Gap, and in the battle of Antietam, September 17, in the latter engagement his horse was shot under him.

In the following month he was promoted to lieutenant-colonel of the regiment. He succeeded to the command of the regiment at the battle of

Col. Hulings Monument — Green Mount Cemetery, Baltimore, MD. – Courtesy David Reese

Fredericksburg, Va., April 29, 1863, when Colonel Irwin was severely wounded. He led his regiment at the battle of Gettysburg, on the 2nd and 3rd of July following. At Rappahannock Station his regiment carried the enemy's works and captured more prisoners than he had men in his command. In October following, Colonel Irwin was compelled

Colonel Thomas M. Hulings Post No. 176, Grand Army of the Republic, at right, as it looked around 1895. The Post was located on the second floor of the Old Town Hall, at the southeast corner of N. Main and East Third streets, where the Lewistown Municipal Building is located (2011). – Courtesy MCHS Archives

to resign on account of the wound he received at Fredericksburg, and thereupon Lieutenant-Colonel Hulings was promoted to colonel.

The campaign of the Wilderness was a final and fatal one for Colonel Hulings. At Spotsylvania, on May 10, 1864, Colonel Hulings received orders to withdraw his command to its previous position; but hardly had he begun to execute the movement, when the enemy, perceiving it, advanced in force to recover the works, firing as they rushed forward. At this moment, while Colonel Hulings stood with his hand on one of the captured guns, cool, collected, and giving orders to his retiring men, he was struck in the head by a musket ball and fell dead inside the fort. His body was never recovered; however, his monument can be found in Green Mount Cemetery, Baltimore, MD.

On December 10, 1868, the Colonel Thomas M. Hulings Post No. 176, Grand Army of the Republic, was organized at Lewistown. Post 176 was located on the second floor of the Old Town Hall, at the southeast corner of N. Main and East Third streets, where the Lewistown Municipal Building is located (2011).

Francis "Frank" R. Sterrett, First Lieutenant

One of the original five men to organize the Logan Guards, Sterrett was a miller by trade. He is listed on the Muster-In roll of April 1861 at age 28. Shortly after returning from Fort Washington, Sterrett married a Kishacoquillas Valley girl, Sallie Hawn, daughter of Joseph Hawn, Esq. of Armagh Township on August 8, 1861. His company gave Sterrett and his new bride a singularly unique, military send off. The couple journeyed to Lake City, Minnesota, being escorted to the station by his comrades of the Logan Guards. He became a captain of Minnesota Volunteers and was an aide to General Stilwell, Minnesota Volunteers, in the Northwest Indian Wars. On July 20, 1876, he and his wife, then of Red Wing, Minnesota made a return visit to Lewistown to see old comrades, according to an item in the local news.

Frank Sterrett is listed as a private in the Logan Guards in Bates' *History of Pennsylvania Volunteers,* however the original roll book distinctly lists him as a brevet second lieutenant, and as being promoted to first lieutenant when Hulings took over command of the company. Copeland notes a contemporary Washington, D.C. , news dispatch lists Sterrett as being the second lieutenant of the Logan Guards upon their arrival in that city.

Robert William Patton

Robert William Patton, Second Lieutenant (Feb. 22, 1834 - Feb. 8, 1912)

Born February 22, 1834, Patton's earlier years were spent in Lewistown. He received his education in the public schools and at the Lewistown Academy. He was one of the small group of young men who conceived the idea of organizing the Logan Guards in 1858 and was a member of the Logans during the entire period of their existence as a unit. Bates' history lists Patton as second lieutenant upon their departure for the war but, here again, we are confronted with a discrepancy. Documents in the possession of Patton's descendants reveal that he was the first sergeant of the Logan Guards and he refers to himself as "sergeant" in recounting the incident of handing the first morning report to Major McDowell — clearly the duty of a first sergeant. The day book shows that he was elected second lieutenant on April 20, 1861, at which time the Logans were guarding the Capitol.

In August 1862, Patton recruited an infantry company in three days time and, as captain, reported at Camp Curtin. Here he was commissioned as major of the 131st Infantry, and his company was incorporated into the same regiment as Company K. His commission dated from August 16, 1862. Major Patton participated in the battles of Antietam, Fredericksburg and Chancellorsville, and was mustered out with his regiment on May 23, 1863. After the war he always maintained a strong friendship for his comrades-in-arms, and was a regular attendee at reunions of the First Defenders and the 131st Regiment.

In a letter to the Lewistown *Gazette* (1904), Patton corrected the error in Bates' history which states that he was mustered in at Harrisburg on the 18th as second lieutenant.

He writes:

I was first sergeant up to April 20 and was elected lieutenant on that date, as my commission, framed at home, shows. I was the first sergeant who made the company report on the morning of April 19 about three or four o'clock in a room of the Capitol to Generals

McDowell and Mansfield (then major and colonel respectively) who each laid a hand on my shoulders, saying, 'Sergeant, that is the first report of any organization in the United States outside of the District of Columbia.' Sergeants J. Ard Mathews and William B. Weber were with me at the time.

Patton Family Monument and Robert Patton's marker, Mt. Rock Cemetery, Lewistown, PA.

Patton served one term as Mifflin County treasurer, and was the Lewistown postmaster for fourteen years. He later took a position in the United States Assay Office in New York City. He died at the family home at 35 W. Market Street at age 78, and buried at Mount Rock Cemetery, Lewistown, PA. Members of the local GAR Post acted as pallbearers, including fellow Logan Guard Frank H. Wentz.

Henry A. Eisenbise, Brevet Second Lieutenant

Promoted from sergeant to private second lieutenant, May 28, 1861. He was elected orderly sergeant upon the occasion of the organization of the Logan Guards in 1858. Marching to the defense of the Capitol as a duty sergeant, he was promoted to brevet second lieutenant on May 28, 1861. Leaving Lewistown with the Second Logan Guards (Company A, 46th Penna. Vol. Inf.), as first lieutenant, he was promoted to the captaincy when Captain J. A. Mathews became major of the 46th. He was twice a prisoner of war. Resigned February 11, 1863.

Joseph Ard Mathews, First Sergeant (1826 - Aug. 24, 1873)

Organizer and captain of the Second Logan Guards (Company A, 46th Penna. Vol. Inf.). Promoted to major, September 27, 1861. Promoted to colonel, 128th Regiment, November 1, 1862. Colonel Mathews obviously enjoyed the high esteem of the men of his regiment and of the citizens of Mifflin County. The former presented him with a hand-

Detail of Joseph Ard Mathews' presentation sword, among the Civil War collection at the McCoy House Museum, 17 North Main Street, Lewistown, PA.

some saddle bearing a silver plate on the cantle inscribed in part "From the Enlisted Men of the 128th Regiment, P.V., Stafford Court House, March 15, 1863." The latter presented him with a dress sword engraved as follows: "Presented to Major J. Ard Mathews of the 46th Regiment, P.V., by the Citizens of Mifflin County, Pa., September, 1862." Saddle and sword are on display in the museum of the Mifflin County Historical Society. Colonel Mathews was captured by the enemy at Chancellorsville and, after a short period of captivity, returned in time to be mustered out with his command at Harrisburg, May 19, 1863. Shortly thereafter, he received a commission as brevet Brigadier General, U.S. Volunteers on April 2, 1865 and given command of the second brigade of General Hartranft's division in the Ninth Corps for "gallant and meritorious services at Forts Stedman and Sedgwick, Va". Mathews was one of the original five men to organize the Logan Guards in 1858. Burial St. Mark's Cemetery, Lewistown, PA.

Joseph S. Waream, Second Sergeant (1832 - 1880)
Afterwards captain, Company K, 131st P.V.I.; mustered in August 18, 1862; mustered out with company, May 23, 1863; wounded at Fredericksburg, Va., December 13, 1862. Mustered in as sergeant, Company C, 78th P.V.I., February 18, 1865; mustered out with company, September 11, 1865. Died 1880, buried St. Mark's Cemetery, Lewistown, PA.

William B. Weber, Third Sergeant
Mustered in as second lieutenant, Company A. 46th P.V.I., August 14,

1861; promoted to first lieutenant, September 27, 1861; appointed regimental adjutant, September 1, 1862; promoted to captain, Company A, February 11, 1863; resigned February 8, 1865. His father operated a store a grocery store at the corner of Market and Brown Streets, where the Lewistown Trust Company was located, according to Jordan's 1913 *History of the Juniata Valley.* Of the six Weber brothers (there were also two sisters), five served in the Army of the Potomac during the war. All five were at Antietam, four were at Gettysburg, all surviving the conflict without a wound. One brother was captured and sent to Libby Prison, and later transferred to Andersonville. Weber was one of the original five men to organize the Logan Guards in 1858, and among the later survivors into the early 20th century, mentioned as participating in funerals of fellow Guardsmen.

Chauncey M. Shull, Fourth Sergeant
(1829 - Sept., 17, 1904)

Mustered in as corporal, Company I, 83rd P.V.I., March 1, 1865; mustered out with company, June 28, 1865. Mr. Shull also served with the independent infantry company from Lewistown at Shade Gap in 1862. He was a native of Perry County, and was universally known as "Squire" Shull throughout the community. After the war, he engaged in the tailoring business, retiring because of "advanced age and infirmities." His store was on Five Points, where the former Headings' Drug Store was located. He also served as a Justice of the Peace for twenty-five years until shortly before his death at the residence of his daughter, Mrs. Joseph L. McKinney, on North Brown Street, Lewistown, September 17, 1904 at age 75. He had been a widower for nineteen years. A native of Perry County, PA, Shull spent his early years in that county prior to the family moving to Lewistown. The *Democrat & Sentinel* commented at the time of his death that:

He was a man of strict integrity and genial social qualities and had very many friends in Lewistown and vicinity.

A quartette including Messrs. Kieferle and Harry Smith, plus Mrs. Harris Mann, and Mrs. Joseph R. Mann sang at the funeral, while a dozen of his former comrades from Company G of the Pennsylvania National Guard fired the salute at the burial at St. Mark's Cemetery, Lewistown, PA.

His grandson, Chauncey E. Shull donated his ancestor's First Defenders' Medal of Honer, plus his musket, during the Civil War centennial years. Both relics are on exhibit at the McCoy House Museum, 17 N. Main Street, Lewistown, PA.

Elias W. H. Eisenbise

Elias White H. Eisenbise, First Corporal (March 11, 1838 - Apr. 18, 1929)

Afterwards captain, Company F, 107th P.V.I.; mustered in March 8, 1862; discharged on surgeon's certificate, April 3, 1863. Captain Eisenbise was the last surviving member of the Logan Guards. Treasurer First Defenders' Association, 1909-1910, 1910-1911. Elias was the son of Henry Eisenbise and Jane McCarty. He married Jane "Jennie" Elizabeth Selheimer (half-sister of Capt. John. B. Selheimer, about 17 years younger than John) Sept. 1863 and they had children; Harry, John, Lousie and Alida. In 1875, Eisenbise was a conductor on the Main Line Pennsylvania Railroad on the Western Division. He edited and published the Wilkinsburg railroad newspaper called "The East Ender," devoted to "Rhyme, Reason and Railroading." Earlier, while still living in Lewistown, he was a frequent contributor of humorous sketches and poems to the local newspapers.

Failing health kept him from attending that year's meeting of the Logan Guards Association in Pottsville. Eisenbise died on the 68th anniversary of the departure of the Logan Guards from Lewistown. The Lewistown *Sentinel* reported he passed away at Landsdowne, near Philadelphia, at the home of his daughter, Mrs. Thomas Criswell, Wednesday, April 17, 1929. He left his home in Chester, PA to live with

Reading Eagle, **April 18, 1906** shows E. W. Eisenbise, then president of the Chester, PA First Defenders Association. – Courtesy Neil Scheidt

Mrs. Criswell just months prior to his death. Eisenbise was the last Logan Guard from Mifflin County. His body was brought by auto caravan to Lewistown. Nine pall bearers from Logan Post No. 90, American Legion, Lewistown, carried him to his last resting place. The Sentinel reported that a firing squad fired a salute at the grave site, followed by a bugler sounding the "last earthly

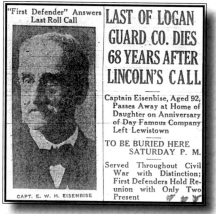

"First Defender" Answers Last Roll Call

LAST OF LOGAN GUARD CO. DIES 68 YEARS AFTER LINCOLN'S CALL

Captain Eisenbise, Aged 92, Passes Away at Home of Daughter on Anniversary of Day Famous Company Left Lewistown

TO BE BURIED HERE SATURDAY P. M.

Served Throughout Civil War with Distinction; First Defenders Hold Reunion with Only Two Present

CAPT. E. W. H. EISENBISE

Front page coverage in the Lewistown *Sentinel* of the passing of Elias W. H. Eisenbise, last Logan Guard from Mifflin County. – Courtesy MCHS Archives

call in honor of the dead First Defender..." Burial St. Mark's Cemetery, Lewistown, PA.

Porter P. Butts, Second Corporal
Further information not available to date.

Capt. John M. Nolte

John M. (Miller) Nolte
Third Corporal
(1835 - April 8, 1890)
Mustered in as first sergeant, Company A, 46th P.V.I., August 23, 1861; promoted to second lieutenant, November 1, 1862; promoted to captain, May 22, 1865; mustered out with company, July 16, 1865. Captain Nolte later became company commander of Company G, 5th Infantry, National Guard of Pennsylvania. Nolte was born in Germany in 1835, and came to the United States when he was thirteen. His family settling near Cincinnati, Ohio, where he learned the shoemakers' trade. He married Mary Christine (Weiderecht) of that city in 1846, later moved to Lewistown, and established a shoe shop. After the war, he served as

Mifflin County Treasurer from 1876 to 1879, and was a member of the local school board for several terms. The couple had five children, the youngest born in 1876, was named John Centennial Nolte, in honor of the 100th birthday of the United States. (The son would go on to operate a successful photographic business on Monument Square as John C. Nolte, photographer.) Captain Nolte operated an "oyster saloon" and restaurant in Lewistown for many years after he left the shoe business. He was taken ill in his Market Street home without any previous illness. His death on April 8, 1890 was sudden, as the *Democrat & Sentinel* lamented:

> *At an early hour Tuesday morning... he was heard moaning, and when Mrs. Nolte went to his assistance shortly after, he was suffering severe pains at his heart. A physician was summoned, but... he had passed the portals of death... His sudden death was a great shock to the community, but much more so to the faithful wife and four children...*

His funeral was one of the largest ever seen in the community, according to the Lewistown *Gazette* and the *Democrat & Sentinel*. A funeral cortege assembled at his home, noted the *Gazette*, and consisted of the Logan Drum Corps; Company G, Fifth Regiment, National Guard of PA; Col. Hulings Post G.A.R.; twelve surviving veterans of the original Logan Guards; Independent Order of Red Men; Independent Order of Odd Fellows; members of the Masonic Order; the hearse with the remains; and his relatives, followed by friends and citizens. Burial was at St. John's Lutheran Church Cemetery, Lewistown, PA.

Death of Capt. Nolte.

Capt. J. M. Nolte, one of the best known citizens of Lewistown, died suddenly and unexpectedly on Tuesday morning last. His death was wholly unlooked-for. Although his health had not been very good the past winter, and he had severe attacks of the prevailing epidemic, yet he was able to be about his business and seen when he retired on Monday even-

News of John M. Nolte's 1890 death, published in the *Democrat & Sentinel,* shocked the town and resulted in one of the largest funerals in the community's history. – Courtesy MCHS Archives

Frederick Hart, Fourth Corporal (? - 1863)

Mustered in as corporal, Company F, 107th P.V.I.; promoted to sergeant, June 11, 1863; killed at Gettysburg, July 1, 1863. Assumed battlefield burial.

David Wasson, Quartermaster Sergeant
No further military record available; died December 30, 1899.

William T. McEwen, Commissary Sergeant
(May 16, 1834 - Dec. 29, 1906)
Mustered in as second lieutenant, Company C, First Penna. Vol. Cavalry, August 10, 1861; promoted to first lieutenant, February 26, 1862; to captain, October 1, 1862; to major, February 23, 1863. Wounded in the ankle at Brandy Station, Va., June 9, 1863; resigned October 17, 1863 following a declaration of permanent disability due to bullet and sabre wounds inflicted in action. Major McEwen had served five years in Texas as a trooper in the Second U. S. Cavalry prior to the outbreak of the Civil War, along side future Confederate general Fitzhugh Lee and others who would side with the South. Military service ran in the McEwen family, with a grandfather, Henry McEwen, on the staff of General Benedict Arnold during the invasion of Canada in the American Revolution.

McEwen was a resident of Wayne Township, Mifflin County and was a cooper by trade in his early years. He returned to Mifflin County in 1860 and briefly worked at the Mann Axe factory prior to the war. After his military service, he and his brother opened a photographic studio in Lewistown, which operated for two years. In 1866, he was elected Mifflin County sheriff on the Democratic ticket for one term. The *Daily Sentinel* reported at the time of his death that McEwen spent time in Indiana and again in Texas before purchasing a small farm near Newton Hamilton, PA where he spent his remaining days. McEwen was in his 73rd year when he died after a short illness, and was buried in the Newton Hamilton Memorial Cemetery, Newton Hamilton, Mifflin County, PA.

Joseph W. Postlethwait, Drummer (Feb. 12, 1841 - June 27, 1912)
Born February 12, 1841 at Newton Hamilton, Mifflin County, PA. Mustered in as musician, band of 49th P.V.I., August 29, 1861; discharged by general order, August 9, 1862. Following his first tour of duty, he re-enlisted for three years in the 49th Regiment of the Pennsylvania Volunteers. Died June 27, 1912 at Great Belt, Butler County, PA. Burial Newton Hamilton Memorial Cemetery, Newton Hamilton, Mifflin County, PA.

William Hopper, Drummer (? - 1863)
Mustered in as sergeant, Company A, 46th P.V.I., September 2, 1861; died May 5, 1863 of wounds received at Chancellorsville, May 3, 1863.

Jesse J. Alexander, Private (1835 - 1866)
Mustered in as private, Company C, First Penna. Vol. Cavalry, August 10, 1861; discharged January 8, 1863, for wounds received in action which later resulted in his death on May 13, 1866 at age 31. Buried Milroy Presbyterian Cemetery, Milroy, Mifflin County, PA.

James D. Burns, Private (? - 1879)
Mustered in as private. Company F, 107th P.V.I., March 8, 1862; discharged on surgeon's certificate, July 26, 1862; M.O. private, Company A, 20th Penna. Vol. Cavalry, January 7, 1864; discharged by general order, June 16, 1865. Burial St. Mark's Cemetery, Lewistown, PA.

William H. Bowsum, Private
Mustered in as private, Company A, 46th P.V.I., September 21, 1861; captured at Winchester, May 25, 1862; returned; mustered out with company, July 16, 1865.

William E. Benner, Private
Further information available to date.

Robert U. Betts, Private (1841 - 1886)
Mustered in as private, Company C, First Penna. Vol. Cavalry, August 10, 1861; mustered out with company, September 9, 1864. Pvt. Betts, his wife, Isabel (1845 - 1910) and children Ellen or Elen K.; Louisa K.; and Harry M. are buried at the family plot Yeagertown Lutheran Cemetery, Yeagertown, Derry Township, Mifflin County, PA.

William R. Cooper, Private (1841 - 1888)
Mustered in as private, Company K, 91st P.V.I., December 21, 1861; wounded May 2, 1864; discharged by general order, January 6, 1865. Buried St. John's Lutheran Church Cemetery, Lewistown, PA.

William Cowden, Private (? - 1862)

Mustered in as private, Company A, 46th P.V.I., September 2, 1861; killed at Cedar Mountain, August 9, 1862. Place of burial not known.

Henry Comfort, Private

Further information not available to date.

Samuel M. Comfort, Private (1843 - 1917)

Afterwards second lieutenant, Company A, Fourth Penna. Militia, September, 1862; sergeant, Company A, 36th Penna. Militia, July, 1863; mustered in as private, Company C, 78th P.V.I., February 18, 1865; discharged by general order, June 7, 1865. Mr. Comfort also served with the independent infantry company from Lewistown at Shade Gap in 1862. Buried St. Mark's Cemetery, Lewistown, PA.

Jeremiah Cogley, Private
(Aug. 12, 1836 - Nov. 2, 1925)

Afterwards sergeant and second lieutenant, U. S. Marine Corps. He spent most of his adult life in Lancaster County, PA, living the final five years with his daughter, Mrs. Mary C. Swope in Mechanicsburg, PA.

During his active years he was a cigar manufacturer utilizing Pennsylvania tobacco in his products, and later he was in charge of the Lancaster tobacco market. He outlived two wives, according to his Lewistown *Sentinel* obituary, passing at age 87. Under the headline, "But One Logan Guard Remains" Cogley's death in 1925 left only Elias W. H. Eisenbise as the sole survivor of the Logan Guards. He was buried in Lancaster Cemetery, Lancaster, PA.

Jeremiah Cogley's grave, Lancaster Cemetery, Lancaster, PA – Courtesy Jeff Burk, 2006

Marker inscription: *First Defender - First to arrive in defense of the Capitol April 18, 1861, Sergeant Co. E. Logan Guards of Lewistown*

Thomas W. Deweese (Dewees), Private (1833 - 1902)

Buried Bull Hill Cemetery, Donnally Mills, Perry County, PA. Inscription: *Priv Co. A, 16 Regt. P.C. DIED July 27, 1902, Aged 69 YRS. 2 M. 5 DAYS.*

Franklin D'Armit, Private

This name also appears as three variants in the old records – Dearmit, De Armint, and Dearment. Further information not known at the present.

James B. Eckebarger

James B. Eckebarger, Private (July 13, 1833 - November 28, 1912)

Mustered in as first lieutenant, Company C, 49th P.V.I., October 2, 1861; promoted to captain, October 16, 1861; discharged November 19, 1863. For forty year after the war, he served as a rail car inspector for the Pennsylvania Railroad., retiring at the age of 70. He died at the home of his daughter, Mrs. John McCord, in Renovo, PA at age 79.

His Lewistown *Daily Sentinel* obituary, dated November 29, 1912, notes:

Another of the ten surviving "First Defenders" or members of the famous Logan Guards of Lewistown, answered the last call yesterday morning at 6 o'clock...He was a member of the Knights of the Golden Eagle and Col. Hulings Post, No. 176, G.A.R., Lewistown, and served as captain of Company C, 49th Pennsylvania regiment...

As befitting a former railroad man, his body was returned from his daughter's home in Clinton County to Mifflin County on the noon train, December 1, 1912, while his funeral plans were in the hands of the J. H. Fretz Funeral Parlor located on North Dorcas Street, Lewistown. His funeral was held in the home of his daughter, Mrs. George W. Springer, at 14 Chestnut Street. Burial was in St. Mark's Cemetery, Lewistown, PA.

George W. Elberty, Private (1844 - 1905)

Mustered in as sergeant-major, 46th P.V.I., August 20, 1861; transferred to Company A as sergeant, April 7, 1862; discharged on surgeon's certificate of disability dated August 29, 1863. Further information not available to date.

William Asbury Elberty, Private
(1844 - 1905)
Mustered in as musician, Company A, Fourth Penna. Militia, September, 1862. He is buried in Woodlawn Cemetery, Wilkinsburg, Allegheny County, PA.

William A. Elberty marker in Allegheny County, PA. – Courtesy George Stoecklein, 2008

William Butler Freeburn, Private
(? - 1863)
Mustered in as first sergeant, Company B, 49th P.V.I., August 10, 1861; promoted to first lieutenant, Company K, January 28, 1862; promoted to captain, September 6, 1862; transferred to Company B, January 11, 1863. Died August 20, 1863 from wounds incurred while laying a pontoon bridge at Fredericksburg, April 29, 1863. Buried First Methodist Cemetery, West Fourth Street, Lewistown, PA. Marker inscription: *Logan Guard Co B 42 Regt PV Died on the field of battle.*

George M. Freeburn, Private
Mustered in as private, Company C, 78th P.V.I., February 18, 1865; mustered out with company, September 11, 1865. Buried First Methodist Cemetery, West Fourth Street, Lewistown, PA. DOB, DOD unknown to date. Inscription on his grave marker simply reads: *34y 1st Defender 1861 Co K 131st & Co C 78th Regts PV*

Joseph A. Fichthorn, Private
(December 15, 1832 - March 10, 1925)
Mustered in as private, Company A, Fourth Penna. Militia, September, 1862; as sergeant, Company A, 36th Penna. Militia, July, 1863; as private, Company H, 195th P.V.I., July 22, 1864; mustered out with company, November 4, 1864; mustered in as private, Company C, 78th P.V.I.,

Joseph A. Fichthorn

February 18, 1865; mustered out September 11, 1865. Born in Lewistown, he was the son of Daniel and Margaret (Smith) Fichthorn. His father was a contractor, who built many Lewistown structures, including the St. John's Lutheran Church. Joseph apprenticed as a tin smith for three years with Daniel Eisenbise and Abraham Blymyer; later served a stint as a hand on the Pennsylvania Canal, and even went to Minnesota as a lumberman for one year just prior to the war.

'GRAND OLD MAN' OF LEWISTOWN DIES, AGED 92

Joseph A. Fichthorn, Only Local Surviving Member of Famous Logan Guards, Passes Away

DEATH FOLLOWS 2 WEEKS' ILLNESS

Manifested Much Interest in Public Affairs During Long Life; Held Public Office

In 1855 he married Sophia Hoover of Lancaster, PA. The couple had two sons and one daughter. After his military service he returned to the tin smith trade and operated a hardware business, retiring at age 78. When he died in 1925 at age 93, Fichthorn was the last surviving Logan Guard living in Mifflin County, and was widely known as Lewistown's "Grand Old Man." Jeremiah Cogley of Lancaster, PA and Elias W. H. Eisenbise of Chester, PA were the only out-of-county Logan Guards still surviving at the time of Fichthorn's death. He was a member of the Ongpatonga Tribe, No. 67, Improved Order of Red Men in Lewistown, as well as a charter member of the Henderson Fire Company founded in 1870. His death notice in the *Daily Sentinel* noted that Fichthorn served as Mifflin County Treasurer from 1878 - 1881, and Chief Assessor for the Second Ward, Lewistown, retiring from that position at age 91, when the stresses of the office became "too tedious for his failing eyesight." He was buried in the St. John's Lutheran Cemetery, Lewistown, PA.

JOSEPH A. FICHTHORN

Joseph A. Fichthorn, Lewistown's "Grand Old Man" died at his home Monday afternoon at the age of 93 years. He was the only member of the Logan Guards, First Defenders in the Civil War, living in Lewistown.

Fichthorn's passing merited front page coverage in the local newspapers. – Courtesy MCHS Archives

In 1987, Fichthorn's First Defenders' Medal of Honor, ribbon from the 46th First Defenders Reunion (April 18, 1907) in Pottsville, PA and a photograph of the old veteran at age 90 were donated to the Mifflin County Historical Society by his niece, Martha Reimer, from Broken Arrow, OK.

Abram Files, Private
Mustered in as private, Company D, 131st P.V.I., August 12, 1862 ; mustered out with company. May 23, 1863.

Joseph Bingam Farer (Farrer), Private
No further military record; killed "in a collision" shortly after the war, according to Willis Copeland.

Daniel Fessler, Private
Afterwards member of Steven's Light Battery; served during entire war according to Copeland; no further detailed record available. May have been buried in Mount Carmel Cemetery, Mount Carmel, Northumberland County, PA.

Owen M. Fowler, Private (1842 - 1874)
Afterwards served as captain of U. S. Colored Troops. According to existing records he was a printer by trade and died in Shamokin, PA. Buried Shamokin Cemetery, Shamokin, Northumberland County, PA.

George W. Hart, Private (1832 - 1904)
Mustered in as private, Company C, 78th P.V.I., February 18, 1865; mustered out with company, September 11, 1865; died August 1904; buried First Methodist Cemetery, Lewistown, PA.

John Hughes, Private
Mustered in as private, Company A, 20th Penna. Vol. Cavalry, February 28, 1864; mustered out with Company A, First Penna. Provisional Cavalry, July 13, 1865; died in Newton Hamilton, Pa., from disease contracted in the field. Place of burial not known.

John T. Hunter, Private
Mustered into service April 18, 1861. Afterwards captain of U. S. Col-

ored Troops; died from wounds received in action. Burial place not found to date.

James William Henry, Private

Mustered in as sergeant. Company H, 149th P.V.I. (Second Bucktails), August 26, 1862; wounded at Gettysburg, July 1, 1863; mustered out with company, June 24, 1865. Place of burial not known.

John W. Jones, Private (1832 - 1889)

Mustered in as sergeant, Company F, 107th P.V.I.; wounded at Fredericksburg, Va., December 13, 1862; later served in 12th Penna. Vol. Cavalry. Burial St. Mark's Cemetery, Lewistown, PA.

James M. Jackson, Private

Afterwards hospital steward (three months service) with Penna. Volunteers, and service in the 12th U. S. Infantry. Further information not available to date.

Thomas Kinkade, Private (? - 1862)

Mustered in as private, Company A, 46th P.V.I., September 2, 1861; died May 11, 1862, of wounds accidentally incurred at New Market, Va.; buried in National Cemetery, Winchester, VA., Lot 1.

John S. Kauffman, Private

Mustered in as private, Company H, 149th P.V.I., August 20, 1862; wounded at Battle of the Wilderness, May 6, 1864; mustered out with company, June 24, 1865. Further information not available to date.

Henry F. Kaiser, Private (Mar. 23, 1835 - Dec. 20, 1906)

Born in Allegheny Co., PA. Mustered in as private; Company E, 49th P.V.I., August 6, 1861; later Co. E; discharged through disability. Burial Main Street Church Cemetery, Fayetteville, Franklin County, PA.

George I. Loff (Loft), Private

Further information not available to date.

John S. Langton, Private

Further military record not available; moved to Decatur, Illinois after the war.

Charles E. Laub, Private

Afterwards sergeant, First Regiment, District of Columbia Volunteers; died from disease contracted in the service. Place of burial unknown.

Elias W. Link, Private

Mustered in as private, Company A, 46th P.V.I., September 2, 1861; died at Harper's Ferry, Va., November 11, 1862. Place of burial not known.

William F. McCay, Private
(May 4, 1842 - Jan. 5, 1901)

Mustered in as private, Company F, 107th P.V.I., March 8, 1862; discharged July 14, 1862; sergeant-major, Fifth U. S. Cavalry. A native of Mifflin County, he was employed in the pension department in Washington, D.C. for many years. McCay was also a newspaper reporter during his working life, and was elected Mifflin County coroner on the Democratic ticket in the 1870s, according to reports in local newspapers. It is not known if he served the full term. For a number of reunions, he later wrote about the history of the Logan Guards, filling the role of company historian. McCay's extensive remembrances of the Logan Guards and Civil War experiences are published in Ellis'

Letter to New York Evening Post, Jan 24, 1896 - Portion of a letter in the MCHS Archives written to the editor by W. F. McCay, taking exception to a Post article lauding the 6th Massachusetts as being the real first defenders of the Union, rather than the five Pennsylvania companies that arrived in Washington, April 18, 1861.

History of the Susquehanna and Juniata Valleys. He was commonly referred to as Major McCay among his army comrades, and those who knew him around Lewistown. Upon his death in 1901 in Washington, DC, his obituary in the *Democrat & Sentinel* noted:

> *He was the son of Abraham McCay (MacCay), deceased, a former merchant tailor of Lewistown and who served a term*

as judge... *the deceased was a man of intelligence, a great reader and well informed, and he always took an active interest in public and political affairs.*

> **Another Soldier Gone.**
>
> The remains of William F. McCay, familiarly known among army comrades as Major McCay, were brought to Lewistown Sunday evening, his death having occurred at Washington, D. C., a day or two previous after an illness of two weeks from disease of the kidneys. The body was conveyed to the home of his mother, Mrs. Martha Forsythe, on West Third street, where funeral services were held on Tuesday afternoon conducted

The *Gazette* dated Jan. 10, 1901 reported McCay's funeral in a page one item. – Courtesy MCHS Archives

Although he lived most of his life in Mifflin County, some years prior to his death, his family moved to Washington, D.C., where McCay held a position in government, perhaps in the pension department.

The Lewistown *Gazette* reported that McCay requested that members of his old company act as pallbearers at his funeral, stating:

> ...*which last sad duty was performed by Comrades Uttley, Fichthorn, Wentz, Weber, Walters and Miller, selected from the few survivors of the original company. A number of G.A.R. veterans were also present, and other First Defenders in addition to the pall bearers...*

W. F. McCay headstone, Mt. Rock Cemetery, Lewistown, PA

Nine Logan Guards, including those mentioned, attended the funeral held at the residence of his mother, Mrs. Martha Forsythe on West Third Street. He was buried in Mt. Rock Cemetery, Lewistown, PA, following what the press termed an "impressive funeral ceremony" observed by the "Masonic fraternity."

Samuel B. Marks, Private

Afterwards second lieutenant, Company A, Fourth Penna. Militia,

September, 1862; mustered in as first lieutenant, Company H, 195th P.V.I., July 22, 1864 ; discharged October 22,1864; private, Company C, 78th P.V.I., February 18, 1865; mustered out with company, September 11, 1865; was a guest at U. S. Military Home in Kansas around 1900.

John S. Miller, Private
Further information not available to date.

Joseph Ard Miller, Private
(Nov. 29, 1833 - Nov. 16, 1916)

Mustered in as private, Company A, Fourth Penna. Militia, September, 1862; mustered in as private, Company C, 78th P.V.I., February 18, 1865; mustered out with company, September 11, 1865. His civilian occupation was that of a plumber, working first with his father George Miller, later carrying on the business on his own. Early in life, Miller served as Burgess of Lewistown for one term. *The Daily Sentinel* noted at the time of his death:

Joseph A. Miller

The duties of office were unattractive to him and he refused to be a candidate for re-election.

He was one of the most active proponents of building the water line which later supplied Lewistown residents with abundant drinking water. When Miller died in 1916 at over 82 years of age, only three local Logan Guardsmen survived. His wife was the former Josephine Fry of Burnham, PA, and they had one daughter, Mrs. Harry F. Conrad. Miller's funeral was held at his home at 1 East Third Street, attended by a large number of friends, relatives and former comrades. Members of the Col. Hulings post of the G.A.R. were in attendance and conducted the service at the grave site, as were the last living Logan Guards in Lewistown - Frank H. Wentz, Henry A. Walters and Joseph A. Fichthorn. The three old comrades headed the procession, along with other members of the local G.A.R. post. *The Daily Sentinel* reported:

...a quartet, G. R. Frysinger, Ben F. Ruble, Mrs. C. W. Hartzell

and Mrs. Geo. T. Hawke sang "One By One" just before the body was lowered to its last resting place.

Burial was in the First Methodist Cemetery, Lewistown, PA. Inscription: *GAR Vet Logan Guard Co E 25 Regt PV*

William McKnew, Private

Afterwards wagon master, 54th P.V.I. Further information not available to date.

Robert A. Mathews, Private

Further information not available to date.

John A. McKee

John A. (Andrew) McKee, Private (1836 - 1904)

Mustered in as captain, Company A, Fourth Penna. Militia, September, 1862. McKee was the son of Thomas R. and Martha (Robinson) McKee, pioneer settlers of Lewistown. His biography in the *History of the Juniata Valley and Its People* notes he was admitted to the Mifflin County bar in 1859, and "until his death continued an active, successful practice." From 1871 to 1873, McKee was a United States assessor of Internal Revenue, overseeing the tax on distilleries, among other duties. He was a proponent of the First Defenders' Medal of Honor in the years after the war, and added his voice in the push to see that commemorative medal struck, and finally presented to the surviving First Defenders. He died June 10, 1904, and is buried in the First Methodist Cemetery, Lewistown, PA.

Robert D. Morton, Private (? - 1864)

Mustered in as sergeant, Company F, 22nd Penna. Vol. Cavalry, March 2, 1864; killed at Berryville, W. Va., August 30, 1864.

William A. Nelson, Private

Mustered in as corporal, Company K, 131st P.V.I., August 7, 1862 ; promoted to first sergeant, March 8, 1863; mustered out with company,

May 23, 1863; mustered in as captain, Company H, 36th Penna. Militia, July, 1863.

Robert Nelson, Private
Further information not available to date.

Thomas A. Nourse (Nurse), Private (? - 1862)
Mustered in as corporal, Company A, 46th P.V.I., September 2, 1861; killed at Antietam, September 17, 1862. Assumed battlefield burial.

John A. Nale (Nail), Private (? - 1862)
Mustered in as private, Company F, 107th P.V.I., March 8, 1862; died October 9, 1862 of wounds incurred at Antietam, September 17; Willis Copeland noted he was buried in the U. S. Military Asylum Cemetery, today known as the U. S. Soldiers' and Airmen's Home National Cemetery, also known as the Soldiers' Home National Cemetery, Washington, D.C.

James Price, Private
Mustered in as private, Company F, 205th P.V.I., September 1, 1864; mustered out with company, June 2, 1865. James' older brother, Charles Price, was a brother-in-law to Private Henry Printz, being married to Henry's sister, Louisa Printz.

Henry Printz, Private
(Feb. 10, 1842 - Oct. 10, 1887)
Joined the Logan Guards at age 19. Mustered in as corporal, Company A, 46th P.V.I., September 2, 1861; promoted to 1st Sergeant; Sgt Printz was wounded at the Battle of Cedar Mountain, Virginia on August 9, 1862. Honorably discharged April 11, 1863 on surgeon's certificate; Col. Joseph Ard Mathews urged Printz to re-enlist, and he mustered in as corporal, Company

Marker of Henry Printz, St. John's Cemetery, Lewistown, PA. - Courtesy Susan Sillence

A, 36th Penna. Militia, July, 1863; promoted to Second Lieutenant by Lt. Melbourne, September 2, 1864 Co. "F" 205 Reg. PA Volunteers.; mustered out with company, June 2, 1865. Lewistown *Gazette* dated June 14, 1865, reported:

Co. F, of the 205th regiment, arrived home last Thursday. On arriving in front of the courthouse, the members of the company presented Lt. Henry Printz with a beautiful gold watch, worth over $125, as a token of their respect and esteem.

Much of what is known about Henry Printz, in addition to his service record, has been revealed through the diligent genealogical research of his descendant, Susan Sillence of Hamburg, NY. For example, (from pension records), at five feet, nine and one half inches tall and weighing two-hundred pounds, Susan notes that Henry was described by Col. Mathews as being, "a hale and hearty individual".

Henry was a brick maker, and apprenticed under his father, Peter Printz (appearing as Prince in the 1850 Census for Lewistown), a master brick maker, and mother Margaret (Lotz/Lutz) Printz. The family lived on Logan Street, and it was from this house Henry likely departed on his way to the company muster on April 16, 1861. There were two sisters, Mary Jane and Louisa, and a younger brother, Albert, who served in the 46th Penna. Volunteers. The oldest child, Mary Jane Printz, was married to William L. Beatty, who later served with Henry in another company. Henry's other sister, Louisa, was married to Charles Price, the older brother of James Price, a member of the Logan Guard.

By the 1880 census, Henry is listed as a constable in Lewistown. Among Henry's Civil War paperwork for a disability pension, his father stated that Henry "cannot do a day's work in the brickyard." Henry's wounds were attested to by his company captain, William B. Weber, also a Logan Guard, and he was certified disabled by Surgeon G. W. Burke. As late as 1882, the effects of the wounds kept him bed-fast for days at a time, according to sworn statements in his pension records. The musket ball passed through his pelvis and exited his hip, with "loss of tissue at both entrance and exit...with...injury to the nerves..." Henry Printz, endured a lifetime of physical sacrifice for their service in the war, as did thousands of his wartime comrades. He died October 10, 1887 in Lewistown. Burial is in St. John's Lutheran Church Cemetery, Lewistown, PA.

John M. Postlethwaite, Private

Mustered in as musician, Band of 49th P.V.I., August 29, 1861; discharged by general order, August 9, 1862.

Bronson Rothrock, Private (Feb. 1836 - Jul. 26, 1906)

Born in Lewistown in 1836, mustered in as private, Company C, 46th P.V.I., September 2, 1861; mustered out with the company, July 16, 1865. Rothrock was a guest at the U. S. Military Home, Kansas in 1900, and died in Vermilion County, IL. Burial Danville National Cemetery, Danville, Vermilion County, IL.

James N. Rager, Private (? - 1864)

A Mexican War veteran who had served in the Juniata Guards which was mustered into Federal service in 1847 as Company D, llth U. S. Infantry. It is interesting to note that Mr. Rager's former company commander of the Juniata Guards, William H. Irwin, marched shoulder to shoulder with him as a private in the ranks of the Logan Guards. Mr. Eager re-entered the army August 20, 1861, as a private in Company E, 49th P.V.I., was transferred to Company D, January 11, 1863, and died at Fort Delaware, May 14, 1864.

James Xenephon Sterrett, Private

Mustered in as second lieutenant, Company D, 107th P.V.I., March 6, 1862; discharged September 29, 1862.

William Sherwood

William Sherwood, Private (1832 - 1914)

Mustered in as corporal, Company D, 49th P.V.I., August 6, 1861; promoted to sergeant, November 25, 1861; to first sergeant, January 8, 1862; to first lieutenant, August 5, 1862; to captain, Company F, March 16, 1864; mustered out February 28, 1865. Captain Sherwood was born in Kensington, England, and emigrated to the United States as a child. He learned the trades of saddler and carriage trimmer. He married Ellen Armstrong of Ferguson Valley. The *Daily Sentinel* described his military career at the time of his death:

Among Civil War veterans he had a record surpassed by few. Although he fought in fifteen of the fiercest battles of the war he was never wounded. A flying shell tore the heel off his right shoe, that being his most narrow escape during the four years of remarkable service in battle.

Sherwood was a widower of eight years at the time of his death, living in a room at the St. Charles Hotel, where the local press noted he could meet with his many friends and reminisce about his "war adventures and experiences." He was survived by two sons William and Charles. Four of the five surviving Logan Guards attended his funeral, including H. A. Walters, Frank H. Wentz, Joseph Fichthorn and Joseph A. Miller. Thomas Uttley was too ill to attend. Sherwood's pallbearers were six Civil War veterans from the Lewistown G.A.R. Post. Burial was in First Methodist Cemetery, Lewistown, PA.

The Daily Sentinel front page notice of Sherwood's passing.
— Courtesy MCHS Archives

Augustus Edward Smith, Private

Mustered in as corporal, Company F, 107th P.V.I., March 8, 1862; promoted to sergeant, April 1, 1862; honorably discharged on surgeon's certificate, June 14, 1862.

Theodore B. Smith, Private (? - 1896)

Mustered in as corporal, Company K, 131st P.V.I., August 7, 1862; mustered out with company, May 23, 1863; mustered in as corporal, Company H, 195th P.V.I., July 22, 1864; mustered out with company, November 4, 1864; mustered in as private, Company C, 78th P.V.I., Feb. 18, 1865; mustered out with company, Sept. 11, 1865. Burial St. Mark's Cemetery, Lewistown, PA.

James P. Smith (Sugar Jim), Private

Mustered in as first sergeant, Company C, 49th P.V.I., August 31, 1861; promoted to second lieutenant, October 26, 1862; to first lieutenant, February 25, 1864; to brevet captain, August 1, 1864; to captain, June

3, 1865; mustered out with company, July 15, 1865. His moniker was bestowed when he shed tears, according to comrades present their first night in Washington, when there was no sugar for his coffee.

Nathaniel Walker Scott, Private

Mustered in as corporal, Company C, First Penna. Vol. Cavalry, August 10, 1861; died July 2, 1863 in Libby Prison, Richmond, Va., of wounds received at Brandy Station, June 9, 1863. Assumed battlefield burial.

Charles W. Stahl, Private (? - Sept. 17, 1874)

Mustered in as private, Company A, Fourth Penna. Militia, September, 1862; mustered in as sergeant, Company A, 36th Penna. Militia, July, 1863; mustered in as corporal, Company F, 205th P.V.I., September 1, 1864; mustered out with company, June 2, 1865. 38 years, 7 months and 1 day. Burial is in the First Methodist Cemetery, West Fourth Street, Lewistown, PA.

George Ard Snyder, Sr., Private (1831 - 1911)

Mustered in as private, Company K, 131st P.V.I., August 11, 1862 ; mustered out with company, May 23, 1863; mustered in as private, Company C, 78th P.V.I., February 18, 1865; absent, on detached service, at muster out. Burial First Methodist Cemetery, West Fourth Street, Lewistown, PA.

Lucien T. Snyder

Lucien T. Snyder, Private (1834 ? - Nov. 16, 1912)

The Logan Guards' day book reveals that Pvt. Snyder, who was a printer and reporter by occupation, had the reputation of being the cleanest soldier at Fort Washington and, on that account, was invariably selected as orderly to the commanding officer when detailed for guard duty. He was a Lewistown resident at the time of enlistment. Private in the 25th Pennsylvania Infantry, Company E. Mustered out on July 26, 1861 at Harrisburg, Pennsylvania.

After the war, he worked in the newspaper business at press offices in Philadelphia and Washington, D.C. At the time of his death at about age 78, he left a wife and two daughters. One daughter, Adele, was a government employee at the US Mint in Washington, however the whereabouts of his wife and other daughter were unknown, according to a local press report.

The *Daily Sentinel* explained the delay in Snyder's death notification in a front page article dated December 10, 1912:

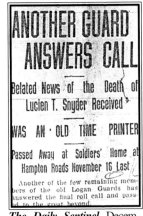

The Daily Sentinel December 10, 1912 front page notice of Snyder's passing. – Courtesy MCHS Archives

Another of the few remaining members of the Logan Guards has answered the final

Snyder Marker, Arlington National Cemetery. – Courtesy Hope, at Find a Grave

roll call and passed to the great beyond. Word was received in Lewistown this morning that Lucien T. Snyder had died at the Soldiers home at Hampton Roads, Va. November 16th. A message announcing Mr. Snyder's death had been sent at the time of his demise, but mis-directed, was returned to the dead letter office at Washington. Capt. Eckebarger at Renovo had also been notified, but owing to the latter's death, information was not received until now.

Snyder was buried with military honors in Arlington National Cemetery, Arlington, VA.

Gideon M. Tice, Private
(1839 - Feb. 27, 1883)

Mustered in as sergeant, Company A, Fourth Penna. Militia, September, 1862; mustered in as private, Company C, 78th P.V.I., February 18, 1865; discharged by general order, May 17, 1865: died March 8, 1883, as the result of disease contracted in the service. A March 1, 1883 item in the Lewistown *True Democrat* announced his death at age 44 years, 3 months and 19 days. Believed to be buried at Mt. Rock Cemetery, Lewistown, PA.

Thomas M. Uttley, Private
(Sept. 5, 1835 - May 20, 1915)

Thomas M. Uttley

Regimental adjutant, Fourth Penna. Militia, September, 1862; regimental adjutant, 36th Penna. Militia, July, 1863; served with independent company from Lewistown at Shade Gap, 1862. When he first entered service, he was detailed to the department of Quartermaster General Reuben C. Hale, a prominent Lewistown citizen. Thomas Uttley was born in Mapleton, Huntington Co., PA, and attended Milnwood Academy, Shade Gap, PA. He later studied law and was admitted to the Mifflin County Bar in 1859. He married Margaret Rebekah Junkin of Lewistown, and they had four sons: Harry, Thomas V., William W., and Ira J. William was also a lawyer, in practice with his father at the law offices of T. M. Uttley & Son on North Main Street. At the time of his death, he was the oldest member of the county bar in both service and age, having been engaged in the law for fifty-six years. The *Gazette* noted that during one of the Cleveland administrations, he served as Lewistown Postmaster for a short time. As a loyal Democrat, he represented his party as state and national conventions throughout his active, professional years.

Uttley was known for his long walks taken for exercise around Lewistown, even into his advanced years, and was often seen in all parts of every neighborhood. He was an elegant speaker and debater, having honed the latter skill during long exchanges at the Apprentices' Literary Society Hall on Third Street. Uttley was especially well versed in logic and oratory.

He died suddenly of heart disease at age eighty in his home at 29 North Main Street. He was walking on the street the day before he died, and felt "indisposed" and went to bed on the morning he passed. According to the *Gazette*, his wife sat by his bedside, talking quietly about what a pleasant life the couple had shared, how he had almost reached his goal of living 80 years, and recalling how many years they had been permitted to be together. She prepared to leave the room to fetch some liquid nourishment, when he suddenly died. Uttley was one of five surviving local members of the Logan Guards when he died. Following an impressive funeral at the family home attended by hundreds, he was buried at St. Mark's Cemetery, Lewistown, PA.

Frank H. Wentz

Franklin "Frank" H. Wentz, Private (Feb. 28, 1844 - May 25, 1917)

Mustered in as sergeant, Company F, 107th P.V.I., January 27, 1862; promoted to first sergeant, March 8, 1862; to second lieutenant, March 25, 1863; to first lieutenant, March 8, 1865; wounded at Gettysburg, July 1, 1863; mustered out with company, July 13, 1865, brevet captain, 1865. He served as Vice President First Defenders' Association, 1909-1910, 1910-1911. He was born in Philadelphia, and came to Lewistown to learn the cabinet-makers trade at R. H. McClintic & Bro. on Valley Street. He was just 18 years old when he enlisted in the Logan Guards. After the war, he joined the Henderson Volunteer Fire Company #1, and was elected chief engineer about 1878, a position he held until his son took over about 1914. He was a dedicated fireman the remainder of his life. He was auditor of Mifflin County for twenty-five years, and held other minor elective offices. Wentz was in the shoe business, but later operated a soft drink bottling works that was so successful over the years, he was known around the county as "Wentz, the Pop Man." His illustrious life and long career came to a sad end, however. The obituary in the *Democrat and Sentinel*, and the Lewistown *Gazette* cited the heartbreaking cause of his death at age seventy-three:

Lieutenant Frank H, Wentz died... at the home of his daughter-in-law, Mrs. George M. Wentz, 132 W. Third Street, after a brief illness. It is not known what diagnosis the man of medicine wrote on the death chart, but those who were about him in the latter days of his life have no doubts in the matter. It is entirely due to worry over the death of his only son, George M. Wentz, whose life was snuffed out in the twinkling of an eye on the afternoon of December 22, 1916, when the chainless tires of the Henderson fire truck skidded madly over the icy streets... *ended the run against a telephone pole... crushing the life out of the man.*

Frank Wentz was so stricken that his beloved son died in service with his cherished fire company. One additional irony occurred on the day of his death, when an invitation arrived at his late home. It was an invitation from the citizens of Allentown, PA inviting him to participate in the dedication of the First Defenders Monument in that city, Wentz being among the few remaining Logan Guards that might be able to attend. He was buried in the First Methodist Cemetery, Lewistown, PA.

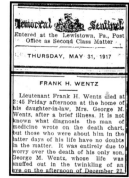

Democrat & Sentinel Front page notice of Wentz's passing. – Courtesy MCHS Archives

Gilbert W. Waters, Private (? - 1863)

Mustered in as first lieutenant, Company L, Ninth Penna. Vol. Cavalry, October 1, 1861; promoted to captain, April 30, 1862; killed at Shelbyville, Tenn., June 28, 1863. Buried at St. Mark's Cemetery, Lewistown, PA.

William B. Weber, Private

Mustered in as second lieutenant, Company K, 131st P.V.I., August 18, 1862; promoted to first lieutenant, March 8, 1863; mustered out with company, May 23, 1863; mustered in as corporal, Company C, 78th P.V.I., February 18, 1865; mustered out with company, September 11, 1865.

Henry A. Walters

Henry Augustus Walters, Private (Jul. 23, 1838 - Sept. 4, 1923)

Signatory to the original bylaws of the Logan Guards August 7, 1858 as a Lieutenant, and sworn in as a Private at Harrisburg, April 18, 1861. Henry was born in 1838 on the Lewistown side of the Long Narrows, now the Lewistown Narrows. Family history tells that his father passed away after a fall from a bridge around 1848, although his burial and location of death is unknown. Henry attended the Lewistown Academy until approximately age 12 years when he quit to work on the Juniata Division of the Pennsylvania Canal as a hoggee (a young boy or youth who rode, drove and tended horses and mules that pulled packet boats) to help support the family. His residence was at 102 North Wayne Street, Lewistown, PA. He operated a grocery store, as well as a wood, coal, and limestone yard plus a store at 116 Pine Street. After the war (1866 to 1871), Henry was helped financially by William Willis (before the war Henry worked for him) and was Captain of a Canal boat. Henry A. Walters was one of the last two surviving Logan Guards living in Mifflin County at the time of his death in 1923. His 3rd great grandson, 1st Sgt. Michael Alan Walters of Lewistown, proudly walked in his ancestor's footsteps during the 150th anniversary march of the Logan Guards, May 7, 2011. Copeland commented in 1962: "We recall Mr. Walters as a portly, phlegmatic (*content and kind*) old gentleman who conducted a small general store at the corner of Wayne and Third Streets in Lewistown and from whom we purchased many a "jawbreaker" and licorice stick. " Henry A. Walters is buried in St. Mark's Cemetery, Lewistown, PA.

(Bates incorrectly lists him as Henry "G." Walters. Thus any list based upon this source continued the error.)

David Wertz (Worts), Private (? - 1862)
Mustered in April 18, 1861 as a private. Died in 1862 as the result of rheumatism contracted in the service. No additional information at this time.

George W. White, Private
Mustered in as corporal, Company C, First Penna. Vol. Cavalry, August 10, 1861; wounded May 9, 1864; taken prisoner June 21, 1864; returned; transferred to Company D, Second Provisional Cavalry, September 9, 1864. No further record available at this time.

Philip Wintered, Private
Mustered in as private, Company D, 49th P.V.I., March 16, 1863; mustered out with company, July 15, 1865; wounded at Spotsylvania and Winchester.

Edwin E. Zeigler, Private
(Sometimes appears as "Edward")
(Nov. 24, 1842 - Jan. 3, 1924)

Mustered in as second lieutenant, Company E, 49th P.V.I.; resigned November 26, 1861; mustered in as second lieutenant, Company G, 107th P.V.I., March 7, 1862; promoted to captain, June 30, 1862; to major, April 18, 1865; to brevet lieutenant-colonel, March 15, 1865; mustered out with regiment, July 13, 1865. For 47 years he was a freight agent for the Pennsylvania Railroad. In 1865 he enter

Edwin E. Zeigler

railroad service at Huntingdon, PA, then moved to the Allegheny City station for 22 years, and was promoted to the Duquesne Station, Pittsburgh until his retirement at age 70. Following his death in Pittsburgh, a special private railroad car was arranged by PRR officials for his final return to Mifflin County. Joseph Fichthorn, age 91, was the only one of the three surviving Logan Guards able to attend Zeigler's funeral. Fichthorn met the funeral cortege in the lobby of the Coleman House on W. Market Street. Burial was in the First Methodist Cemetery, West Fourth Street, Lewistown, PA.

For a number of years following Col. Selheimer's death, Zeigler had possession of the original company flag given by the ladies of Lewistown. With the consent of his living Logan comrades, Zeigler decided to donate the old banner to the State Museum in Harrisburg. The fragile, tattered silk artifact remains a tangible reminder of the men and times of the Logan Guards, Mifflin County's own First Defenders of the Civil War.

SOURCES & BIBLIOGRAPHY

MIFFLIN COUNTY SOURCES:

* Morning Report and Muster Book of the Logan Guards for May, June and July 1861 kept by First Sergeant J. A. Mathews kindly shared by the late Joseph B. Heitman, grandson of John B. Selheimer.

* Roll Book of the Logan Guards for 1858, 1859, 1860 kindly shared by the late Mrs. James T. Sterrett, granddaughter of Robert William Patton and related correspondence and papers.

* George R. Frysinger Papers - Not just one single collection, but a wide-ranging resource of extensive files, the Civil War editor of the Lewistown *Gazette* providing materials including: Civil War correspondence, post-war correspondence on the First Defenders Medal of Honor Commission; correspondence with the First Defenders Association; contemporary news stories, personal recollections and editorials, 1861 - 1933, including extensive commentary on the Logan Guards spanning seventy-two years.

* Soldiers' letters, whole or in part, as published in local newspapers in the Mifflin County Historical Society microfilm archives.

* Manuscript: *First Defenders Medals Number one - The Pennsylvania First Defenders Medal of Honor, Parts One & Two* by Anthony R. Margrave, Sussex, England, 1974. Related 1970s-era correspondence between Margrave and J. Martin Stroup, MCHS.

* C. Eugene Miller, PhD, Professor Emeritus, University of Louisville, a monograph: "A Exoneration of a Gentleman from Pennsylvania," defending Brig. Gen. William Howard Irwin's war service, 1992; correspondence with MCHS Research Librarian Jean Aurand Laughlin; news clippings from *The County Observer*; (Lewistown) *Sentinel* news release, "Louisville Armed Forces Committee" dedication of Brig. Gen. W. H. Irwin memorial, 1993.

* J. Martin Stroup papers; Mifflin County Historical Society secretary and editor of the (Lewistown) *Sentinel,* 1930s - 1970s; extensive files and correspondence related to the 1961 Civil War Centennial and First Defenders' commemorative activities; Logan Guards Memorial Plaque Committee materials.

* Correspondence with Michael Alan Walters concerning his 3rd great grandfather Henry Augustus Walters, Private in the Logan Guards.

* Additional contemporary newspapers from the vertical archive files in the Mifflin County Historical Society Research Library.

* Photographic archives of the Mifflin County Historical Society.

* Civil War artifacts and ephemera from the Mifflin County Historical Society collections, McCoy House Museum, 17 N. Main Street, Lewistown, PA.

MIFFLIN COUNTY BOOKS:

Commemorative Biographical Encyclopedia of the Juniata Valley: Comprising the counties of Huntingdon, Mifflin, Juniata and Perry, Pennsylvania. Containing sketches of prominent and representative citizens and many of the early settlers. Chambersburg, Pa.: J. M. Runk & Co., 1897. (Common reference, *The Valleys*)

Copeland, Willis R. *The Logan Guards of Lewistown, Pennsylvania – Our First Defenders of 1861*: Lewistown, PA, Mifflin County Historical Society, 1962.

Ellis, Franklin. *History of that part of the Susquehanna and Juniata Valleys, Embraced in the Counties of Mifflin, Juniata, Perry, Union and Snyder in the Commonwealth of Pennsylvania*, Philadelphia: Everts, Peck and Richard, 1886 (1602 pages in 2 vols. Reprinted Unigraphic, Inc. 1975 Juniata County Bicentennial Commission with extensive 173 page index compiled by Stella Benner Shivery and Shirley Garrett Guiser)

Frysinger, George R. and Eleanor M. Aurand, *Mifflin Countians in the Civil War*: Lewistown, PA: Mifflin County Historical Society, 1996. (Compilation of Frysinger's Civil War rosters)

Jordan, John W. *History of the Juniata Valley and Its People*, Volume I, II & III, New York: Lewis Historical Publishing Company, 1913. (Extensive biographical encyclopedia)

Kauffman, Donald R. *Mifflin County Cemetery Records Vol. I & II*. Lewistown, PA: Mifflin County Historical Society, 1978. (The only extant compilation of Mifflin County Cemeteries.)

ADDITIONAL SOURCES:
These Pennsylvania historical societies aided with documenting the June 1914 transfer of Civil War battle flags to the State Capitol involving Logan Guards and other Mifflin County Veterans, or provided additional information on the First Defenders.

* Historical Society of Berks County, Special Collections and Archive, Henry Janssen Library, 940 Centre Ave., Reading, PA 19601

* Historical Society of Dauphin County, 219 South Front Street, Harrisburg, PA 17104 (microfilm archives of Harrisburg newspapers, 1914)

* Lehigh County Historical Society, 501 Hamilton St., Old Courthouse, Allentown, PA 18105-1548

* Historical Society of Schuykill County, 14 North 3rd St., Pottsville, PA 17901

BIBLIOGRAPHY:
Beckwith, George Cone *The Peace Manual: Or, War and Its Remedies*. American Peace Society, 1847.

Barney, William L. "The Confederacy," article in *Series: A MacMillan Information Now Encyclopedia*, Macmillan Reference USA, Simon & Schuster Macmillan, 1998.

Bates, Samuel P. *History of Pennsylvania Volunteer*s: Harrisburg, PA, B. Singerly, State Printer, 1870.

Billings, John D. *Hardtack and Coffee or The Unwritten Story of Army Life*. Boston: George M. Smith & Co., 1888.

Boatner, Mark M. *The Civil War Dictionary*. NY: Randon House, 1991.

Brown, George William. *Baltimore and the 19th of April, 1861*. Baltimore, MD: Johns Hopkins University, 1887.

Cullum, George and Wood, Eleazer: *Campaigns of the War of 1812-1815, Against Great Britain: Sketched and Criticized*. J. Miller, 1879.

Cuthbert, Norma B. *Lincoln and the Baltimore Plot 1861 from Pinkerton Records and Related Papers*. San Marino, California: The Huntington Library, 1949.

Detzer, David. *Allegiance: Fort Sumter, Charleston, and the Beginning of the Civil War*. New York: Harcourt, 2001.

Eicher, David J. *The Longest Night: A Military History of the Civil War*. New York: Simon & Schuster, 2001.

Fisher, H. L. *Olden Times: Pennsylvania Rural Life*. York, PA: Fisher Brothers, Publishers, 1888.

Gilham, Major William. *Manual of Instruction for the Volunteers and Militia of the United States*. Philadelphia, PA: Charles Desilver, 1861.

Graeff, Arthur, Ralph Dunkelberger, and Wayne Homan. "Four Firsts in Berks County - 1861." Reading, Pennsylvania: Historical Society of Berks County, 1961.

Holzer, Harold and Craig L. Symonds, *The New York Times Complete Civil War, 1861 - 1865*. New York: Black Dog & Leventhal Publishers, 2010.

Hoptak, John David. *First Defenders of the Union - The Civil War History of the First Defenders*: Author House 2004.
____ "The Union's Forgotten First Defenders." The Bivouac. Web. 20 Apr. 2010. <http://www.bivouacbooks.com/bbv4i2s6.htm>.

Jepsen, Thomas C. *My Sisters Telegraphic - Women in the Telegraphic Office 1846 - 1950*. Athens, OH: Ohio University Press, 2000.

Lossing, Benson J. *Pictorial History of the Civil War* Hartford, Conn.: T. Belknap, Publisher, 1866.
____ *The Pictorial Field Book Of The Civil War In The United States Of America*. Hartford: Thomas Belknap, 1874.

McPherson, James M. *Battle Cry of Freedom – The Civil War Era*: New York, Oxford Press 1988.

Pennsylvania Capitol Preservation Committee "Pennsylvania's Historic Civil War Flags." Web. 22 Feb. 2011. <http://cpc.state.pa.us/cpcweb/flags_about.jsp>.
___ "Pennsylvania Militia Color, 109th Infantry Flag" Web. 22 Feb. 2011. <http://cpc.state.pa.us/cpcweb/flag/showflag/1985.008>.

Pennsylvania National Guard "Guard History." Web. 21 Feb. 2011. < http://www.paguard.com/html/guard_history.html>.

Sauers, Richard A. *Advance the Colors! Pennsylvania Civil War Battle Flags Vol. I & Vol II* Capitol Preservation Committee 1987, 1991.

Story, Joseph: *A Familiar Exposition of the Constitution of the United States. Boston*: T. H. Webb & co., 1842. (Associate Justice of the Supreme Court of the United States, November 18, 1811 – September 10, 1845)

Thompson, Heber S. *The First Defenders*: n.p., 1910.

US War Department *Revised Regulations for the Army of the United States, 1861*. Philadelphia: J.G.L. Brown, Publisher, 1861.
___ The 1863 *U.S. Infantry Tactics, Infantry of the Line, Light Infantry and Riflemen*. Philadelphia: J. B. Lippencott & Co, 1863.

Wilson, James Grant and John Fisk, Editors. *Appletons' Cyclopædia of American Biography*. New York: D. Appleton & Company, 1900.

SELECTED NOTES

Chapter 1

The Thompsontown Patriotic Blues and Millikin's Troop of Horse of the Kishacoquillas Valley, both volunteer units from the War of 1812, are discussed in some detail in Ellis' *The Valleys*, Chapters V. Chapter VI includes company rosters and Mifflin County militia units for the Mexican War.

William F. McCay's story of militia life, and his recollections of the Logan Guards, are both reprinted in Ellis's *The Valleys*. However, many of his recollections first appeared in the Wed., April 20, 1881 edition of the Lewistown *Gazette*.

Chapter 2

In 1864, Benson J. Lossing recorded a lengthy comment by President Lincoln about the would-be Baltimore assassination attempt. Lossing's *Pictorial Field Book of the Civil War* recounts the president's remarks, which state, in part:

The next morning I raised the flag (included a 34th star for the new state of Kansas) *over Independence Hall, then went on to Harrisburg... There I met the Legislature and people, and waited until the time appointed for me to leave... In New York some friend gave me a new beaver hat in a box, and in it had placed a soft wool hat. I had never worn one of the latter in my life. I had this box in my room, Having informed a very few friends of the secret of my new movement, and the cause, I put on an old overcoat that I had with me, and putting the soft hat in my pocket, I walked out of the house at a back door, bareheaded, without exciting any special curiosity. Then I put on the soft hat and joined my friends without being recognized by strangers...*

We went back to Philadelphia and found a message from Pinkerton (who had returned from Baltimore), that the conspirators had held their final meeting that evening, and it was doubtful whether they had the nerve to attempt the execution of their purpose. I went on to Baltimore. I heard people talking around, but no one particularly observed me. At an early hour on Sunday morning, at about the time I was expected to leave Harrisburg, I arrived in Washington.

The plot on Lincoln's life in 1861 was dramatized in the occasionally telecast *The Tall Target*, a 1951 M-G-M thriller, starring Dick Powell (1904 - 1963). The actor plays a detective, John Kennedy, no less, who tries to stop the assassination of Abraham Lincoln on the train taking the newly-elected president to his Washington, D.C. inauguration. It is loosely based on the Baltimore Plot, the conspiracy to assassinate the President-elect in that Maryland city. The portrayal of hauling the trains through Baltimore provides authenticity, as the engines are uncoupled and the passengers cars drawn through the city by horses. During this transfer process, the disguised president is portrayed in one of the cars. Movie reviewer, Leonard Maltin states on the TCM web site: "Gripping suspense as detective Powell follows tip that Abraham Lincoln is going to be assassinated during 1861 train ride." Although the characters are fictional, with the exception of Lincoln and wife Mary, the film shows Hollywood's take on this "footnote" to early Civil War history.

There was a real New York policeman named John (Alexander) Kennedy.. He was born in Baltimore, Maryland on August 9, 1803. His father was a native of Ireland who became a teacher in Baltimore. John moved to New York City and worked with his brother. In 1849 he was appointed a commissioner of emigration. In 1860 he became superintendent of the New York City Police. During the New York Draft Riots, aged 59, he was severely beaten by a mob, while protecting the office of the provost-marshal at 46th Street and 3rd Avenue, on the morning of 14 July 1863. (In part from *Appletons' Cyclopædia of American Biography, 1900.*)

Chapter 3
☛ The history of Mifflin County recounts many notable women, including Elizabeth Cogley. The railroad began using the telegraph for dispatching, where many women were later employed in that capacity. Cogley, referred to in the town as Miss Lib, was an operator for the Atlantic and Ohio Telegraph Company when that office merged with the PRR operation. She began working for the Pennsylvania Railroad in 1855, about six years after the railroad laid tracks to Lewistown. At that time, she was the first female telegrapher known to be working for a railroad. She trained her younger brothers, including Elias Cogley, both of whom was involved in the excitement of the back-and-forth messages of April 16, 1861. The Cogley family's story is detailed in *It Happened in Mifflin County, Book 1* in the chapter "R. B. Hoover and the Lincoln Stone."

Chapter 4
☛ During the Baltimore Riot of April 19, 1861, Union soldiers and city residents were killed, including Francis X. Ward, a friend of native Marylander James Ryder Randall. Randall was a college teacher in Louisiana, and was moved by the news of his friend's death. He wrote the nine-stanza poem, "Maryland, My Maryland" as a plea to his home state to secede from the Union and join the Confederacy. The Maryland State Archives notes that the song is set to the tune of "Lauriger Horatius" better known as the melody of "O Tannenbaum", and became the official state song in 1939.

☛ George R. Frysinger tells about his attempt to acquire a copy of George William Brown's *Baltimore and the 19th of April, 1861* while in that city shortly after the book was published in 1887. (Brown was Baltimore mayor during the April riots of 1861). He read a newspaper notice while in the city announcing Browns' books were available at public libraries. With money in hand, Frysinger said a young man came forward to "learn my errand." Told to wait, the young man entered a side room and shortly an elderly gentleman appeared. Frysinger was interrogated with a "set of questions in catechetical fashion, asking if I lived in Baltimore or Maryland, etc., etc."

Frysinger answered negatively to all questions, and was bluntly told no books would be sold to anyone from out of state, Frysinger explaining:

This aroused my suspicion that for some sinister reason this book was withheld from general circulation, and my desire to own a copy was increased manyfold. Yet not until nearly 40 years passed was I able to procure one through a friend in Baltimore after a search of several book stores in the city.

That copy of the book is now in the Mifflin County Historical Society Research Library. In it is a typewritten note from Frysinger, that states, in part:

The peculiar circumstances under which this book came to have a place in our society library have been narrated at length in a paper read before the members at the regular meeting on May 5, 1932, and therefore need not be enlarged upon in this Book Note, except to refer to the fact that the author does not do justice to the five companies of Pennsylvania Volunteer infantry of which the Logan Guards was one... The sequel to the story is that our society is in possession of this book in spite of adverse circumstances, but by comparison with the opening chapter in Bates History of Pa. Volunteers it is easy to see why a sparse mention of the gallant First Defenders from Pennsylvania is all that is to be found in its pages.

Chapter 5

Three books of note on the topic of the Civil War army life: *The Story of a Common Soldier of Army Life in the Civil War, 1861–1865*, (1920) by Leander Stillwell; *Hard Tack and Coffee: The Unwritten Story of Army Life* (1887), a memoir by John D. Billings; and Samuel "Sam" Rush Watkins' *Company Aytch: Or, a Side Show of the Big Show.*

Leander Stillwell was an American lawyer and judge. From 1861 to 1865 he was with the Union army joining as a private of Company D, Sixty-first Regiment, Illinois Infantry Volunteers. He was appointed Corporal, then Sergeant and later First Sergeant in 1863, and re-enlisted in 1864, at Little Rock, Arkansas. He participated in the battle of Shiloh, the siege of Vicksburg, and several minor engagements. His experiences were published 1917 - 1920. His description of lying on the deck of a steam boat in transit, covered in cinders, living on "hardtack and raw sow-belly with river water for a beverage..." He recalled looking down through the cabin window into the cabin with officers at table being served by waiters in white uniforms. The officers dined on "fried ham and beefsteak, hot biscuits, butter, molasses, big boiled Irish potatoes steaming hot, fragrant coffee served with cream, in cups and saucers, and some minor goodies in the shape of preserves and the like."

John D. Billings was a veteran of the 10th Massachusetts Volunteer Artillery Battery in the American Civil War. *Hard Tack and Coffee* quickly became a best seller, and is now considered one of the most important books written by a Civil War veteran. Re-enactors find it a valuable resource. The book is profusely illustrated with pen and ink drawings by Civil War veteran Charles Reed, who served as bugler in the 9th Massachusetts Battery. Reed received the Medal of Honor for saving the life of his battery commander at Gettysburg. Billings' memoir is not about battles, but rather about how the common Union soldiers of the Civil War lived in camp and on the march. Humorous prose and Reed's superb drawings, based on the sketches he kept in his journal during the war, make for a compelling read. Many modern reviewers comment that it's like sitting on the porch listening to a sage old uncle weaving his stories about life during the Civil War.

Sam Watkins was a noted Confederate soldier during the Civil War. He is known today for his memoir, *Company Aytch: Or, a Side Show of the Big Show* often heralded as one of the best primary sources about the common soldier's Civil War experience. It was originally serialized in the Columbia, Tennessee *Herald* newspaper. "Co. Aytch" was published in a first edition of 2,000 in book form in 1882. One Amazon.com book reviewer noted that Sam's writing style is quite engaging and skillfully captures the pride, misery, glory, and horror experienced by the common foot soldier. Watkins is often featured and quoted in Ken Burns' 1990 documentary, *The Civil War.*

Chapter 6

The Milroy Zouaves preformed the Ellsworth drills, named for Col. Elmer Ephraim Ellsworth, who was known for the Zouave craze that swept the county prior to the Civil War. Precision drills and drill teams were all the rage. On July 2, 1860, Ellsworth and 50 of his best men embarked on a six-week tour that took them to 20 cities, including Detroit, Cleveland, Boston, Pittsburgh and Baltimore. Ellsworth's Zouaves humbled their competitors and awed thousands who came to watch their choreographed exhibitions. Newspapers described Ellsworth as "the most talked-of man in the country."

The day after Virginia voted to secede from the Union, eight regiments of Union infantry were sent across the Potomac River to seize Arlington Heights and Alexandria. Colonel Ellsworth, (mentioned above) the leader of the Eleventh New York Volunteer Regiment, saw a Confederate flag flying over the Marshall House hotel. Ellsworth charged up the stairs and cut down the flag, only to be shot by James Jackson, the hotel proprietor, who was then killed by Francis Brownell, one of Ellsworth's soldiers. The Smithsonian Institution's Legacies exhibits explain:

The incident electrified Washington, D.C. Ellsworth lay in state at the White House, Brownell received the Medal of Honor, and everyone wanted relics of the Marshall House incident. Over the years the Smithsonian acquired Jackson's shotgun and Brownell's rifle and Medal of Honor as well as this piece of the flag in 1961. (The online exhibits is at: http://www.smithsonianlegacies.si.edu/objectdescription. cfm?ID=34 Retrieved: August 18, 2010)

Chapter 7

Upon their return, members of the Logan Guards were constantly asked about life in the army, and most, to a man, were eager to recount the experience. One story told in 1881 by William McCay, on the 20th anniversary of the Logan Guards leaving for Washington, was about a soldier dubbed with a sweet nickname by his comrades. The account appears in the April 20, 1881 issue of the *Gazette*:

We were silently marched to the Capitol building... That night was our first real experience in the art of eating wormy pork and hard-tack. Rations were issued and in the spacious cellars under the Capitol we took our first meal of coffee, hard-tack and pork. One of our members, who was fully six feet in height, shed tears because he had no sugar on his bread. This young man was afterwards a captain in the gallant Forty-ninth Pennsylvania Volunteers, and a brave soldier. He is, however, called "Sugar Jim" to this day.

Chapter 8

Heber S. Thompson(1840 - 1911) is the author of the first book on the First Defenders, also titled *The First Defenders*, 1910. Thompson was also the author of a Civil War diary during the time he was a prisoner-of-war in South Carolina. His papers are held by the University of South Carolina, titled: "Heber S. Thompson Papers, Aug.-Dec. 1864." Capt. Thompson served with the 7th Pennsylvania Cavalry, while his diary focuses upon his experiences at the 1st South Carolina Hospital located four miles from Charleston at Rikersville, South Carolina. The diary indicates that the hospital was not for Federal officers alone but admitted "private soldiers black & white." "They by this I suppose consider that they are putting into practice our ideas of negro equality," Thompson mused. Regarding his surroundings, Thompson recorded: "everything is clean, clothing, bedding & victuals." Several entries refer to hospital food. Early in his confinement he noted that the "quantity is ample & the quality good," but later in the diary he talks about the shortages of rations he and fellow prisoners received. Dr. George Rogers Clark Todd (1825-1900), brother-in-law of Abraham Lincoln, is mentioned by Thompson, who indicated that the doctor was good to his Union patients whenever he was not drinking. At one point, the diary records, Dr. Todd administered a few grains of opium to a patient suffering with a leg wound, and Thompson himself had a malarial fever broken through a quinine regimen. (See: http://library.sc.edu/socar/uscs/2007/thomp07.html Retrieved: Aug 7, 2011)

Thompson is buried in the Charles Baber Cemetery, Pottsville, Schuylkill County, Pennsylvania.

Chapter 9

William F. McCay was from Jack's Creek, east of Lewistown, the family home was where the Glick Farm is located in 2011. McCay's Jan. 24, 1896 letter to the editor of the *New York Evening Post* supported the position of Pennsylvania's First Defenders as first to protect Washington, D.C., and deserving of a Congressional medal of recognition, through a bill introduced by U.S. Rep. Constantine J. Erdman, 9th Congressional District of Pennsylvania around that time. McCay also took exception to having the Pennsylvania companies compared to "The Wide Awakes," in the previous *Post* column of January 20, 1896. This group was a paramilitary campaign organization affiliated with the Republican Party during the 1860 election, known for massed torch light parades in support of Abraham Lincoln, and party candidates.

He continued:

These First Defenders, the advance of a mighty host of the loyal and patriotic who wore the Blue, who fought to maintain the Union & Integrity of the Gov't., has not received that recognition which is there due...

McCay's letter elicited a pointed, some might assert condescending, response from B. F. Watson, of New York, a former officer of the 6th Massachusetts, which he termed the "Old Sixth" in his response to McCay. The 6th lost men during the Pratt Street Riot of April 19, 1861. These mere civilian volunteers, Watson averred, unarmed and without proper military gear, hardly counted as true defenders.

The "Old Sixth" fought its way through Baltimore, Watson declared, his lengthy two column response continuing, in part:

The only casualty ever reported or claimed before by the "First Defenders," and received at the hand of some Baltimorean was a bloody nose, belonging to a colored attendant of the "First Defenders," who did not fancy a "Defender" of that particular complexion... A defender is one who defends." Whom did these unarmed companies as such defend? The moral influence of their presence, however reassuring to the capital and creditable to themselves, could hardly be included in the category of defense in time of war.

The *Evening Post* followed the letter with an editor's note:

Having given both sides to this controversy a hearing, we must now consider the discussion closed so far as our columns are concerned.

It was a controversy, to be sure, among the various veteran groups or units of the era. Some might say, just as the Civil War itself, is still being refought today.

Chapter 10

☞ There exists a national color flag inscribed, "Logan Guards". The Pennsylvania Capitol Preservation Committee notes in its collection description, that Company A of the 46th PA was nicknamed the "Logan Guards," however, the Preservation Committee cautions the flag could belong to an Illinois regiment inscribed in honor of Major-General John A. Logan. The CPC also states that this flag was carried by a "Logan" in the 1914 procession, as Copeland asserts, that honor went to Logan Guard Frank H. Wentz. Lewis H. Ruble, of the Second Logan Guards, likely carried one of the other flags bearing the 46th identification. Regardless of the true origin of the flag, Mifflin County's own Frank H. Wentz marched proudly with the colors firmly gripped in his right hand.

The Capitol Preservation Committee undertook the task of preserving these Pennsylvania flags in the 1980s. The CPC's web site describes the 1914 ceremony and the national flags:

In a heartrending ceremony, the aged warriors placed the colors in custom-

made flag cases in the main rotunda. The flags were kept virtually untouched until 1982 when the Capitol Preservation Committee initiated its "Save the Flags" project. Throughout the years dust had accumulated on the rolled flags, and the long-term vertical display of the flags had placed severe stress on the brittle silk fabric and painted designs. Textile conservators carefully removed the flags from the rotunda and transported them to a state facility near the Capitol.

Over a period of five years, 390 Civil War and twenty-two Spanish-American flags were conserved. CPC notes each flag is now kept on an acid-free panel stored in custom designed, stainless steel storage units. The flags are protected from light, dust, fluctuating temperature, humidity, and excessive handling.

Chapter 11

☞ The Centennial of the First Defenders in 1961 brought out a number of Civil War artifacts, many donated to the Mifflin County Historical Society. Two items came from descendants of Robert W. Patton. These items included his First Defenders cap, worn at all survivor reunions. The other item was a thirty-four star US flag. The Lewistown *Sentinel* article dated April 13, 1961 explained;

... a 34-star flag that belonged to Second Lieutenant Patton of the Logan Guards, later major of the 136th Regiment of Pennsylvania Volunteers. The number of stars indicates it is of 1861. Kansas, admitted to the Union in January of that year, made the 34th state. These two relics (including the cap) are from granddaughters of Maj. Patton, Mrs. Charles Robert of Carlisle and Mrs. James Sterrett of Mifflintown. They do not know the history of the flag, but the manner in which it was preserved in their grandfather's home indicates it held some special significance.

Chapter 12

☞ Reenacting the events of the Civil War is a significant means of maintaining our knowledge and understanding of life during the 1860s. Activities include: living histories, public demonstrations and scripted battles. Thousands representing both sides of the conflict participate in reenacting everything from major engagements, camp life and battlefield medicine, to the civilians' role during the period. Some area units include: 147th PA Volunteer Infantry Regiment, McClure. PA; 148th PA Regiment Field Hospital & Venture Crew, Lewistown; 149th "Bucktails" PA Volunteer Infantry Regiment, Lewistown, PA; and the 46th Pennsylvania Regimental Band, Logan Guard, Altoona, PA

According to a May 14, 2010 article in the Lewistown *Sentinel*, the 148th PA Regiment Field Hospital & Venture Crew of Lewistown present the life of the Civil War era through Living History Encampments. The combination of the re-enactment group with a Venture Crew is a first-of-its-kind entity. Venture Crews are elements of the Boy Scouts of America that are open to young men and women ages 14-21. The 148th's Venture Crew, which is sponsored by the Burnham Lions Club, provides area youth with an opportunity to get out of the house and learn valuable lessons about team work and Civil War history,

From the 46th Pennsylvania Regimental Band web site:

Our Reenactment Unit, known as the 46th Pennsylvania Regiment Band (The Logan Guard) was formed in December 1995 by a group of musicians from the Altoona Area of Central Pennsylvania. The band is now run by President, Lt. Rick Long and Principal Musician, Sgt. Maj. Bob Myers.

It is our desire to honor the Logan Guards Militia from Lewistown, the 46th PA Regiment, and the musicians from the Birdsboro Community Band who enlisted as a group and maintained the morale of the troops with their music throughout the war.

Each of our members is both a talented musician and a gifted living historian who brings to life the typical soldier/musician of the American Civil War. The 46th takes the field with instruments, as well as under arms. We also reenact Confederate, as the band of the 17th Mississippi Volunteers.

The group's web site is at http://46thparegband.50webs.com/index.html (Retrieved: Aug 7, 2011)

Motion picture and television producers often turn to reenactment groups for support; films like *Gettysburg*, *Glory* and *Gods and Generals* benefited greatly from the input of reenactors, who arrived on set fully equipped and steeped in knowledge of military procedures, camp life, and tactics, according to behind the scenes documentaries included in DVD editions. Actor Sam Elliott, who portrayed Union General John Buford in the film *Gettysburg*, said of reenactors in a documentary about the making of the film:

I think we're really fortunate to have those people involved. In fact, they couldn't be making this picture without them; there's no question about that. These guys come with their wardrobe, they come with their weaponry. They come with all the accoutrements, but they also come with the stuff in their head and the stuff in their heart.

Chapter 13

Pensions became a political issue after the Civil War, and the greatest proponent for the veteran was the G.A.R. or Grand Army of the Republic, the preeminent Union veterans' organization with 500,000 veterans in 1890. Six US Presidents, from Grant to McKinley, were Civil War veterans. The first pension law for service in the Civil War came on July 14, 1862, allowing only soldier with combat related injuries, monthly payments ranged from $30 down to $8 depending on rank. Another act in 1890 modified the law to include all soldiers of the Civil War who served 90 days or more and who were suffering mental or physical disabilities of a permanent nature. In 1907, the monthly pensions increased by age to $12 to veterans 62 years and older; $15 per month for those over 75 years of age. By 1920, the Fuller Act for all veterans passed, allowing $50 per month, and with disabilities, $75 per month. Pension records remain today a valuable research tool for genealogists and historians.

Additional information can be found in *It Happened in Mifflin County, Book 2*,

Chapter 6, "The G.A.R. & Mifflin County," published by the Mifflin County Historical Society.

Genealogist Susan Sillence, a descendant of Logan Guard, Henry Printz, donated copies of his Civil War pension documents to the Mifflin County Historical Society in 2011. Susan is the self-described "Nancy Drew" of her family, always on the lookout for information to fill in the branches of the family tree. Civil War pension records, like those of Henry Printz, show the process veterans followed while seeking a pension of that era, including disability documents with wound diagrams, letters and surgeon's statements. Such documents are a wealth of personal data on Civil War ancestors. County historical societies hold a wealth of specific information on residents, such as obituaries, cemetery records and newspaper files. Reconstructing the records of a Civil War ancestor can be made less tedious with online sources, and visits to local historical societies.

Pennsylvania Volunteers of the Civil War at http://www.pacivilwar.com/nara.html is just one valuable online resource. The site notes: *Look for your ancestors in this PA genealogy database of American Civil War soldiers - infantry, cavalry & artillery rosters, histories, biographies, draft, journals, letters, medal of honor recipients, prisoners of war (POWs), & pensions of our Pennsylvania military ancestors. Use this free Pennsylvania database to help with your genealogy search.*

Two of four Mifflin Countians received the Congressional Medal of Honor for Civil War service, though neither served in the Logan Guards, include:

James P. Landis, Chief Bugler, 1st Pennsylvania Cavalry. In action at Paines Crossroads, Va., 5 April 1865. Citation given: 3 May 1865. Capture of enemy flag.

John Lilley: Private, Company F, 205th Pennsylvania Infantry. Petersburg, Va., 2 April 1865. Citation given: 20 May 1865. After his regiment began to waiver he rushed on alone to capture the enemy flag. He reached the works and the Confederate color bearer who, at bayonet point, he caused to surrender with several enemy soldiers. He kept his prisoners in tow when they realized he was alone as his regiment in the meantime withdrew further to the rear.

Additional information on Mifflin Countians and the Medal of Honor can be found in *It Happened in Mifflin County, Book 1*, Chapter 18, "County Medal of Honor Recipients," published by the Mifflin County Historical Society.

APPENDIX

MIFFLIN COUNTY VOLUNTEERS IN OTHER UNITS

Although the Logan Guards may be the best-known Mifflin County military unit of the Civil War period, other companies and groups also originated in the county. Willis R. Copeland's *The Logan Guards of Lewistown, Pennsylvania* included a chronologically service summary (1861 through 1865) of enlisted companies and groups as they left Mifflin County. Copeland's listing follows, and includes the emergency troops of 1863, as well as volunteers for long and short terms. Copeland noted, "The list is given so far as we are able to gather the facts in each case, and should inaccuracies be discovered, they must be attributed to lack of information." Presented here chronologically, corrections and supplemental information has been added.

– 1861 –

APRIL - 1861

The Burns Infantry of Lewistown left town early in the morning of the 20th of April 1861. They became Company I in the 7th Pennsylvania Infantry. Term of service, three months. Thirty men from McVeytown enlisted in this company.

A small squad of Mifflin County men were in Company I and perhaps other companies of the 15th Pennsylvania Infantry, organized for three months service. Left April 20, 1861.

A few men from the county enlisted in Company B. 11th Pennsylvania Infantry, for the three months term. Left April 26, 1861.

A small squad were in the 10th Pennsylvania Infantry, a three months regiment. Left in April 1861.

JUNE - 1861

A large squad of Mifflin County men enlisted in the original Bucktail Regiment, known as the 42nd of the Pennsylvania Line, and also as the 13th Reserves, First Rifles and Kane Rifles. Left early in June 1861.

Mifflin County men formed parts of companies in the 34th Pennsylvania Infantry, known as the 5th Reserves, a three years regiment. Left the middle of June 1861.

Mifflin County men unlisted in the 36th Pennsylvania Infantry, known as the 7th Reserve, for a three years term. Left in June 1861.

JULY - 1861

A few men from the county were in the 62nd Pennsylvania Infantry, organized in July 1861, for three years service.

Men from Mifflin County were in the 31st Pennsylvania Infantry, known as the 2nd Reserve. Three years term. Left Harrisburg in July 1861.

Some men from the county were in the 51st Pennsylvania Infantry, organized late in July 1861, for three years.

AUGUST - 1861

The Mifflin County Dragoons of the Kishacoquillas Valley, with headquarters at Reedsville and Milroy, believed to be the first company in the state to tender its services to the Governor — date of offer, January 28, 1861. The 44th Regiment of the Pennsylvania Line and the 15th Reserve, but best known as the 1st Pennsylvania Cavalry, mustered in the Dragoons as Company C. This was a three years regiment. The company left on August 7, 1861, mounted on Mifflin County horses, under Capt. John P. Taylor.

A few Mifflin County men enlisted in Company C of the 52nd Pennsylvania Infantry, recruited in August 1861, for three years.

Second Logan Guards, Lewistown, Company A of the 46th Pennsylvania Infantry, three years service. Left August 26, 1861. The first full company to report to the Governor under the second call for troops in 1861.

Milroy Zouaves, or Potts Guards, Company H, 49th Pennsylvania Infantry. Three years term. Left August 29, 1861.

SEPTEMBER - 1861

Second Burns Infantry, Lewistown, Company E, 49th Pennsylvania Infantry. Three years term. Left September 3, 1861.

Governor Guards, McVeytown, Company K, 49th Pennsylvania Infantry. Term, three years. Left September 11, 1861.

Belleville Fencibles, Company C, 45th Pennsylvania Infantry. Three years term. Left September 27, 1861.

OCTOBER - 1861

A few men from the county enlisted in the 77th Pennsylvania Infantry which left Harrisburg for the southwest in the middle of October 1861.

A group of fourteen men from Newton Hamilton, under Captain David B. Jenkins, were in Company F, 12th Pennsylvania Cavalry, the 113th Regiment of the Pennsylvania Line. Term of service, three years. Left in October 1861. Company I also had a squad from this county.

A squad of Mifflin County men under Captain Seth Benner was recruited for the 110th Pennsylvania Infantry for three years service. They left in October 1861.

A few men in the 79th Pennsylvania Infantry, three years term. Left Pittsburgh for the southwest, October 18, 1861.

A small squad from Mifflin County was in the independent cavalry company known as the Anderson Troop, recruited for escort and headquarters duty with Generals Anderson, Sherman and others in the fall of 1861.

NOVEMBER - 1861
A few men in the 55th Pennsylvania Infantry, throe years term. Left Harrisburg on November 22, 1861.

Companies in the 53rd Pennsylvania Infantry, three years term, organized in the fall of 1861, had recruits from Mifflin County.

Mifflin County men, enlisted in 1861, joined the 12th U. S. Cavalry and the 18th U. S. Infantry.

Men from this county were in the 84th, 87th and 93rd Pennsylvania Infantry, all recruited in 1861.

A large group under Captain Gilbert Waters enlisted in Company L, 9th Pennsylvania Cavalry, the 92nd of the Pennsylvania Line, known as the Lochiel Cavalry. Three years term. Left Harrisburg for the southwest, November 20, 1861.

– 1862 –

Mifflin County men enlisted in the 126th, 130th, 143rd and 148th Pennsylvania Infantry, recruited in 1862.

FEBRUARY - 1862
Nale Light Infantry of Lewistown, Captain E. W. H. Eisenbise, Company F, 107th Pennsylvania Infantry, enlisted for three years service. Left February 11, 1862.

Some men from the county were in the 157th Pennsylvania Infantry. Left in February 1862. Three years term.

AUGUST - 1862

Company K, 131st Pennsylvania Infantry, Captain Joseph S. Waream, enlisted for nine months term. Left August 6, 1862.

Company D, 131st Pennsylvania Infantry, Captain David A. McManigal, enlisted for nine months term. Left August 9, 1862.

A group of thirty-five men under Captain George W. Soult enlisted in Company H, 149th Pennsylvania Infantry (Second Bucktails), for three years service. Left August 23, 1862.

SEPTEMBER - 1862

Keystone Guards, Lewistown, Captain John A. McKee, Company A, 4th Infantry, Pennsylvania Militia. Emergency men to protect the southern border of the state. Left September 13, 1862.

Irwin Guards, McVeytown, Captain William Macklin, Company C, 4th Infantry, Pennsylvania Militia. Emergency men to protect the southern border of the state. Left September 14, 1862.

Company F, Milroy, Captain James M. Brown, 18th Infantry, Pennsylvania Militia. Emergency men to protect southern border of the state. Left September 16, 1862.

Kishacoquillas Cavalry, Captain John Stroup, headquarters in Belleville, Company M, 16th Pennsylvania Cavalry, 161st Regiment of the Pennsylvania Line. Three years term. Left September 19, 1862.

OCTOBER - 1862

A small group of men from the county were in Company D, 151st Pennsylvania Infantry. Nine months term. Left in October 1862.

– 1863 –

Some in the 19th Pennsylvania Cavalry, the 180th of the Pennsylvania Line, organized in the summer of 1863

JUNE - 1863

Independent militia company, infantry, Captain Absalom B. Selheimer, volunteered to repel invaders in an attempt to reach and destroy the Pennsylvania railroad at Mount Union via Shade Gap. Left June 16, 1863.

Independent militia company, infantry, Milroy, Captain James E. Johnson. Garrisoned the block house at Mount Union for protection of the Pennsylvania railroad and defended the roads southward. Left June 19, 1863.

Independent militia company of cavalry, Kishacoquillas Valley, Captain William Mann, Jr., on duty as mounted scouts in Fulton County. Left June 17, 1863.

Independent militia company of cavalry, McVeytown and vicinity, Captain J. Trimble Rothrock. Left June 16, 1863, on scout duty at Mount Union and vicinity. Entered the service for a six months term, then re-enlisted for three years. Became Company E of the 20th Pennsylvania Cavalry, the 181st Regiment of the Pennsylvania Line.

Independent militia company, infantry, Lewistown, Captain David B. Weber. Left for six months service in June 1863.

Some men in the 21st Pennsylvania Cavalry, the 182nd of the Pennsylvania Line, six months term, re-enlisted for three years. Mustered in June 23, 1863.

Company A, Lewistown, Captain H. A. Eisenbise, 36th Pennsylvania Militia. Three months term. First company in the state to report at Harrisburg for "Gettysburg militia campaign." Provost guard at Gettysburg after the battle. Left June 28. 1863.

Company H, Milroy and vicinity, Captain Ralph Maclay, 36th Pennsylvania Militia. Three months term. Engaged in clearing up the Gettysburg battlefield. Left June 30, 1863.

JULY - 1863
Company F, Newton Hamilton and vicinity, Captain James C. Dysart, 46th Pennsylvania Militia. Left July 1, 1863.

– 1864 –

Companies H and I, 210th Pennsylvania Infantry, recruited in the summer of 1864, had a large number of Mifflin County men in their ranks.

Company H, Captain Moses F. Cunningham, 184th Pennsylvania Infantry, three years service, was mainly recruited in Mifflin County. Mustered in during the fall of 1864.

JANUARY & FEBRUARY - 1864

A group of twenty-eight men from the county were in the 3rd Pennsylvania Heavy Artillery, the 152nd it the Pennsylvania Line. Left in January and February 1864.

APRIL - 1864

Company D, Lieutenant James C. Dysart, 184th Pennsylvania Infantry, three years service, was composed largely of Mifflin County men. Left in April 1864.

JULY - 1864

Group of over forty men from Newton Hamilton and vicinity under Captain Edward B. Purcell united with a Johnstown infantry company and formed Company F of the 194th Pennsylvania Infantry; one hundred days men. Left July 19, 1864.

Company H, Lewistown, Captain Absalom B. Selheimer, 195th Pennsylvania Infantry; one hundred days men. Left July 20, 1864.

A group of seven men in Company K, 195th Pennsylvania Infantry; one hundred days men. Left July 22, 1864

AUGUST - 1864

Group of over forty men from Newton Hamilton and vicinity under Captain Edward B. Purcell united with a Johnstown infantry company and formed Company F of the 194th Pennsylvania Infantry; one hundred days men. Left July 19, 1864.

Company F, Lewistown, Captain Jacob F. Hamaker, 205th Pennsylvania Infantry; one year men. First group, forty men, left August 23, 1864. Balance left August 29.

Company K, Kishacoquillas Valley, Captain Frank B. McClenahen, 205th Pennsylvania Infantry; one year men. Left August 30, 1864.

Companies D and G of the 205th also contained men from this county, who left about the same time.

– 1865 –

A number of men enlisted for one year in Company I, 83rd Pennsylvania Infantry, in the spring of 1865. Also groups in two of the companies recruited in the spring of 1865 for one year and assigned to the 101st Pennsylvania Infantry.

FEBRUARY - 1865

Company C, Lewistown, Captain Absalom B. Selheimer, 78th Pennsylvania Infantry; one year men. First company to enter Camp Curtin in response to the last call made for volunteers. Left February 6, 1865.

1863 - 1865

USCT - United States Colored Troops

On May 22, 1863, the United States War Department issued General Order 143, establishing the "United States Colored Troops" (USCT). This order hastened the recruitment of black soldiers in support of the Union war effort as the Civil War.

While recruitment of former slaves to the Union Army was authorized as early as July 1862, it began in earnest after the Emancipation Proclamation in January 1863. The "Bureau of Colored Troops" established by this General Order was considered necessary to manage the growing numbers of black soldiers. By the end of the war, more than 178,000 former slaves served in the Union Army, constituting about 10% of all Union troops.

In accordance with General Order 143, Mifflin County's men of color joined various units, including the 54th and 55th Massachusetts Infantry, enlisted in June 1863; in the 5th Massachusetts Cavalry, enlisted January 1864; also the 3rd, 5th, 6th, 8th, 22nd, 24th, 25th, 32nd, 41st, 43rd, 45th and 127th regiments of USCT, recruited in Pennsylvania in 1863, 1864 and 1865.

The Molson family of Lewistown, Mifflin County, Pennsylvania had four members join the Union cause, including: David W. Molson, PA 48th Reg't., Co. B; James S. Molson, NY 107th Reg't., Co. F; William Nelson Molson, USCT 43rd Reg't., Co. B; Samuel B. Molson, USCT 43rd Reg't., Co. D.

INDEX

M

Marks, Alfred 22
McClay, Dr. Samuel 89
McClenahen, Daniel M. 19, 147
McCoy, Thomas F. 14, 22
McNitt, Garver M. 131, 136, 144
Mexican-American War 14, 105, 161

MIFFLIN COUNTY NEWSPAPERS
  Daily Sentinel 116, 117, 175, 178, 180, 185, 189, 190, 192
  Lewistown Gazette 20, 33, 34, 56, 57, 78, 79, 85, 90, 91, 93, 100,
      105, 112, 128, 164, 168, 174, 184, 188, 194
  Lewistown Republican 16, 90
  Lewistown Sentinel 157
  True Democrat 62, 67, 192

MILITARY UNITS, MIFFLIN COUNTY, OTHER
  Anderson Troop 214
  Belleville Fencibles 32, 85, 213
  Burns Infantry 86, 97, 98, 101, 212, 213
  Captain Millikin's Troop of Horse 14
  Ellsworth Cadets 95
  Governor Guards 213
  Irwin Guards 32, 215
  Juniata Guards 14, 25, 104, 161, 189
  Keystone Guards 215
  Kishacoquillas Cavalry 215
  Lewistown Artillerists 14, 16
  Lewistown Guards 14, 16
  Mifflin County Dragoons 32, 34, 85, 213
  Mifflin County Zouaves 84
  Mifflin Guards 14, 25, 104, 161, 189
  Nale Light Infantry 214
  Potts Guards 213
  Second Brigade (Mifflin County) 32
  Second Burns Infantry 213
  Slemmer Guards 51, 84, 85, 96, 98, 101
  Teacher's Company 101
  Thompsontown Patriotic Blues 14
  USCT - United States Colored Troops 218
  Washington Guards 14

About the Author

Forest K. Fisher's association with the Mifflin County Historical Society began in 1996, when he joined the board of directors. The next year he started editing the society's newsletter, a job he's held ever since, dubbing the quarterly publication *Notes from Monument Square*. Fisher served as society first vice-president, a term as society president that ended in 2004, followed by serving as the board's second vice president. He also chairs the Scholarship Committee, serves on the Library and Museum committees, plus develops the society's annual "Picture the Past" pictorial calendar. In 2005, the historical society recognized him as the Juniata Valley Real People - Real Connections Volunteer of the Year.

In addition to writing the *It Happened in Mifflin County* series (Book 1 - 2004, Revised, 2009; Book 2 - 2005; and Book 3 - 2006) for the historical society, he also wrote *Images of America - Mifflin County* through Arcadia Publishing in 2008. Fisher's articles on Mifflin County history have appeared in *Historic Chronicles of Pennsylvania* and is a regular contributor to *Common Ground Magazine* (McVeytown, PA). Articles on the historic building of Mifflin County appear annually in *The Sentinel* (Lewistown, PA) and *The County Observer* (Lewistown, PA). Fisher is a contributor to the Pennsylvania Railroad Technical & Historical Society's *Lewistown and the Pennsylvania Railroad From Moccasins to Steel Wheels* in 2000, and to the Mifflin County School District's 1993 local history, *Mifflin County Yesterday and Today*.

Born and raised in Reedsville, Mifflin County, Pennsylvania, his interest in history stems from being raised in a multi-generational family, listening to the recollections of great-grandparents born during the Civil War period. He attended Mifflin County schools, and is a graduate of Penn State University, teaching at the elementary level in the Mifflin County School District from 1975 until his retirement in 2009. Fisher and his wife Dot live along Honey Creek, near Reedsville, Pennsylvania.

PRESERVING THE PAST FOR THE FUTURE

ounded in 1921, the Mifflin County Historical Society operates under this motto, endeavoring to conserve the heirlooms of a county established in 1789.

The Society's museum, the McCoy House, is located at 17 North Main Street, Lewistown, Pa. The house was the birthplace of soldier-statesman Major General Frank Ross McCoy. The 1841 McCoy House was acquired and restored by the Pennsylvania Historic and Museum Commission. McCoy House is host to periodic special exhibits and is the permanent home of the society's collections. McCoy House is listed on the National Register of Historic Sites and the Pennsylvania Trail of History.

McCoy House - 17 North Main Street, Lewistown, Pa.

Seasonal Hours from mid-May through October: Every Sunday 1:30 to 4 PM. Special holiday hours in December. Call the Society office for arranging group or special tours.

Mifflin County Historical Society
Office & Library

Historic Mifflin County Courthouse
1 West Market Street, Lewistown, PA 17044
Telephone: (717) 242-1022
FAX: (717) 242-3488
E-mail: info@mifflincountyhistoricalsociety.org
Web Site: www.mccoyhouse.com
Hours on Web Site or call the Society office.

Mifflin County Historical Society

presents ...

It Happened in Mifflin County
American History with a Central Pennsylvania Connection
By Forest K. Fisher
MCHS Past President & Newsletter Editor

Mifflin County possesses a unique history, connected in many ways to the broader history of the United States. The books in this series detail many of these connections through expanded essays originally appearing in the Mifflin County Historical Society's publication, Notes from Monument Square, written from 1997 to the present by its editor, Forest K. Fisher. Each book is illustrated with approximately dozens of vintage and contemporary photos, etchings, and early maps. Read about Mifflin County's connections to US history, plus excerpts from local newspapers, history trivia, and extensive notes, too. All combine to reveal daily life in bygone days ... It Happened in Mifflin County.

Includes index, extensive notes and bibliography
Book 1 - $15.75
Book 2 - $15.75
Book 3 - $15.75
(PA Sales Tax included + $3.50 S&H)
* To purchase online, visit www.mccoyhouse.com and click on STORE *

1 West Market Street, Lewistown, PA 17044
Telephone: (717) 242-1022   FAX: (717) 242-3488
E-mail: info@mifflincountyhistoricalsociety.org